From Immigrant to Ethnic Culture

American Yiddish
in South Philadelphia

Stanford Studies in Jewish History and Culture
Edited by Aron Rodrigue and Steven J. Zipperstein

From Immigrant to Ethnic Culture

*American Yiddish in
South Philadelphia*

Rakhmiel Peltz

Stanford University Press
Stanford, California 1998

Stanford University Press
Stanford, California
© 1998 by the Board of Trustees of the Leland Stanford Junior University
Printed in the United States of America

CIP data are at the back of the book

With all my love, to Hannah, who best understands the hard work necessary to grasp the story that grows within us from generation to generation. She joyfully embraces our legacy and culture.

To Bill Labov:
Thank you for introducing me to South Philadelphia and for teaching me so much —
Rakhmiel Peltz

Acknowledgments

My work has benefited from the support of many individuals and institutions. I am grateful for their assistance.

Laura Bloch, Janet Mowery, and the staff of Stanford University Press helped make this a better work.

I thank the Lucius Littauer Foundation, and in particular its director, William Frost, and program officer, Pamela Brumberg, for a grant for the preparation of this book.

My original dissertation research was subsidized in part by fellowship grants from the American Jewish Archives in Cincinnati, the Brookdale Institute on Aging and Adult Human Development of Columbia University, the Max Weinreich Center at Yivo, the Memorial Foundation for Jewish Culture, and the National Foundation for Jewish Culture.

During subsequent years, I received financial assistance from several sources for my research and writing, for which I am most grateful: the Boston University Graduate School, the Columbia University Council for Research in the Humanities, the Memorial Foundation for Jewish Culture, the Starkoff Fellowship of the American Jewish Archives, and the Yivo Institute for Jewish Research.

I acknowledge the valuable comments on my dissertation by my adviser, Mikhl Herzog, as well as by Barbara Kirshenblatt-Gimblett and Deborah Dash Moore. As my research matured, I profited from the criticism of colleagues, including that of anonymous reviewers of the manuscript for this book. However, no one understood the whole enterprise as completely as my wife and colleague, Hannah Kliger, who helped me at every step of the way.

South Philadelphia was introduced to me by Bill Labov of the University of Pennsylvania, who generously welcomed me as a full-time guest participant in his graduate field course in 1982–83. I was encouraged by the staff of the Senior Center of the Jewish Community Centers of Philadelphia: Addy Sugarman, Bobby Rosin, and the director, Fran Kleiner. Most important, my stay in South Philadelphia was made more serious, meaningful, and pleasurable thanks to the Jewish residents of the neighborhood. They shaped this project with me, paradoxically making me their teacher by letting me sit and listen to them. Though many are no longer alive, they breathe life into this book.

Over the years, Yiddish seminars and workshops as well as seniors groups in Holyoke, Northampton, and Worcester, Mass., have continued to teach me the lessons of the cultures that are within all of us.

I thank Tsofi Mitnick, who generously typed the original dissertation. I always feel the devotion and support of my parents.

Last, I have learned most about the ever-connecting life cycles that link the past with the future from my children, Binale and Eliezerl. The Yiddish spirit is alive in them.

I acknowledge permission by the publishers to reprint materials from articles that I have written in the following publications: *International Journal of the Sociology of Language* 67 (1987): Mouton de Gruyter, a division of Walter de Gruyter & Co.; *Traditions in Transition: Jewish Culture in Philadelphia 1840–1940*, ed. G. Stern, © 1989 by the Balch Institute for Ethnic Studies, Philadelphia; *Studies in Yiddish Linguistics*, ed. P. Wexler, © 1990 by Max Niemeyer Verlag GmbH & Co. KG, Tübingen; *Language And Ethnicity*, ed. J. Dow, © 1991 by John Benjamins B.V., Philadelphia; *The Labyrinth of Memory: Ethnographic Journeys*, eds. M. C. Teski and J. J. Climo, © 1995 by Marea C. Teski and Jacob J. Climo, reproduced with permission of Greenwood Publishing Group, Inc., Westport, Conn.

Contents

A photo section follows p. 112.

Note to the Reader

System for Transcribing Yiddish

a	similar to a in father, but shorter
ae	similar to a in and, bath in Philadelphia English pronunciation
aw	similar to ow in cow, now
ay	similar to i in fine
e	similar to e in bet
ey	similar to ey in grey
i	between the i of fit and ee of feet
iy	similar to ee of tree and street
kh	like ch in German ach
o	between aw of dawn and o of done
ow	similar to aw of awful, dawn, awning
oy	shorter than oy in boy
r	produced by trilling either the tip of the tongue or the uvula
th	like th in thin, or that
tsh	like ch in church
u	similar to oo in book, with lips slightly rounded
uw	similar to oo of school
w	similar to w in wonder

Symbols and Punctuation

:	long vowel
(?)	sound or word not clear, cannot resolve

( )	sound omitted by speaker usually in fast speech, not detected by investigator; introduced in transcription to improve intelligibility of passage
—	pause that is a sharp break in speech; realization of previous sound is less than full; hesitation
,	phrase-final intonation (more to come)
.	sentence-final falling intonation
..	medium pause
...	lengthy pause
?	end of a question that terminates with rising pitch
!	end of a statement that is emphasized and said with great emotion
CAPS	mark very emphatic stress
[	Brackets between two lines indicate overlapping speech, two people talking at the same time
´	stressed vowel

This system has been adapted from U. Weinreich 1968: xx–xxv; 1971: 19–24; and Tannen 1984: xix. Consonants and consonant combinations correspond roughly to pronunciation in English if they are not listed. Additional symbols provide for sounds present in the Yiddish speech of South Philadelphia Jews: ae, aw, iy, ow, th, tsh, uw, w.

Translations

Translations of short Yiddish excerpts are in parentheses after the Yiddish phrase. Longer Yiddish passages (which may contain English) appear as paragraphs or dialogues, and are followed by my English translation. The Yiddish texts and my translations appear in the same typeface.

קלײנגלײק

אזא נס,
ברויט און זאַלץ אויפן טיש,
אַ ווינקל באַוואַרנט פון קעלט און פון רעגן,
לופט פאַר די לונגען וויפל דו ווילסט,
און דער נס פון אַ ציכטיק געלעגער.

און דער נס פון אַ בריוו,
וואָס דערגרייט צו מען טיר
דורך בריקן פאַרוואָרפענע איבער תהומען,
און דער נס פון אַ שכנה, וואָס ווינט איבער מיר
און רופט מיר אויף יודיש בײַם נאָמען.

זאָל נאָר מיר נישט ווערן, חלילה, פאַרשטערט
מײַן שטילער,
בענשוועליקער יום־טוב.
פאַר עמעצן קלײנגלײק,
פאַר מיר — גאָרע וועלט,
אויסגעחלומטע, אויסגעטרוימטע:

Hadassah Rubin, *In tsugvint: Lider*, p. 103. Tel Aviv: Farlag yisroel-bukh, 1981.

Preface

Writing now, so many years after my almost daily visits to South Philadelphia, a gnawing fear rises within me. Have I forgotten what happened? Is this book different from the one I planned to write in 1988, three years after my departure? Is there only one story to tell? Have I somehow betrayed the neighborhood's Jewish residents, many of whom are no longer living? I was always sure that I would tell my story, and I had confidence in what I found; however, I could not be certain that mine would be the story the South Philadelphians would want to tell. It took me a long time to accept that what I have to convey is my experience, my interaction with the place and people, and the memories that ricochet back and forth through time.

One of the members of my dissertation committee referred to my work as a "love affair," a judgment I interpreted at the time as derogatory, as if the stuff of which dissertations or books are made should have nothing to do with relationships. Over time, however, I have come to accept the term as something close to the truth—indeed, my "love affair" with South Philadelphia has not weakened over the years. But the lessons and images I took from South Philadelphia have changed with time, and this book reflects these changes. My views have been altered by my own writing—fieldnotes, transcripts, articles, a dissertation, and talks for various audiences, including people who grew up in South Philadelphia. And, of course, I have kept in touch with and occasionally visited my friends in South Philadelphia.

When all is said and done, the predominant sentiment I associate with South Philadelphia is not fear—of forgetting, of misstating—but joy. This book, in great part, is a quest to articulate the joy the South Philadelphians transmitted to me even as we shared sad feelings and sad tales. They helped me to see my history through theirs, and they guided my understanding of myself as a person, a Jew in America, a man, a father, and a son. The South Philadelphia experience also guided my reinterpretation of the lives of American Jews in general. To be sure, this was far from my mind the first day I ventured onto the streets of Jewish South Philadelphia in

1982, or even when I left in 1985. As I continued my work in other American Jewish communities, I told and retold the stories and lessons of South Philadelphia, and a new truth and understanding emerged. From the South Philadelphia Jewish story, we can learn about the motives and desires of Jews in America; and if we listen closely, we can also learn about the cultures and legacies of other ethnic, racial, and religious groups.

From the beginning, I made it clear that I wanted to hear the story of South Philadelphia. I listened, and the residents called me teacher. Not until the end of my intensive year in South Philadelphia did I grasp the power of that paradox. Despite my inclination to avoid the limelight, and despite the fact that I shunned public visibility because I believed it would hinder the formation of intimate relationships, I became known to many residents throughout the neighborhood as the leader—the teacher—of a Yiddish discussion group at the local senior center. But in fact, what I did primarily in that group was listen. Somehow, this made me their teacher.

I had never been to South Philadelphia or to any neighborhood like it, but the Jews I met there were familiar to me. Their stories were not unlike the ones I had heard as a child, when I absorbed the Yiddish conversation of my grandparents and the landsleit (fellow townspeople) who came to visit. As a little boy who sat but said little, I learned to listen. More than thirty years later, as the South Philadelphians told stories and I listened, I was reminded of my childhood.

And what about Yiddish? Yiddish drew me to South Philadelphia; it determined my activities in the neighborhood and how I conducted my ethnographic research and analysis. Although I had studied Yiddish from age seven and had heard it from birth, especially from my grandparents, not until my time in South Philadelphia did I connect the Yiddish of the family elders with the academic and literary world of Yiddish high culture that I had studied while growing up and adopted as my own in young adulthood. This synthesis turned out to be crucial, for my scholarly work and for my personal sense of self. South Philadelphia was the laboratory where this newly fashioned unity would be put to a test: the private world of grandmothers woven together with the ideas of the academy, the Yiddish of everyday life as a subject for the Yiddish intellectual present. How would these develop in one and the same project?

When I first went to the neighborhood in 1982, I had been pursuing graduate-level Yiddish Studies at Columbia University for three years while earning a living in biology. Since 1966, when I entered graduate school in biology, I had been in some way connected to scientific research, first as a student, then as a postdoctoral fellow, then as an independent investigator in charge of a basic research laboratory, and later, during my early studies in Yiddish, as a part-time researcher and university lecturer. For many years before embarking on a program of formal study of Yiddish culture, I worked in biology in the daytime and pursued my Yiddish interests into the wee hours of the morning. I was never concerned about explaining my commitment to biology to my Yiddish colleagues. No explanation is needed when the lines are drawn so clearly: Yiddish, after all, is at the periphery, and I was solidly positioned in a high-status field. Once I started my formal Yiddish graduate studies, it became difficult for me to lead a double life. I had no way to share my Yiddish studies and future career plans with my colleagues and teachers in biology.

When I left my professional association with the scientific establishment at the time of my first visit to South Philadelphia, I was not thinking of how my investigation of Jewish life in South Philadelphia would be affected by my training in molecular biology. Only later, when I was reviewing my fieldwork and data analysis in an attempt to find meaning in the overall endeavor, did the role of the biologist within the Yiddishist begin to loom large. My penchant for empirical research in the field of Yiddish, a field largely dominated by text and historical studies, might well have stemmed from my love for the laboratory bench, I realized. My shunning of hypothesis testing, a hallmark of much social science research, no doubt reflected the world of contemporary biological research, where I learned to constantly recast theoretical formulations on the basis of experimental results. Moreover, my major research tool was the use of Yiddish speech, speaking Yiddish where Yiddish was generally not spoken. This technique felt familiar to me; it hearkened back to inhibitor studies I had performed. (These studies involve the addition of a chemical substance known to inhibit a specific biochemical process and the subsequent measurement of its effect on the biological system.) Although I had been a diehard patriot of observation and analysis of naturally occurring systems, at times the only tool I could use to pursue a question in biology involved the controlled perturbation of a system. Adding Yiddish to my interactions with the Jews of South Philadelphia was a similar strategy.

Although it did not occur to me at the time, my work was converging around the intersection of the natural sciences (methods and organization), the humanities (Yiddish language, literature, and folklore), and the social sciences (the structural variation of a cultural phenomenon in its social setting). In my own mind I remained a biologist, always fascinated by the dynamism and creativity of life. Biology had taught me that all processes are in a state of becoming, that all structures are in a state of flux. These convictions were going to be tested by the lives and behaviors of the South Philadelphia Jews.

While conducting the research for my first dissertation, in biology, I began every day by observing the first synchronous cellular divisions after the mixing of sea urchin sperm and eggs. I have never experienced anything more aesthetically beautiful and awe-inspiring than the quickly changing beginnings of this stunning batch of organisms. In South Philadelphia, too, I would be viewing life in its stages of development. Although most of the residents I came to know were elderly, their growth and their change were no less fascinating or amazing.

I went to South Philadelphia to research the almost-ignored field of spoken Yiddish in America. Indeed, my first experience in the neighborhood was as part of a graduate-student team in a year-long graduate field course on "the speech community" taught at the University of Pennsylvania by William Labov. I had studied Yiddish language and general linguistics, in addition to history and literature, and was searching for training in empirical sociolinguistics. Labov's work in Philadelphia had been greatly influenced by Erving Goffman, who on occasion had co-taught the same field course. Goffman's fine eye for the symbolic in human interaction had a great impact on those convinced that language should only be studied in its social setting. Labov's earlier work had developed under the influence of his teacher at Columbia University, Uriel Weinreich, the structural dialectologist who specialized in Yiddish culture. By making Labov's intensive field course part of my graduate training, I was setting the groundwork for my dissertation agenda: studying Yiddish language in terms of dynamic social structure and interaction. What started out as a plan to investigate language grew in an integrated fashion into a study of identity and culture. Language provided a method, a lens through which to look at what is meaningful to members of an ethnic group, to residents of a neighborhood. But it was not possible to focus only on language, especially after the South Philadelphia residents showed me how deeply language was connected to their view of themselves, to their personal and group identity, and to their behavior.

I had not formally studied the culture of American Jews in graduate school. My training was focused on the history of Jews in Eastern Europe. The research for my master's degree utilized published as well as archival historical documents from the Soviet Union. Choosing now to focus on America was not an insignificant step. Students of Yiddish, myself included, had always been drawn to Eastern Europe, the Yiddish heartland. America never had the same romantic lure or symbolic importance. No achievement could measure up against the venerable and heroic Old Home. Eastern Europe took me far away from my Bronx. By the time I started this project, I was willing to examine territory closer to my life history, a landscape much more familiar than Poland. Like some anthropologists, I too was pointing my telescope closer. I was coming home.

This account necessarily reflects the research, thinking, and teaching I have done since leaving South Philadelphia. In my more current research on Jewish life in smaller New England cities, as in South Philadelphia, I have found that the culture and the legacy of the people I am studying—the children of immigrants as they age—have generally not made their way into the standard story we tell ourselves about the American Jewish experience. Although I was originally trained with an eye toward Eastern Europe, I have become familiar with the histories, community studies, and ethnographies of Jews in America. The priorities of the ordinary people, and their visions of themselves, are not usually present in these works. But the typical progression we read of—from Yiddish to English, city to suburb, immigrant to ethnic, segregation to assimilation—does not describe the story of the South Philadelphia Jews. This study highlights the transitions that individuals experience as they age, the characteristics of institutions whose life cycles are synchronous with those of its members, and the features of neighborhood life and the culture of an ethnic group through the voices of South Philadelphia Jews.

It was there, in South Philadelphia, that I learned I could become a teacher by being a good listener. I hope that I have been a good learner and that this book does justice to the South Philadelphia story of which I am a part.

From Immigrant to Ethnic Culture

American Yiddish
in South Philadelphia

PART I

Getting to Know the Residents

CHAPTER ONE

Walking into the Neighborhood

My first impressions upon entering South Philadelphia on a Friday in September 1982 were formed by my part in a student group that had been assigned to study the Jews. We were searching for a city block to observe. Here is what I recorded then in my fieldnotes:

As we turn the corner . . . , we come upon an open-air fruit stand. This is the beginning of a busy shopping block, with stores on both sides. The people walking the street are mostly white and not too well dressed: men and teenagers in T-shirts and jeans, older women in housedresses. The street contains old stores selling varied products and services: hardware, housewares, toys, clothing, shoes, fruit and vegetables, linoleum, custom-made draperies; cleaners, laundromat, pizza parlor, luncheonette, upholsterer. Displays of goods overflow from the stores onto the sidewalk.

At first glance, 7th Street looks like a normal, old, diverse city shopping street. But as we walk farther up the block, we see a few boarded-up stores. We cross to the next block; there are no occupied stores. On one building there is a sign for a church; one open doorway reveals a Vietnamese child peering out from his bed. The next block of 7th Street makes a comeback with a cluster of stores, including one with double-showcase windows displaying lingerie, another selling elegant shoes. Three black teenage girls walk out of the shoestore. But on this block too we see one burned-out store, and several that might have been vacant for ten minutes or ten years.

It is difficult to decide what types of people shop and own stores on 7th Street. There are some black and Asian faces, but most people look like working-class whites, maybe Irish American, maybe Italian American. We see a smoked-fish store, one indication of a Jewish storekeeper and customers. Then we hear Yiddish from a merchant selling her wares to passersby. As we look at names on windows and go into the stores, we discover more Jewish shopkeepers, some with heavy accents, some clearly American-born.

We walk off the shopping street in search of more Jews. We stroll down narrow, dead-end blocks of low row houses, elegant porch-lined streets, and long, nondescript blocks of brick row houses. We do not see many people, but the faces and voices of those we do see are not particularly Jewish. There are no mezuzahs on the doorposts. To the east, we find a few blocks that contain burned-out and boarded-up row houses. This is not our idea of a Jewish neighborhood. There aren't any trees on the streets. Stripped cars are parked on many blocks. No one is sitting in the neighborhood park. Some blocks are strewn with trash; other blocks have houses with rebuilt facades, and trash bags are put out neatly for the day's collection.

We see more Jewish names (a realtor, a few doctors, the state representative's office), and more indications of Jewish residents: a massive synagogue with cupolas on four corners, with a peeling sign over the front door; another synagogue three blocks away, more modest than the first; to the north, yet another synagogue in a converted corner house. Some of the streets contain small houses that must have once been synagogues, as evidenced by the star of David on the window and the ten commandments over the doorpost. Then we see a sign proclaiming "Jewish Community Center." The door opens and three gray-haired women emerge, carrying shopping bags and talking about a friend who had just moved to a senior citizens home in the Northeast.

We had found our neighborhood. (Knight, Peltz, and Pintzuk 1983: 8–10)

Many of those remarks still pertain today. Jews are not visible on the sidewalks of South Philadelphia. The Jewish population is largely an elderly one that does not walk the streets. And the Jews are few in number. Unless one goes to a synagogue, the senior center, or an organizational meeting, the human Jewish presence (discounting the historically Jewish edifices) is not obvious. At the time of my first observations, the ownership of the stores was still largely Jewish; this is no longer true.

When I first went to the area, it seemed unfamiliar, not the kind of place with which I associated Jewish residence. It was too run down, not aesthetically pleasing. Instead of tree-lined streets, I saw a park only one block square and an array of homes and vehicles. The residents were not especially well dressed and were part of a different socioeconomic class from most Jews I knew. Before I met them, I felt distant from the local Jews, whoever they might be. In order to establish any rapport or alliance with them, I would have to explore possible new spheres of shared experience. This was my thinking when I embarked on my work in 1982.

In August 1984, I began the intensive period of fieldwork that lasted until September 1985. This book is based mostly on that year-long adventure. Although this ethnographic study includes observations about non-Jews, it focuses on the Jewish residents and institutions.

I spent most weekday mornings and afternoons in the neighborhood. My aim was to get to know the Jewish inhabitants of South Philadelphia as well as possible, to interact with them in a casual and friendly manner, and to participate in and observe situations that would reveal the character of the Yiddish they spoke and their attitudes toward the language. I needed to become known, accepted, and trusted in the neighborhood in order to get them to talk freely with me. Very soon I realized I could not isolate language from life, and although I used Yiddish constantly and focused on its use, I cast my net more widely. I became determined to try and understand the people's lives, their personal, family, and group histories. I began to wonder how and in what sense they were their parents' children.

In a neighborhood in which Jews are a dispersed minority, the senior center was an excellent location for meeting Jewish South Philadelphians. Members congregated in the lunchroom to talk and play cards every morning and afternoon. Many of my casual meetings with members took place there and in two other lounges in the building. I did not attend most of the regular programs at the Center, and I tried not to interfere with the serving of the daily subsidized hot kosher lunch. However, I was present at special events, such as the bazaar, holiday celebrations, birthday parties, and awards presentations for my friends.

I also met South Philadelphians at Izzy's luncheonette and hot dog stand on the *zibete* (Seventh Street). There I usually ate lunch and socialized for an hour or two. I had met Izzy, a lifelong Jewish South Philadelphian, in 1982. He introduced me to his neighbors, who came to his small, rather bare store to drink a cup of coffee, eat a sandwich or a hot dog, or order hot pretzels Philadelphia-style (with mustard) from the window that opened from the store onto the street. Izzy's place served as the second Jewish community center in South Philadelphia. One of my other favorites on the shopping street was Libe and Izhak's linoleum store, which rarely attracted a customer but was well supplied with chairs for visitors. If I dropped by in the morning I was usually invited to their house for lunch, across a yard shared with the store; a bell rang in their kitchen when a customer entered the store.

At Malke and Abram's store, where they sold notions, crockery, and hardware, most of the social and business interactions took place on the doorstep, where Malke reigned. She sat alongside a chair set aside for guests, greeting passersby and selling *khazeray* (various items of little worth) that were displayed outside the store.

I spent most of my time on the zibete in public space, on the street or in stores, areas that customers and neighbors entered on their own and without invitation. One exception was Basye A.'s upholstery store, where business was so slow that, during my visits, we sat at the kitchen table upstairs, where she lived.

On a few occasions I entered other stores and eating places, but I did not conduct a systematic survey of the shopping street or an interview with each Jewish proprietor. I preferred to cultivate friendships with selected individuals, to meet people through them, and to frequent the same few places repeatedly for longer periods of time. I did, however, attend each of the three synagogues for various services and activities. Since I observe the Jewish Sabbath and all religious holidays and do not travel on those days, my appearance at the local synagogues was limited. On occasion I went to the neighborhood in the evening or on the weekend, but my main exposure was on weekdays. As it happened, that was when the neighborhood's largely elderly population was most active. Eventually, residents who saw me several times a week at the Center or at Izzy's luncheonette assumed I belonged and accepted me as a neighborhood insider.

Visits in people's homes were not always as spontaneous as my forays on the zibete, and often arrangements had to be made in advance. In other words, most of the Jewish residents did not sit outside on the front stoop, available for conversation. When I wanted to interview people, I needed to make appointments over the telephone. In some cases, the people I interviewed were individuals I had known for a few years and with whom I kept in touch by telephone and letter. Since the people I met at the Center spent most of their days there, there was little reason or opportunity for me to meet with them in their residences as well. If the occasion warranted, such as an illness or an operation, a death in the family, or a holiday, I sometimes asked to visit at home. However, I called on two residents, Yisrul and Marye, without advance notice, and they invited me back repeatedly. In all, I was in the houses of more than twenty neighborhood residents.

As I got to know some people better, we talked occasionally on the phone. I sent greeting cards in connection with birthdays, illness, new jobs or achievements, and the birth or death of loved ones. Although I recorded conversations with residents throughout the year, more than half of our conversations took place during July 1985, by which time I felt well acquainted with my interviewees. After September 1985, when I moved to Massachusetts, most of my communication with my neighborhood friends was by letter, in Yiddish and English.

Meeting the Residents: The Investigator as Subject and Object

I was able to conduct pure observations of the neighborhood on many occasions, but in most instances I was also a participant, usually speaking Yiddish with Yiddish speakers. Thus, much of the information I gathered was about the responses of the community to my use of Yiddish. Of course, all ethnographic study reflects the context in which the ethnographer and the residents interact; the aim to study behavior that exists in the absence of the ethnographer is a fantasy of the ethnographer that can lead to creative thinking, but seldom to a grasp of the situation at hand.[1] Although all aspects of my self-presentation in the South Philadelphia Jewish community could be relevant to an evaluation of the information I collected on the vitality of the neighborhood, I limit the discussion here to my own background in Yiddish language and culture and my involvement in Jewish neighborhood life.

I grew up in a Bronx, New York, neighborhood that was heavily populated by Jews. My parents and grandparents spoke Yiddish, as did my older sister when she was a child. My parents spoke mostly English at home, and not until I started to attend Yiddish afternoon school at the age of seven did I begin to understand and speak Yiddish. Even after that I continued to converse in English with my grandparents, though they usually spoke Yiddish. In addition to attending public school, I took courses in a Yiddish-language high school and teachers seminary, but it was not until college that I started to speak Yiddish with Yiddish speakers, first with my grandparents and then with my friends and parents. This change in language behavior came about through my involvement with Yugntruf, a youth organization founded in 1964 that was committed to the perpetuation of Yiddish language and culture. I became a reader of the daily Yiddish press and literary journals and was an active member of Yiddish cultural organizations.

But it was not only my ability to talk freely in both the Yiddish of my family and the language of high culture that enabled me to get along in Jewish South Philadelphia. I felt comfortable when interacting with Jewish storekeepers and other residents because the neighborhood residents bore some similarity to the neighbors of my youth. Furthermore, having lived in different areas of Philadelphia for seventeen years, I was well acquainted with the city and its Jewish community. Even so, my feelings of familiarity and freedom were more closely tied to my childhood memories of the conversation of my immigrant grandparents. The capacity and desire to sit at length while old folks told Yiddish stories returned as I talked and listened to my elderly South Philadelphia friends.

My motivation to conduct this investigation was rooted in an interest in the continuity of immigrant culture. I had found little scholarly work on the influence of American Yiddish culture on American Jewish life. In Jewish South Philadelphia, an active community that unfolded in a neighborhood of primary immigration, I had a unique opportunity to contribute to an uncharted field and, at the same time, to delve more deeply into the American ethnic experience relevant to my own background.[2]

In anthropological field research, it is not uncommon for the ethnographer to induce the performance of a custom that is long out of use. This practice has been used to evoke linguistic forms. But in my case in South Philadelphia, I was a native son with greater fluency in the ethnic mother tongue than many of the native speakers themselves. What I evoked were not linguistic forms, in most cases, but associations that speaking Yiddish held for the residents and for myself. In this recounting of my interaction with the residents, the connections between our past and our present become evident.

During 1984–85, my first encounter with the Jewish residents of South Philadelphia was at the Center. After describing to the director and program head my plan to study Yiddish in South Philadelphia, I expressed my desire to organize a weekly Yiddish conversation group to study how Yiddish is spoken in that setting. I did not plan to administer tests or questionnaires but to observe language behavior and record speech. In addition, I explained that I wanted to talk informally to members at other times elsewhere in the neighborhood.

The two staff members thought that the conversation group would fit well into their program and supported the plan enthusiastically. They reserved 10:30 A.M. to 12:00 noon on Fridays, a day with good attendance, for the Yiddish group. They suggested that initially I meet with members to read and discuss Yiddish stories. Reading stories had been an occasional activity at the Center, but regularly scheduled discussion groups were rare. The first Yiddish conversation session took place three weeks after our story reading. The staff invited those they thought would be interested, and I announced it to members sitting in the lunchroom that morning. In addition, the conversation group was listed in the *South Philadelphia Review East* along with the other Center activities for the week. We called the group *A gleyzele tey* (a glass of tea).

At the session, I introduced myself as a student interested in Jewish life in South Philadelphia and in Yiddish. I pointed out the tape recorder, explaining that without the recording I might forget some things that happened. I repeated this explanation many times over the course of the year, as needed, so that my purpose would be clear. I suggested that all those present volunteer their Yiddish names. They did, and from that moment on, I addressed and referred to them by their Yiddish names. Most Jewish neighborhood residents used their English names, and many had not heard their Yiddish names since their parents died or even since childhood. As Lehiste (1975) found for second-generation Estonian American bilinguals, identity is tightly bound to personal names, and emotional reactions are strong when questions are raised about ethnic-language personal names. I found that a warm atmosphere was facilitated by our use of Yiddish names, in itself a declaration of a shared identity.

From that day on, most of the neighborhood residents linked me to the Center and the *Gleyzele tey* group. In my conversations in the neighborhood, I did not usually bring up the session or the Center, but people read the weekly paper and the Center's monthly *Beacon*, and they frequently mentioned the group to me when we met on the zibete. I never delivered lectures and tried to speak as little as possible in the Friday morning sessions, but even the people who socialized with me mainly in their homes believed that my official role was as a Center staff member and a teacher, despite my repeated explanations of my mission as a student.

My intention was not to be an interventionist, neighborhood organizer, or social worker. I stayed out of the limelight and never entertained at Center performances or local organizations. My policy was to show no favoritism and to treat everyone as a friend, even those who were not liked by most neighbors, who disrupted group discussions, and who remained indifferent and uninterested when I was present. I did not hide any of my past or current interests, however, and I presented myself to people as I would in most other social situations.

Shaffir, in his reflections on fieldwork in Hasidic communities, noted that the participant-observer should tell the subjects of the study something about the research, but rarely all (1985: 124). Because the Jewish communities he studied were much more closed to outsiders than Jewish South Philadelphia was, condoning only the behavior of Jews who are pious, he felt it necessary to feign religious observance. In one instance, he identified himself as a sociology student but withheld the fact that he was collecting data about the community. Herein lies one of the ethical dilemmas in field research: the investigator must ensure the informant's right to privacy; yet if the researcher continually reminds the informant that he or she is collecting information it is unlikely that the two will establish a rapport. Chrisman points to the dual obligation of the researcher to remain visible without neglecting the "value of 'melting' into the research sample in order to collect data relatively unbiased by observer presence" (1976: 141). Chrisman, who was a Danish American, tried to gain entry into the fraternal societies of elderly ethnic group members. He believed that his identity as a "young Dane" would mean more to the association members than his identity as an anthropologist. And indeed, despite his note-taking, tape-recording, and questioning, they seemed to concentrate on the fact that he was the only "young Dane" willing to take responsibility in running their organization (1976: 139).

Similarly, in my study, community members rarely commented or asked about my project but reveled in my interest in their personal lives, in Jewish culture, and in Yiddish language. Our good rapport made it unnecessary for me to repeatedly explain my work, although at one time or another I announced my purposes to almost everyone I met. Consequently, I knowingly ran some risk that neighborhood friends who confided in me about personal problems would forget that I was collecting information from them. At the opposite extreme, it was conceivable that some residents would be eager to tell me a personal story in hopes that it would go beyond the confines of South Philadelphia. Rarely did our conversations peruse our shared ethnographic experience. In many instances I remain unsure what neighborhood residents thought about "this new experience . . . in the context of their everyday lives" (see Page 1988: 165).

Avenues of communication were both facilitated and hindered during this fieldwork by differences in the life experiences of the residents and myself. These included extent of formal education, cultural interests, gender (most residents were women), and financial status. Two realms of difference, age and place of residence, provide good examples. Because of demographic changes over the years, this Jewish neighborhood consisted mostly of Jews older than 60 (see Appendix B). Although I had contact with people of all ages, I spent most of my time with individuals 20 to 60 years my senior. On the one hand, the elderly Jews relished the attention I gave them, which they often did not get from younger family members or friends. On the other hand, the fundamental activities that defined our lives were very different: for me, being a graduate student; for them, eating a subsidized lunch and sitting home alone for most of the week.

I lived in Center City Philadelphia, about two and one-half miles from the center of Jewish South Philadelphia. A few of the South Philadelphians associated my neighborhood with the *hekhe fentster* (high society).[3] But most simply appreciated that someone from the outside cared about South Philadelphia. Although I did not live in the neighborhood, opportunities to talk were still plentiful; many of the older residents stayed home most of the time and talked to friends on the telephone. As I got to know people better, I also called them from time to time. This part of our relationship was largely nonreciprocal: they rarely phoned me.

I did not accentuate the differences between myself and the South Philadelphians but attempted to construct close bonds based on common concerns. One affinity that tied us was an interest in aspects of Jewish culture. We could talk about a holiday, a traditional delicacy, an item of Jewish news, or reminiscences of a former, old-fashioned way of life. Except at the Center, Jewish residents usually did not have neighbors with whom to share such ethnic interests. Although a shared Jewish ethnic consciousness helped us feel related, these topics were not the only or even the typical subjects for interaction. We shared a general desire to talk to each other—about matters that worried us, joyous events, friends, neighbors, and family members. Like Chrisman with his Danish research subjects, I believed that the interactional turf I shared with my elderly Jewish research subjects would overshadow their awareness of our different ages and places of residence.

My knowledge of the residents' cultural assumptions and shared histories, which Merritt has termed "mutual biographical context," made it possible for me to better evaluate communication in the neighborhood. Our common ethnic concerns, my interest in the neighborhood and its history, my fascination with the residents' personal stories, and my worry about their continuing well-being created a common base of knowledge that was open to expansion.[4]

Speaking Yiddish Some of the Time

"Initially, keep your eyes and ears open but keep your mouth shut" (Ned Polsky, quoted by Shaffir 1985: 129). Although I did not follow this dictum of field research to the letter, I do not believe I ever monopolized conversation, though sometimes when I planned to remain silent I found it difficult to do. In this South Philadelphia Jewish community, speech was the major facet of sociability, and to have refrained from speaking would have labeled me an antisocial type who could not participate in the life of the community.

People seemed to accept and like me, but I was marked as having an unusual trait: I spoke Yiddish most of the time with Yiddish speakers. This was unusual in that most Yiddish speakers in South Philadelphia, at least in public, ordinarily spoke English. But I felt comfortable speaking Yiddish, and Yiddish became the bond and matrix out of which my friendship with many South Philadelphia Jews grew. I believe that Yiddish became a key to insider status for me. By speaking mostly Yiddish to Yiddish speakers, I was able to broadcast my Jewish identification simultaneously to Jews and non-Jews. My behavior was a signal for Jews to relate to me in a similar fashion if they were able and willing to do so. In retrospect, I realize that not only was I not keeping quiet—that is, merely watching and listening, a role that might single me out as an observer in this talky neighborhood—but my way of talking made me conspicuous.

During my earlier brief visit in the neighborhood, I had noted that Jewish residents seldom spoke Yiddish except when they were addressed in the language. So I spoke Yiddish and they responded in kind. In this respect, my study is atypical: the subjects of the research often accommodated to my speech and thus exhibited behavior not common to their daily lives. Although the practice in anthropological linguistics of eliciting remembered speech elements is well established, in South Philadelphia, Yiddish ways of talking were alive enough that community members could share them both with the investigator and with one another. As a native-son ethnographer I was able to introduce everyday use of a minority language, thereby opening doors that revealed behavior, emotion, and identification.

My decision to speak Yiddish in the neighborhood, and the concomitant effects on the behavior of the residents, led to the emergence of specific patterns of language choice on both our parts. In other words, my own language choice was not uniform. In fact, my conversations seemed largely determined by the response I received to my initiating exchanges in Yiddish. Thus, although at first I used Yiddish when I knew the other person understood, I eventually shifted to the language chosen by the other person. Sometimes the configuration of participants in a discussion or a specific setting itself, such as the *Gleyzele tey* discussion group, swayed conversation toward Yiddish. Generally, however, I matched the language of response or the language that I sensed would provide my interlocutor with the most comfort.

My influence on the residents' behavior was, of course, limited. Many took a liking to me and in numerous ways identified with me, but even those who were old, sick, and fairly immobile had other, separate interests. Sometime, for example, I had to wait quite a long time until they were free for us to meet. In all, my experience suggests that I was more interested in using Yiddish than the residents were.[5]

What Was I Searching For in the Neighborhood?

It is with language that we present ourselves to others and formulate our feelings of self. In this South Philadelphia ethnic community, therefore, there was no way that I could tease language free from culture, communication free from identity, and individual stories free from family and neighborhood history. So, despite the fact that I was looking at South Philadelphia in the late twentieth century, I necessarily also became a student of history. As a developmental biologist, I know that at any point in time processes are in flux, whether the object of study is molecular structure, an organism, or a social group or society. So an approach to the South Philadelphia Jews that took account of their cultural and linguistic pasts as well as the present seemed entirely appropriate to me.

I collected whatever information I could get my hands on to broaden and deepen my diachronic and my synchronic perspective on the Jews of South Philadelphia. To this end, I searched through the archives and libraries of individuals and organizations, reading maps, newspapers, and official documents.[6] Except for the Neighborhood Center Collection, the South Philadelphia materials were scattered and scant, a neighborhood and Jewish community largely overlooked.[7] During my fieldwork, I subscribed to the *South Philadelphia Review East* to keep abreast of the important local news. The Jewish community was not a major focus of this newspaper, but perusing the contemporary Philadelphia press gave me some degree of confidence that I was not enveloping myself in a world of interpersonal relationships restricted to the residents and myself.

Although I was identified in the neighborhood, at least in part, by my concern for Yiddish language and Jewish culture, the relationships I developed there transcended the bounds of my research. In short, regardless of the language we spoke together, I became friends with many of the residents, and our conversations reflected our level of comfort with each other. Friends dwell on that which they share, that which yields a response. Gossip and narratives figure strongly in my notes. After each meeting with a neighborhood friend or after attending a local event, my fieldnotes contained a melange of news about mutual acquaintances and family, stories from personal and family history, as well as descriptions of neighborhood history. Through diverse sources, I searched for corroboration and gradually formed a picture of the world of South Philadelphia Jews. How they reacted to the world of their parents and composed their own Jewish personal and group identities is what my analysis is, ultimately, all about. Moreover, the ideas and emotions they conveyed formed the building blocks for my understanding of the historical forces that drive individuals and groups to constantly reformulate their sense of self.

CHAPTER TWO

"It Used to Be Like Jerusalem"
History and Institutions of the Jewish Community of South Philadelphia

Rivke A., who came to America in 1923 at the age of twelve, remembers the bustling Jewish life in South Philadelphia: "O se flig zan vi Dzheruzalem" (Oh it used to be like Jerusalem).[1] Shmuel-Arn was born in South Philadelphia more than 70 years ago and has lived there all his life. In the mid-1980's he was the president of Conservative congregation Adath Shalom at Marshall and Ritner Streets (in years gone by, known as Beys Shmuel, or the *litvishe shul*).[2] At a meeting of the Philadelphia Jewish Community Relations Council, Shmuel-Arn does not feel it at all necessary to qualify his statement, "Judaism started in South Philadelphia." The distinct Jewish nature of the neighborhood looms large in the consciousness of the residents. Moreover, in Philadelphia as a whole, foreign-born Jews represented the largest immigrant group as late as 1920 and 1930 (Varbero 1975: 15, 30).

South Philadelphia is the area of the city immediately to the south of Center City Philadelphia, bounded on the east and west by the Delaware and Schuylkill Rivers respectively. It is the home of many ethnic groups, including Italian, Jewish, Irish, and Polish immigrants and their descendants, as well as a long-standing African American community. The largest settlement of East European Jews in Philadelphia during the period of mass immigration was in South Philadelphia, just below South Street. This area became home to Jews who settled on the streets close to the docks that welcomed their ships. Because its population was replenished by new arrivals through the 1920's, South Philadelphia continued to be a major Jewish neighborhood until mid-century, even though the older immigrants started moving out to Logan, Parkside, Southwest Philadelphia, Strawberry Mansion, and Wynnefield in the early 1900's.

South Philadelphia's Jewish population, estimated at 55,000 in 1907, reached almost 100,000 around 1920. A Philadelphia Housing Association Survey reported a drop of 41 percent in the number of Jews between 1920 and 1930, but in 1930 South Philadelphia was still the most populous Philadelphia Jewish neighborhood, numbering close to 50,000. Various reports estimated the area's Jewish population at 35,000 in 1942, 15,000 in 1958, and 3,000–4,000 in 1980.[3] After World War II, Jews continued to leave for other neighborhoods, including Mt. Airy, Overbrook Park, and especially Northeast Philadelphia; often they moved again to suburban communities in Pennsylvania and southern New Jersey. The neighborhood's Italians had a higher birthrate than the Jews and tended to stay put (Varbero 1975: 183). The Jewish population of South Philadelphia declined more rapidly than that of the neighborhood's other ethnic groups, yet the ironies of Jewish geographic mobility would have it that the five communities of secondary settlement that were spawned largely by Jewish South Philadelphia at the beginning of the century today contain fewer Jews than South Philadelphia. It is important to remember that although Jewish South Philadelphia has undergone changes, in many ways it is a continuation of the community of primary immigration.

Jewish South Philadelphia, a neighborhood analogous to New York's Lower East Side, has received scant attention in both scholarly and popular works. Because the little that has been written has focused on the original community of one hundred years ago, I describe here the richness of Jewish life that evolved during succeeding years in Philadelphia's long-standing Jewish neighborhood.

The massive immigration of East European Jews to the United States commenced with the assassination of the Russian Tsar Alexander II in 1881 and the pogroms and repressive May Laws of 1882 that followed. The first ship carrying Russian Jewish immigrants that reached the Christian Street wharf arrived on February 23, 1882. In those early years, most of the immigrants entering through the port did not stay in Philadelphia, but those who did remain quickly set up a Jewish community in the northeastern section of South Philadelphia, near South Street, between Third and Sixth Streets. Although a small number of Jews had lived there earlier, by the time the new immigrants arrived, the area was mainly known as a slum and home to the underworld. Nevertheless, since the choice of immigrant residence during this period was most greatly influenced by the proximity to employment, South Philadelphia remained a popular choice. For the almost

40 percent of the immigrants employed in the garment industry, and for others working as peddlers, in cigar factories, or as keepers of stands and shops, South Philadelphia was a suitable home.

Poor working conditions and the presence of Jewish anarchists and socialists quickly made the community ripe for union organizing. Yiddish writer and journalist Moses Freeman operated a newsstand at Fifth and South and reported on the activities in full view at this busy and infamous corner, known by the immigrants as the *khazer-mark* (hog market). Needle trade contractors and bosses could acquire Jewish immigrant labor there for a pittance. On weekday evenings and Sundays, meeting rooms in the neighborhood were full of Jewish workers intent on building unions. During the first major strike by Jewish clothing workers, for example, a mass meeting was organized on August 4, 1890, by Cloakmakers Union No. 1 at Wheatley Hall, at Fifth and Gaskill Streets, to protest the arrest of workers. Soon South Philadelphia would be dotted by the headquarters of workers' associations and unions with an overwhelmingly Jewish membership, such as the Bakers Union, the Philadelphia Men's and Kneepants Makers Union, the Vestmakers Union, and the Agudes hashokhtim defiladelfya (Philadelphia Association of Ritual Slaughterers) (Freeman 1929: 72, 63, 65; Whiteman 1977: 122–35).

South Philadelphia housed the citywide headquarters of numerous Jewish organizations for many years afterward. The proximity to Center City made the neighborhood a convenient locale for meetings. As organizational life developed in the city, South Philadelphia branches of organizations often acquired the designation "Downtown" as part of their name. This was to distinguish them from "in town," the term South Philadelphians used to refer to locations in the central part of the city.

The new immigration also brought with it the development of a diverse religious community. On the same block where the mass cloakmakers' rally took place, the Hungarian Synagogue (Emunas Israel Ohev Sholom) opened in 1888 in the former Garrick Theater. One of the founders pawned his gold watch in order to buy a Torah scroll for the new synagogue. In its heyday the shul had three weekday morning services plus three evening study groups, and on Saturdays several hundred people attended services. It closed in 1967.[4]

Still functioning, however, are three large synagogues established in the original immigrant quarter in the 1880's. The first Russian synagogue in Philadelphia, B'nai Abraham, was begun in 1882 and moved to its present location at Sixth and Lombard in 1885. In 1891, Rabbi Bernard Levinthal arrived in Philadelphia to serve the congregation, and for the next 60 years he led Philadelphia's Orthodox Jewish life and was a figure of national prominence as well. Kesher Israel at Fourth and Lombard represents the union in 1894 of B'nai Jacob, founded in 1883, and Rodfey Tsedek, founded in 1887. The Roumanian American Congregation (Oir Chodash Agudath Achim) was founded in 1886 at 512 S. Third Street and moved to Fourth and Spruce Streets in 1901, calling its synagogue *Di groyse rumeynishe shul* (The Great Roumanian Synagogue). Currently the congregation is known as the Society Hill Synagogue.

In 1905, Charles Bernheimer wrote that Jews were already moving to the more southern streets near Moore Street, but his list of nineteen local shuls does not include any located that far south (1905: 52). It is certain that several years later a sizable number of Jewish institutions had opened their headquarters there. For example, nine branches of the Workmen's Circle, a Jewish fraternal organization, formed a labor lyceum on Sixth and Tasker Streets in 1912. The Downtown Jewish Orphanage opened on the same street during an influenza epidemic after World War I, but moved further south to Ninth and Shunk in 1925. The two largest Orthodox shuls in the expanded region of secondary settlement in South Philadelphia, Shaari Eliohu and Shaari Israel, were erected at Eighth and Porter and Fourth and Porter in 1912 and 1913. Several residents remembered that their families moved to the shopping street at Seventh (*di zibete*) near Porter during World War I, and the area was already mostly Jewish. It is exactly here that most Jewish residents of South Philadelphia were concentrated 75 years later (see map, Appendix A).

The area of Jewish residence in the southeastern part of South Philadelphia, south of Snyder Avenue, was inhabited by Jewish families by World War I and became the major Jewish sector of South Philadelphia by the late 1940's. The gravitation of Jewish life toward this southern region seems to have occurred gradually. Even in the 1980's, several Jews still lived at addresses north of Snyder Avenue. In addition, the only Jewish bakery and the one remaining Orthodox synagogue in South Philadelphia were away from the southern reaches of the district, just to the north of Snyder Avenue (see Appendix A).

Financial constraints prevented all institutions from following their clientele and relocating their headquarters. For example, the Neighborhood Center, an important settlement house that remained a Jewish recreational and cultural center for immigrant families, did not move from its first site at Fifth and Bainbridge Streets to its Marshall and Porter Streets location until 1948. Reincorporated within the Federation of Jewish Charities in 1918, the Neighborhood Center was previously known as the Young Women's Union. It was one of the original Jewish Federation constituents in 1901, which had pioneered the first kindergarten, nursery school, day-care center, and probationary supervision and foster homes for children of immigrants (P. Rosen 1983: 200–201). In 1900 the public school enrollment near the settlement house was 85–95 percent Jewish, but by 1948 that number had diminished to only 10–15 percent. In 1923 and 1925 the Neighborhood Center's board of directors considered new locations farther south at Fourth Street and Snyder Avenue and at Eighth and Wolf Streets, but it was not able to move nearer to the area's Jewish population center until 1948 (Greifer 1948: 135, 144, 246, 264–66).

In its new location, the Neighborhood Center shared the building of a religious school, a modern Talmud Torah not affiliated with a synagogue, which had opened its doors in 1928 as the Jewish Educational Center No. 2 (Center No. 1 was established at the same time at Fifth and Moore Streets; B. Rosen, ed., 1938). The descendant of this institution today is the Stiffel Senior Center of the Jewish Community Centers of Philadelphia, which I refer to as the Center throughout this book. The Center was the major research site for this study, and it was where I convened the weekly Yiddish conversation group, *A gleyzele tey*. The Center at Marshall and Porter was the only Jewish institution open daily during the course of my work.

The former Neighborhood Center offered programs for all ages but emphasized social, cultural, and athletic activities for young people. *The Review*, the newsletter of the Jewish Y's and Centers of Greater Philadelphia, the network resulting from the union of the Neighborhood Centers and Y's in 1965, documented the transformation of the South Branch into a full-fledged center for senior adults between the years 1966 and 1976. The Talmud Torah no longer existed. Starting with only seventeen senior members, an array of nutritional, educational, health, and counseling programs for several hundred seniors gradually developed. Many of the senior center's members had attended the Talmud Torah more than 50 years earlier in the same building. Their children studied at the Talmud Torah too, in addition to going there to day camp, religious services, teen dances, and basketball games. Beyle, for example, recalled teaching there as a teenager and having singer Eddie Fisher as one of her student cantors. In some cases the parents of the members I met had been the first members of the newly converted senior center twenty years earlier. The life cycle of the institution has coincided with the personal and family life cycles of the Jews of South Philadelphia. The Center, a new-world, American institution, remains a living remembrance of their mortality and the persistence of their Jewish community.

To counter the influence of the Protestant Bethel Mission, which offered attractive recreational activities for youths in a heavily populated Jewish area, the Jewish Federation opened a Neighborhood House at Sixth and Mifflin Streets from 1922 to 1943, at the border between wards 1 and 39. Throughout its existence the Neighborhood House was in poor physical condition, and it was supervised by the Neighborhood Center from 1930 to 1940. Nevertheless, in 1937, the Neighborhood House had more than a thousand members: 95 percent were Jewish, 97 percent were native-born, and 93 percent lived in row houses with restricted play spaces (Greifer 1948: 267–71). The community strove to provide a congenial general and Jewish environment for the Jewish youth of South Philadelphia.

During most of the period since the beginning of mass immigration, South Philadelphia was the hub of Jewish organizational, religious, and business life. In 1948, Greifer reported that the majority of buildings used for the meetings of Jewish beneficial, fraternal, and Zionist groups in Philadelphia stood in South Philadelphia (1948: 135). A survey of four weeks of the Philadelphia Yiddish daily, *Di yidishe velt*, of April 1941 finds the meeting announcements of 31 different Jewish organizations in the neighborhood. A sampling illustrates their diversity: mutual aid societies such as the Heysiner Independent Young Men's Association, United Ezras Akhim Ahaves Sholem Beneficial Association, and Banos Sholem Free Loan Society; charitable groups, including the Downtown Froyen Lekhem Oniyem Fareyn and the South Philadelphia branch, which raised money for the Philadelphia Psychiatric Hospital; branches of Zionist organizations like Hadassah and Poaley-tsiyon; and the Anshey Zhitomir branch of the Jewish Nationalist Workers Alliance. Established by immigrants soon after they came to this country, these organizations conducted most of their affairs in Yiddish. The participation of children of immigrants was not precluded, but for Jews and many other immigrant groups, South Philadelphia continued to be the main home of those born in the old country. In the 1980's, the only Jewish associations that met in the neighborhood were very American in character: the Jewish War Veterans and its ladies' auxiliary.

Some of the principal Jewish social service agencies in Philadelphia continued to maintain their headquarters in the neighborhood. Besides the Neighborhood Center, also functioning in South Philadelphia as late as 1948 were the Jewish Welfare Society (a family casework agency), the Downtown Hebrew Day Nursery, a residence hotel for young Jewish working women, the Home for the Aged and Infirm Hebrews, the Downtown Hebrew Orphan Asylum, and Mt. Sinai Hospital (Greifer 1948: 335). In a neighborhood with a shrinking Jewish population, the staff and administration of those institutions often struggled with the Jewish funding agencies to maintain their presence in South Philadelphia. Records show, for example, that this was true in 1961 for the Albert Einstein Medical Center— Southern Division, the successor to Mt. Sinai Hospital (Weber 1962). This hospital managed to survive and has expanded its facilities in its present location. Shortly after my research was completed, it finally dissolved its association with Jewish agencies.

South Philadelphia was also the home of myriad synagogues and religious schools. Citywide registers for 1934 and 1943, a period when the neighborhood accounted for less than 15–20 percent of the city's Jewish population, locate one-third of Philadelphia's synagogues in the area (*Seyfer Hazikorin* 1934: 45–47; Malamut 1942–43: 286–89). At that time, the local synagogues were more traditional than those in any other neighborhood. Not only were they all Orthodox, but the names reflect the oldest kind of synagogue founded by East European immigrant Jews, the *anshey*, whose members came from the same hometown. One observer commented, "South Philadelphia . . . once contained as many Jews as Italians (if not more), but the area shows no evidence of ever having been a Jewish ghetto, so complete was the out-migration" (Golab 1977: 165). This is, however, not true: the buildings that housed scores of synagogues and former Jewish institutions still stand as the most obvious reminders of the prevailing Jewish community of yesterday.

The active congregations in the neighborhood have gone about their business quietly, invisible to the rest of Philadelphia's Jewry. Largely unaffiliated with federated synagogue bodies, they did not publicize their activities in citywide papers after the demise of Philadelphia's extensive Yiddish press. Thus, a March 27, 1969, article in the *Jewish Times* mentioned that five or six synagogues functioned at that time in South Philadelphia. Records in the Philadelphia Jewish Archives and residents' reports of their involvement in specific synagogues suggest to me that the actual number of synagogues in 1969 was ten or twelve. In 1983, during my fieldwork for this project, four synagogues operated in the neighborhood.

As of this writing in 1996, three congregations—one Orthodox and two Conservative—still meet (see Appendix A). The Orthodox one, Congregation Shivtei Yeshuron-Heisiner—Ezras Israel, whose name reflects the amalgamation of formerly independent synagogues, has as its president a man in his thirties who lives nearby and is sentimentally attached to the place because his grandfather was the shames (sexton) there. The two Conservative synagogues symbolize the modernizing tendencies in the South Philadelphia Jewish community today. Both arose as young people's congregations (Y.P.C.s) in the late 1940s when American-born South Philadelphians rebelled against the prevalent Orthodox institutions. Congregation Adath Shalom had a female rabbi in the 1980's and allowed women full participation in the service. Congregation Y.P.C. Shari Eli sponsored the only Jewish religious school in the neighborhood, a Sunday School with ten pupils at the time of my fieldwork, nine of whom had one non-Jewish parent. In short, through the matrix of the older immigrant culture, the threads of change and contemporary development emerge.

Home to a diverse assortment of institutions fostering the continuity of East European Jewish culture, South Philadelphia also included the adult branches and children's schools of organizations that advocated the perpetuation of Yiddish language and culture: the Workmen's Circle, the Jewish Nationalist Workers Alliance and, until it fell victim to Senator Joseph McCarthy's anticommunist crusade in the 1950's, the communist-leaning Jewish People's Fraternal Order of the International Workers Alliance.

Prominent leaders of the city's Jewish community are not residents of South Philadelphia today. This is in contrast to 1942–43, when a compendium of "eminent citizens and industrialists" included no fewer than eleven South Philadelphians (Malamut 1942–43: 109–74). However, the neighborhood can still boast of other Jewish newsmakers and professionals. For example, the shingles of a large number of Jewish medical professionals—physicians, osteopaths, dentists, podiatrists, and chiropractors—still hang from neighborhood houses.

Jewish residents active in politics report that as late as the 1960's the majority of the Democratic committee in South Philadelphia was Jewish. During my fieldwork I found some continuity of that political tradition. The 44-year-old city councilman from the eastern part of South Philadelphia, son of a former Republican judge, was Jewish. He resided on Eighth Street and was known for his "well-organized and responsive ward machinery, one of the most powerful in the city," as well as for an attempt to extort a million dollars from a developer of a proposed Center City retail complex (*Philadelphia Inquirer*, June 28, 1986, 6A). Many city leaders who no longer reside in South Philadelphia got their political start in the neighborhood. In former mayor Frank Rizzo's attempt at reelection, his 46-year-old campaign manager and his 49-year-old chief fund-raiser were Jews who grew up in the neighborhood. The father of the former had been a city councilman and ward leader for 40 years; the mother of the latter was an active Center member when I worked there (*Philadelphia Inquirer*, April 23, 1983, 1B).

In earlier times, the Jewish nature of the neighborhood was conveyed as much by the diversity of stores that spilled over onto street stands as by the synagogues and institutions, doctors and politicians. Jewish shopkeepers sold their wares throughout the area, but the concentrated shopping streets were Fourth Street (*di ferde*) in the north, and the zibete in the south. In contrast to the once boisterous hub of South Philadelphia Jewish immigrant life, today the *ferde*, though still largely Jewish-run, is very subdued, specializing in dry goods and surrounded by the gentrified Queen Village neighborhood.

The zibete, in contrast to the *ferde*, is in the core of the present-day South Philadelphia Jewish neighborhood, but it has experienced hard times. Advertisements in the Philadelphia edition of the daily *Forward* of 1946 promoted a variety of commercial enterprises on the zibete, and there was an active South Seventh Street Business Association. The stores sold furniture, children's clothing and toys, dresses, linens, delicatessen, lumber, and almost everything else. My acquaintances there remembered that in the 1940's there were four kosher butchers on a single block of the zibete. Many of the shopkeepers were immigrants; their children were not interested in maintaining the family business. The residents recalled with nostalgia the stores that stayed open past midnight—the *kvas* (cider) stand and the peanut store with the pinball machines—as well as the Saturday promenades, where they socialized and showed off their best. And they remembered the flowing Yiddish speech, the language of commerce on the zibete. The last blow to the vitality of this shopping street came in the late 1970's with the construction of one of Philadelphia's largest shopping centers just a few blocks away on Oregon Avenue, between Third and Fifth Streets (see Appendix A).

A walk today on the zibete between Porter Street and Snyder Avenue will reveal more boarded-up stores than functioning enterprises. An article in the January 28, 1985, *South Philadelphia Review East* reported on an attempt to revitalize business on the block of the zibete between Ritner and Porter Streets by sponsoring a flea market. It was spearheaded by a group of fourteen businesses, only four of them owned by Jews; other Jewish merchants on the block declined to participate. Once, this commercial street consisted entirely of businesses whose Jewish owners lived over their stores. During the years of my work in South Philadelphia, I myself witnessed the inevitable transformation: the closing of two delicatessens, one luncheonette, and other establishments that sold smoked fish, shoes, lingerie, wholesale groceries, hardware, and upholstery. The zibete is the most obvious locus of change in the neighborhood.

During the time I spent on the zibete, I heard many more complaints about the new residents on the street, immigrants from Southeast Asia, than about the developers and real estate agents who were responsible for the neighboring shopping center. It was difficult for neighborhood residents to recognize an absent agent as the villain responsible for change that they did not want.[5] Although Jewish family businesses would probably not have survived on the zibete, even in my short time in the neighborhood I sensed the rapid transfiguration of the shopping street. This predominant transformation in the neighborhood had a ripple effect on all activities.

Contrasting the present with the time when Jews constituted a majority in their neighborhood may give the impression that current Jewish activity is in a state of disintegration. On the contrary, the institutions that do function, including the Center, have a strong group of dedicated leaders and members and support an array of well-attended projects and events. It is interesting that, although the Jewish residents often have close relations

with their non-Jewish neighbors, facilitated by the proximity of their attached row houses, their organizational affiliations, both within and outside the neighborhood, are solely Jewish. Thus, the intensity of Jewish culture that is evident is far more vigorous than one would expect from a
community of its size.

Investigators of ethnic affairs and Jewish life in Philadelphia have almost
always overlooked the Jewish community in South Philadelphia, perhaps
because Jews constitute only a small fraction of the neighborhood population. However, given the fact that this is the oldest continuous Jewish community in Philadelphia, the neglect of the qualitative importance of the
continuity of this urban community is unfortunate. A dissertation on synagogue life in Philadelphia in 1958, which dealt with 50 synagogues and 327
individuals, wholly neglected South Philadelphia (Porter 1958). The Philadelphia Jewish population survey also ignored the area and imprecisely sub-
sumed South Philadelphia with Center City and University City (Yancey
and Goldstein 1985).

During my year in South Philadelphia, press coverage of contemporary
Jewish South Philadelphia was uneven and most often inadequate. Only
the somewhat unusual or sensational news made its way into the general
city papers—for example, the hundredth birthday celebration of a Center
member (*Philadelphia Inquirer*, January 12, 1985, 3B) and an arson incident
at the Center (*Philadelphia Daily News*, December 13, 1985). The citywide
weekly *Jewish Exponent*, despite its mandate to cover Jewish Philadelphia,
provided not much more coverage than the larger city papers. In fact, it
also reported on the same two events.[6] Very seldom did the papers run articles about local organizations. An exception was the feature on the Center's Yiddish discussion group. Except for three pieces describing food
collection in Center City and Elkins Park for the South Philadelphia Jewish poor, no other articles during the period of my fieldwork focused on
the lives of local residents.[7] This reveals a great deal about how the city's
Jewish community views South Philadelphia, as an area of poor residents
left behind and in need of a handout.

The *JCC Impact*, on the other hand, included articles on major events
at the Jewish centers throughout the city, including the South Philadelphia
Center. The nonsectarian *South Philadelphia Review East* contained weekly
notices contributed by the Center and the two Conservative synagogues,
but only rarely did Jewish individuals place birth, death, or other personal
notices in this tabloid. It ran an occasional feature article, such as a description of an intergenerational program at the Center with local elementary school pupils and a report on an award-winning artist who belonged
to the Center.[8] On the whole, however, newspaper readers in Philadelphia
might have been left with the impression that South Philadelphia consisted

of residents of Italian extraction, and that a local Jewish community was nonexistent.[9] In fact, the Jewish community in South Philadelphia is largely invisible today, both within the neighborhood and in the city at large, most likely because of its relatively small population, which is predominantly elderly.

When South Philadelphia is described by people not living in the area, it is most often depicted as a depressed, slum-like neighborhood. Few know that, despite considerable change, it has exhibited more stability and continuity than any other Philadelphia Jewish neighborhood over the past hundred years. Reports from the past forty years have focused on the neighborhood's decline: "We need to educate our people to help them live in a depressed area and to help in redeveloping it" (Greifer 1958). Similarly, "South Philadelphia, once a thriving Jewish community has few Jews there presently and a mere handful of synagogues. The few remaining are open at limited hours, mainly only for the Sabbath. These are attended by a few elderly men still living in South Philadelphia and some business men commercially active in the area" (*Jewish Times*, April 3, 1969, 1). And elsewhere: "Today's Jewish community exists as a ghost of its former self. Most of those who were financially, psychologically, and emotionally able to leave, did" (Rotman 1980: vii). For many years after these statements were written, South Philadelphia Jews have continued to live rich and varied lives, to be creative in the arts and politics, and to provide comfort and support for friends and family members. Certainly many of the residents were financially able to leave but chose not to. Their tenacity and loyalty to their community deserve to be noted.

The residential area is dominated by two-story brick row houses. Yisrul, a 95-year-old immigrant from Volhynia who worked as a carpenter, lived for 70 years on a street of such houses built just before World War I. Khatshe, a 100-year-old immigrant baker, moved into his house in 1918 at the age of 33, close to the only Orthodox shul that still functions, Congregation Shivtei Yeshuron–Heisiner–Ezras Israel, built in 1913. Roze was born at Fourth and Bainbridge Streets in the center of the original immigrant area. She attended the Jewish Day Nursery and Neighborhood Center. When she was very young, she and her family moved farther south but never left the neighborhood. Izzy spent all of his years in South Philadelphia. Born in the more northern section of the neighborhood, he and eight family members moved in 1924 to the building on the zibete that housed his luncheonette in the 1980's.

Feygl-Asye lived in South Philadelphia her entire life. She recalled: "I used to look at the whole neighborhood as I walked home, I liked it here, here were *mentshn* (real people); in other places, *hot men gehot fley in de nuz* (people were stuck up) . . . Here were the best Jews in all of Philadelphia."

Although South Philadelphia was changing and dynamic, it retained the image of the immigrant area, a place about which up-and-coming young Americans felt ashamed. Scorn for the old neighborhood was expressed, especially by residents who had moved to greener pastures. Tsipe-Khashe, who never left, remembered that in the 1930's South Philadelphia Jews were labeled poor. Her girlfriends were happy to move away because they feared that otherwise they would not find boys from proper backgrounds to marry. In reaction, those who remained developed a fierce neighborhood pride.

The ethnic groups of South Philadelphia resided on ethnically homogeneous streets: the Jews lived between Third and Eighth running in a north-south direction; the Italians lived to the west and the Irish and Polish immigrants to the east along the waterfront (Greifer 1948: 141, 322).[10] Ethnic relations were far from peaceful, and territory was often defended. Jews have tended to enjoy better relations with their Italian American neighbors than with other ethnic groups, and some have intermarried. By contrast, the most vivid memories of American-born Jewish residents are of the attacks by Irish American children on the way to school. Jews still live on those same streets, but mostly in the southern reaches of the area. In many instances only three or four Jewish families reside on blocks that were once completely Jewish (see Appendix A).

South Philadelphia's Jewish community today is minuscule in comparison with its size at the turn of the century. Nevertheless, the innovative dedication of the "young people's congregations," which started in South Philadelphia in the 1930's and 1940's, the flurry of activities at the Jewish war veterans groups and ladies auxiliary and at the local Jewish Masonic Square Club, and the day-to-day vibrancy of the senior center all speak to the continuity of an intense Jewish neighborhood tradition.

By stressing the present-day activity and attitudes of South Philadelphia Jews in this study, I do not mean to de-emphasize the diminution in both the size of this Jewish community and the diversity of its institutions. Like Gallaher and Padfield, who have contributed much to our understanding of small rural communities on the decline, I am committed to analyzing the factors that decrease "the character and intensity of psychocultural identification that the residents of a particular community feel for it" (Gallaher and Padfield, eds., 1980: 4). To be sure, South Philadelphia Jews are faced with a complex construction of neighborhood identity that is influenced simultaneously by the low prestige accorded to South Philadelphia by outsiders and the loyalty and familiarity fostered by continuity in faces and places known from childhood.

CHAPTER THREE

Izzy's Luncheonette
The Neighborhood's Center

It is Wednesday, October 17, 1984, and the door of Izzy's eating establishment, which is usually locked on Wednesdays, is opening and closing with regularity. The door is protected by a gate on the outside, ready to shield those on the inside from a potentially hostile eruption on the zibete. The main link to the outside street is a sliding window through which Izzy delivers coffee, pretzels, hot dogs, and an occasional sandwich to a teenager, neighboring store worker, or delivery person. Customers seated inside can catch only a glimpse of the passing trade on the street. From the outside, people see little of Izzy's store or his customers—just his chest moving across the window counter as he slices, squirts mustard, turns a fish cake in the broiler, or stirs sugar into coffee.

At first sight, a visitor might wonder just what kind of an establishment this is. Is it a private house, a warehouse, a clubhouse? The typical accoutrements of a modern commercial restaurant are nowhere present; there are only some small tables and chairs, dishes, glassware, a cash register. At best, the place is nondescript. The walls have not been painted for years, and worn linoleum covers the floors. Some sunlight manages to make its way in through the front window. Izzy is surrounded by the wooden counter along the front that supports his pretzel display; a coffee urn in the corner; a machine that turns hot dogs without cooking them, for the heating element does not work; and plastic margarine containers that hold relish and sliced onions. A kitchen toaster is next to the urn, and on the side wall is an old broiler that Izzy uses to heat food. In back of him are two old ice-cream freezers. They function as storage space for a few packages of supermarket bread, bagels, and three or four boxes of muffins and doughnuts. In a second room, a kitchen, Izzy boils water for tea in a pot on the stove and cooks hardboiled eggs. This kitchen probably looks much as it did around 1925, when Izzy and his eight family members moved into the house. Today, however, the staircase from the kitchen leads to an empty second floor.

Back in the eating room, customers sit at an old formica-topped kitchen table that stands against the ice-cream freezers, leaving room for four seats—four wooden chairs with peeling paint. A large old refrigerator holds the cans and bottles of soda to which customers help themselves. Next to it, in the far corner, is a small sink. There is another table along the side wall and, along the back wall, a container for refuse and a lone chair for another patron if all the chairs at the two tables are filled. Everything in this store is time-worn. And yet the atmosphere supports a lively level of conversation.

Though usually closed on Wednesdays, the store is open today because it will be closed for the next two days, the end of the sukkoth (*sukes*) holiday. I enter the store just before noon to find only one seated customer, a delivery truck operator who knows Izzy. Izzy is preparing a hot dog and coffee to hand through the window to the woman from next door who sells used clothing. He has on a white apron over his plaid shirt and gray trousers. Izzy smiles and we greet each other. As usual, he slurs his words; although he does not speak quickly, he does not articulate precisely. Izzy has finished at the window and turns around toward me. I sit down with my back to the wall and a full view of the room. At a right angle next to me is the other customer, whom I have also greeted.

Izzy starts to tell me about Yom Kippur (*yonkiper*) at his shul. The small building was filled upstairs and downstairs. For yizkor (the memorial service), he carried a Torah upstairs and led a separate service, even though there were speakers there connected to a microphone downstairs. His animated description reveals his joy at attracting a full house to shul, if only once a year. "Why only on yonkiper?" I ask. "Zey hobm meyre" (They are afraid), he answers in Yiddish. "They think, efsher" (They think, maybe). He thinks the Day of Atonement inspires fear in the hearts of South Philadelphia Jews. But it is not only Jews from South Philadelphia who come on yonkiper. Former residents from all over the Philadelphia area return home for this day of judgment and memorial. Izzy tells us that one fellow who lives in Cherry Hill, New Jersey, showed up in shul. Izzy had not

seen him for more than 40 years, when they played ball together at Southern High. Betty, a quiet-mannered woman, enters while we are talking and
seats herself at the second table next to the kitchen door.

Izzy asks us what we want. I tell him to serve Betty first, because I have
time. She orders a fish cake with mustard and relish and a cup of coffee. He
removes the frozen fish cake from its package and puts it on tinfoil in the
broiler, serves her the coffee, and says to me, "Rakhmiel, what can I get
you? I have fresh egg salad." I remember that I had the egg salad last week.
He prepares it freshly in the kitchen for each sandwich. Izzy can move
quickly, but he limps. He is always busy, so, in general, I had decided to
avoid making him walk back to the kitchen. That is also why I do not order
tea anymore. Before I have a chance to answer, a young woman comes up
to the window for six pretzels with mustard. After preparing those, he
turns Betty's fish cake over and turns to me. I say that I'll have a toasted
bagel and cream cheese and a glass of milk. He says, "How about a slice of
fresh tomato from my sister's garden?" I say, "That sounds great."

Izzy then tells me that he has invited the Sunday School children to shul
tomorrow night for the joyous celebration of Simchas Torah (*simkhes toyre*).
Now the driver is finishing up and says to Izzy, "How about making me a
hot dog for tomorrow when you'll be closed?" My toast pops up at the
same time that a small Vietnamese boy, who was playing near the front of
the store, walks in, with two quarters in the palm of his hand. Izzy asks
him what he wants, a fish cake? The boy nods. Izzy puts one more in the
broiler and prepares Betty's sandwich. He serves it on a napkin and tells
her, "Watch the fish cake. It's hot." The driver leaves after paying. The boy
comes in with more money for a soda. Soda in one hand, fish-cake sandwich in another, he is soon on the doorstep again. From the corner of my
eye I see the fish cake on the pavement. In a few minutes his father is in the
store, wearing shorts and a T-shirt, cursing and giving Izzy another 50 cents
for a second fish cake. I now remember that I had heard that the man who
runs the laundromat is white and is married to a Vietnamese woman. Izzy
tells him to watch his kids and not to curse. The father answers, "We are
two different kinds." I think that he is pointing to Izzy as a Jew. The father
sits the little boy down at the table and tells him to wait and eat at the table.

As this exchange takes place, a slight gray-haired man with glasses sits
down at the edge of the side table and orders a doughnut and coffee. Izzy
serves him but does not talk to him. The man keeps muttering to himself
about the weather. Then I hear him talking about the little boy in Yiddish,
but I cannot make out his words. I am surprised that he is Jewish. Betty
tells Izzy that her sister has just left for two weeks in Israel. Izzy is busy
again at the window. Betty and I talk about Israel, since I have spent time
there. While we talk, three women enter the store. Two sit at the table next

to me. Etta has short gold-colored hair and sits rather rigidly, with little facial expression and slow speech. Gloria, with short, jet-black hair, is overweight and talks quickly. They order a lox and cream cheese sandwich on pumpernickel and a fish cake. They are talking about the drugs their doctors have put them on, Thorazine and lithium. The third woman, Dot, seems much younger, probably in her early forties. She sits at the table with Betty and orders a lox sandwich, but I cannot hear or see her clearly. Betty and I continue to talk.

I order a second bagel with cream cheese. In walk two women, one in her late sixties, the other in her forties, a mother and daughter. They stand near the door and look at the doughnuts. They want to buy all that are left. When the younger one hears that each costs 25 cents, she says that at the supermarket they are 17 cents. Izzy retorts quickly and with irritation, "Who will pay for my electric bill?" They buy all the doughnuts and leave the store. Later, through the open doorway, I see the younger woman sitting on a chair in front of the hardware store across the street, eating her doughnuts. The mother returns and starts talking nonstop. She asks, "Is *sikes* (*sukes*) over yet?" I tell her there are two more days. She is surprised that I am Jewish and know of such things. Izzy says to her, "And how is he Jewish!"

When she leaves, Izzy says to Betty, "You know what they say in Yiddish, *vos ir felt, zol ikh hobm*." He then translates, "I should have what she's missing," and explains to Betty that she is not too bright. He says he feels sorry for the woman's daughter, who has a retarded son. Before I leave, he tells me that they have little money and no car, so he drove them to the cemetery and performed the service for the gravestone unveilings of the mother's two brothers. He advises people who have money to call the rabbi for such services.

This description summarizes some details of the setting, activity, and conversation during one and one-half hours at Izzy's hot dog stand. A few of these people became my frequent lunchmates. I discovered that Betty is a non-Jewish woman who has lived in the neighborhood for a long time with her husband and children and remembers quite well when the zibete was all Jewish. Her sister went to Israel with a church group. A few months later I met Dot again at Izzy's, and she remembered that I had visited Israel many times. We had not chatted initially, but when I met her the second time she told me that she grew up in South Philadelphia and went to Talmud Torah. Her mother still lived in the neighborhood, and she herself lived near the Center. Etta is 58 and spoke only Yiddish until age five. Her second husband is an Italian American, as is her friend Gloria, with whom she frequents Izzy's luncheonette.

Izzy's luncheonette and hot dog stand was a neighborhood center, a meeting place, a focal point for residents. Its nondescript nature allowed people to make of it what they needed at the time. Often the serving of food seemed incidental to the patrons' need for communication. It was an ideal spot for me to meet both Jewish and non-Jewish residents.

I realized from Izzy's account of yonkiper at the shul that South Philadelphia was still a place to come home to. Frequently, I met people who had returned to live or to visit, seeking nostalgia, yearning for the living remnant of an earlier period in their lives. South Philadelphia allowed them to maintain a tie with the past. Izzy himself symbolized the experience of those who stayed in the neighborhood. He was surrounded by mementos of his family life from 60 years earlier, when his family moved in.

The diversity of people who went to Izzy's place was striking. Did Jews feel more at home there than non-Jews? There is no question that I separate Izzy's customers along those lines—not old and young, not men and women, not those on drugs and those not. I do not know whether I was more sensitive to the Jewish/non-Jewish divide than the neighborhood people were. Is that the lens I always apply, or is that how I saw my task in South Philadelphia? Probably both. I went into a neighborhood that was predominantly non-Jewish, and I studied the Jews. I analyzed their contact with non-Jewish neighbors, but I did not inquire further into the laundromat owner's meaning when he told Izzy: "We are two different kinds." Most likely, he was reacting to Izzy's criticism of his child-rearing practices. He was discriminating between Izzy's quiet, gentle manner and his own style. But at the time I construed his words to mean "you are a Jew and I am not."

My Jewishness became a topic at Izzy's. I talked about my Jewish experiences there, and Izzy told people about me. I do not always do this, especially not in a new environment, but there, in the neighborhood, I wanted to be labeled an active, self-identifying Jew. When Izzy spoke Yiddish in the store, I wondered whether my presence there encouraged him to do so.

At Izzy's I met poor people and people who were not getting along well in the world because of mental illness, neglect, isolation, or a combination of factors. Izzy took it all in stride. He did not seem to pay attention to an old man's mutterings in Yiddish, although they were of great interest to me. I was surprised when Izzy retorted forcefully to the mother and daughter about the price of doughnuts. He was quick to express anger, yet he also showed great sympathy toward those less fortunate than he—indeed, he had taken the women to the cemetery without charging a fee. I realized that I needed to stop thinking of Izzy as the neighborhood guardian angel. In a neighborhood of contrasts he was also a man of contrasts.

Keeper of the Community

It is 11:00 A.M. and Izzy walks quickly up the zibete toward his lun-cheonette. He should be stationed at the window, selling pretzels, hot dogs, and water ice, but his wife, Sure, has replaced him at the store for a while, so that he can take some food to a sick neighbor a few blocks away.

Izzy has spent all of his 75 years in South Philadelphia. His parents, both from Pruzhan in Belorussia, were married in Philadelphia. After graduat-ing from Southern High, he worked at many occupations: running a fish and fruit store with his mother at the present location of his luncheonette, owning a wholesale fruit business, selling life insurance, selling soft ice cream, and manufacturing and wholesaling his own water ice, an occupa-tion usually associated with South Philadelphia Italians. For the past 40 years, Izzy and Sure, who came to America at age ten from Urinyen near Kaminets-Podolsk in Ukraine, have lived in a nicely furnished house with a large front porch a few blocks from the luncheonette. This is where their son and daughter grew up. Their children, grandchildren, and great-grandchildren live in Northeast Philadelphia.

Izzy is more active than many men half his age. He is the main orga-nizer of Y.P.C. Shari Eli synagogue, and although he received almost no formal Jewish education, he delivers a talk at his synagogue every Friday night and teaches each week at the Sunday school he organized. Izzy par-ticipated in severing the ties of his Young People's Congregation with the Orthodox Shaari Eliohu synagogue in the early 1950's. But up until 1983 when the Orthodox shul closed, whenever he had time he would wait with the few remaining male members, insisting that they have the re-quired ten men for a minyan. On Sundays, after teaching the six-year-olds, he might have to leave quickly to deliver a eulogy and prayer at the grave-stone unveiling of the great-grandfather of one of the children, in ex-change for a donation to the synagogue.

Sure did not go out to work after they were married, but helped with synagogue secretarial work and bookkeeping, as well as similar tasks for the *landsmanshaft*, the fraternal hometown organization originally formed by immigrants from Pruzhan (the Prushin-Shershow Beneficial Association), for which Izzy now serves as secretary. In addition, Izzy has been an of-ficer of the four different Masonic groups to which he belongs. But for the neighborhood people his station is the window of the store on the zibete, where he serves up a hot cup of coffee and a warm hello. The el-derly residents appreciate his concern and charity, his dedication to people and social groups. Izzy's strength and influence help to define this Jewish community.

Jewish South Philadelphia has two physical centers with an open door for community members to socialize and come for help, the Senior Center of the Jewish Community Centers of Philadelphia and Izzy's store. Even though Izzy does not belong to the senior center (in his case a statement of independence), he is a major organizational leader in Jewish South Philadelphia, heading both his synagogue and his Masonic group. But through the store and the countless neighborhood residents he meets and helps daily, he is the most influential leader in the community. He is an organization man, a kind and generous personality, devoted to those close to him, as well as to South Philadelphians in general, Jews and non-Jews alike. By observing and participating in the lunchtime culture of Izzy's center, his luncheonette, and by getting to know Izzy and his activities, I tried to uncover the heart of this Jewish community and to grasp how it is structured and nurtured. Izzy was a key to my study.

A Mutual Admiration Society

The better I got to know Izzy, the more I respected him and appreciated his interest in me. But it took time to get to know him. In 1982, other members of my fieldwork team first chanced upon the hot dog stand and started to talk. About a month later when, for the first time, I walked in with my class partner, Lisa, it was not convenient for Izzy to talk. It was 3:00 P.M. on a Friday, when he has to close the store and prepare to lead Friday-night services at his shul, to which, of course, he invited us. Several times in subsequent years, Izzy let me know that he had been very impressed by that first research group. Our group of four consisted of three women, two of whom were not Jewish (one was a French Canadian), and myself. Izzy occasionally asked me later if I ever heard from anyone in the original group, and to others in the store he would explain how interesting it was to meet students who were studying the neighborhood, "looking for a thesis." When he expressed his gratitude to me for his meeting such a group, I realized that we had probably broadened his horizons, making connections for him to other parts of the country, the academic world, and cultures foreign to South Philadelphia. Izzy had traveled some, but we certainly differed from his regular clientele.

I was the only member of the original group of graduate students to continue on in South Philadelphia. Izzy's place became my place, where I ate and hung out. Neighborhood people saw me there, even those just passing by the window. An active senior center volunteer asked me one day why I did not eat in the Center lunchroom. Before I could decide whether to confess that I wanted to meet people outside the Center, and that I did not want to be seen as a Center staff member, she told me she had thought it might be because I thought the lunchroom was not kosher (which it is), but then she saw me eating on the zibete. She knew Izzy well, she said, and I assumed she was telling me she now knew I ate in nonkosher restaurants. At the Center, people had come to associate me with yiddishkeit and religiosity. Izzy's luncheonette did not coincide with this image. I appreciated the feedback on how I was viewed. Altogether, the neighborhood people had a narrower picture of me than I would have liked to project, but I had become associated with the places I frequented and the people with whom I spent time.

Izzy viewed me differently as he got to know me. At first, I was part of a group of students. Later I spent more time with him, often when the two of us were alone in the store. He had observed that I ordered only dairy food, never the frozen fish cakes or the hot dogs, and he concluded that I kept kosher. When his synagogue planned a trip to Lakewood, New Jersey, he invited me and my wife to come along, with the enticement that we would enjoy the kosher meal at the hotel. One day when I ran out of snacks for the Center conversation group, I rushed out into the bad winter weather looking for kosher cookies, and Izzy directed me to the grocery store where I could find them. The Center's policy was to observe the Jewish dietary laws and I respected that. So, when Izzy turned to the woman in his store to state, referring to me, "And how is he Jewish!" he confirmed that the Center and neighborhood people thought of me as a young person dedicated to Jewish ways.

As time went on, I shared more and more about myself with Izzy and his wife. I felt close to them and wanted them to be my friends. With other people in the neighborhood, I had a more calculated agenda—that sharing something about myself would in turn draw something out about them for my study. With Izzy and Sure, I wanted a more equitable relationship, marked by mutual respect and closeness. I talked about my thyroid operation, the family of my wife, Hannah, and of course my research. With others, I always talked first about my project, but I rarely brought it up again. With Izzy I had so much interaction that I did not fear my project would become a barrier between us.

His responses confirmed this intuition. On one occasion, when I told Izzy I had received a fellowship to study Yiddish in South Philadelphia, he not only noted this piece of news enthusiastically, but soon thereafter began to tell people in the store. Several months later, I told Izzy over the phone that I thought it would benefit my studies to talk to Sure about Yiddish and South Philadelphia. Sure downplayed any contribution she could make to my study, but when we sat down to talk, she had many things to say about her life and the neighborhood. During that conversation, I told

Izzy and Sure that my research fellowship supported my work but that people at the Center had the mistaken notion that I was on staff. At the Center, I never went out of my way to make that point.

As we talked that day, both Izzy and Sure seemed to enjoy reminiscing about family and local history; there might not have been too many other listeners for such stories. Izzy was more talkative and dominating than in the store. Although Sure had much to say, afterward as I reviewed the tape recording, I worried that I had not paid enough attention to her.

Even though I was trying to maintain a low profile in the neighborhood, it felt good to hear from a congregant that Izzy spoke about me at shul Friday night, or to hear from a Center member that Izzy thought highly of me. Izzy, in addition, did not hesitate to tell me directly that he liked my commitment to Yiddish culture, encouraging me to "keep up the good work." I, in turn, let him know that I appreciated and admired his lifelong dedication to Jewish institutions and Jewish life, especially his work in the shul with young children. We became a kind of mutual admiration society, perhaps because we both were exceptions in our generations. In June, when an article appeared in two citywide Jewish publications about my Yiddish group at the Center, Izzy took pride in it. By then my year was winding down, and I did not object to such publicity. Izzy told me that they discussed the article at his Masonic meeting, and he brought it up again at the lodge meeting I attended. I was unsure exactly how to respond to him about the piece and finally said that some visibility for South Philadelphia was a good thing. Throughout my year of fieldwork, what Izzy thought of me was always very important.

The Center on the Zibete

It seemed that virtually everyone came to Izzy's. I had never before seen such an operation, and it took time to figure out its purpose and rules of behavior. In October 1982, on my first visit, I was shocked to see a woman eating food she had brought herself. Later, I realized that the absence of most familiar signs of commerce allowed me to view the place as private space, someone's living room or kitchen. I even thought for a while that Izzy fed the people for nothing and was surprised when a woman handed him 75 cents. Two years later, I was not taken aback when Izzy gave a woman a spoon for her yogurt and told her to wash it when she was finished. And, indeed, she did as he asked. Then there was the day when Izzy closed early to go to his sister-in-law's funeral. His words were telling: "I only opened because these people would have no place to go." Izzy's was a center for people who had no place to go, but I also met people there who led active lives.

One January day, when the senior center's boiler broke, I found Center regulars who normally did not go into his luncheonette sitting at Izzy's. Although the two places attracted some of the same people, they also had separate clienteles. At Izzy's I met congregants of Izzy's shul and members of the Masonic club—people I did not see at the Center. A friend of Izzy's, a Jewish man who used to play in a local string band associated with the Mummer's Parade (not a typical Jewish activity), asked me about the senior center. Although a lifelong resident of the neighborhood, he had never been there.

Neighborhood gossip came my way at Izzy's. I learned about the closing of the practice of a local Jewish doctor. I sat with a non-Jewish young man who knew about Izzy's shul because his sister converted and started attending services on Friday nights. It turned out that I knew his sister's Jewish husband and family. At Izzy's, Jews and non-Jews talked about Jewish affairs. One elderly woman even tried her Yiddish out on us: "Kik im un" (Look at him). More than anyplace else, Izzy's conveyed the Jewishness of the neighborhood. The zibete bespoke little of the neighborhood's Jewish character, but from inside Izzy's luncheonette the world was a different place.

My mission in the neighborhood was to study Yiddish, particularly the spoken language. For this, I needed opportunities to record the language. Yet at the beginning of November 1984 I remarked in my notes, "I cannot figure out the Yiddish angle to record in Izzy's store. No Yiddish is spoken." In fact, some Yiddish talk did occur, but there never was enough to warrant turning on the tape recorder. On one occasion, a customer told a Yiddish joke. "Do you understand?" he asked me. Izzy's response was quick: "Not only does he understand it, but his wife teaches Yiddish at the university and he studies it in South Philadelphia." Another time, Izzy himself turned to me and two other women when a little Vietnamese boy from next door walked in, to say teasingly: "Er iz a shlekhter" (He is bad). Once, Ezra, a Center member, entered the store and talked to me in Yiddish, before switching to his theatrical Yiddish performance style to humorously bless one of the Jewish women who was seated. I never knew for sure whether people spoke Yiddish in the store only because I was present.

Izzy's luncheonette—if not a Yiddish center, and if only in part a Jewish center—was for all a friendly gathering place. An older Jewish woman who used to live in the neighborhood before moving to Atlantic City periodically returned to spend the day holding court at Izzy's, knowing that her old friends would surely stop by. People constantly asked Izzy for help filling out forms. When Sure was ill with cancer during the summer and Izzy closed the luncheonette in order to help her, people continued to come over to his house to get help with their paperwork. Izzy always took care of those who needed him.

Izzy the Man

In contrast to the drabness of the store, Izzy and Sure's house was the most attractive one I saw in South Philadelphia—well designed, with white walls, paintings and wall hangings, carpet throughout, and an up-to-date kitchen. They raised their twin children here, when the block was inhabited only by Jews. Going by Izzy's estimate that the street was 40 percent Jewish even at the time I knew him, it must once have been the most Jewish block in the neighborhood. It was physically more attractive than most because all of the row houses had front porches. At the time of my fieldwork, the block was at the western edge of the Jewish neighborhood, next to the Italian area, but Izzy and Sure recalled that in years gone by Jewish people had lived farther west as well. Although many of the older Jews had grown fearful of crime in the neighborhood, Izzy always felt safe walking there at any hour and still thought of the neighborhood as a Jewish area.

Both of Izzy and Sure's children had settled in the northeast section of the city. They received their schooling in South Philadelphia, including their formal Jewish education, which consisted of Hebrew school at the Center. When that school was closed, they attended three days a week at the more distant Center City Y and went to Sunday school at Izzy's shul. My preconceptions of Jewish geographic and economic mobility led me to assume that the children who moved away from the neighborhood would represent a higher class and culture. Consequently, when I met Izzy and Sure's son-in-law one day at the store, I was surprised to find out that he was a prison guard, who spoke and dressed in a much rougher manner than his in-laws. Izzy had mentioned to me that he had a young great-grandchild who was the product of a mixed marriage. He did not approve of his daughter's attitude that children should choose whomever they wanted to marry. But Izzy and Sure kept up contact and visited every Sunday evening to spend time with the new baby.

Izzy distinguished himself as a leader in the Jewish community through his organizational skills and devotion, his luncheonette, and his charismatic personality, and also because he shared the values of the residents. Like most of his neighbors, Jewish and non-Jewish, Izzy voted for Ronald Reagan for president. Izzy approved of the effort by the business association on the zibete to attract new customers to the street, as long as it would not bring people from north of Snyder Avenue, meaning African Americans. On other occasions, I heard similar conservative, sometimes racist, views in South Philadelphia, not only in reference to African Americans but also about the most recent immigrants to the area, Southeast Asians.

Izzy did not have much leisure time, busy as he was with his organizations and his store, so I was surprised to find out at the end of March that he and Sure had spent five hours in Atlantic City one day. Free buses took the residents to the casinos to gamble; many went just to walk the board-walk and chat. During the eight days of Passover, Izzy closed his store so that he would not have to make the store kosher for the holiday. He told me that he was bored then. The store normally did not close, not even on the Sabbath, when Sure took over its operation while Izzy attended shul services. As was the case for most Jews in South Philadelphia devoted to religious life, Izzy did not strictly observe Jewish law. In part, his partici-pation in establishing the Young People's Congregation in the late 1940's was a revolt against the orthodoxy of the older generation.

Izzy and Sure, in contrast to many of the older people who required at-tention but could not reciprocate, were independent. When I sent them a Jewish New Year's card, they responded in turn. Izzy always thanked me for calling when I telephoned. When I sat down in the store with a staff mem-ber from the Center, he immediately asked her about herself. Further-more, he had a sense of humor—when I asked him once how Sure was, he replied that he would not trade her in for two eighteen-year-olds, because he was not sure what they would do to him. Yet he could also speak di-rectly about difficult matters in life. After Sure was diagnosed with stom-ach cancer in May, Izzy was depressed but was able to talk about the cancer, the chemotherapy, and his hope that the treatment would work. During the next few months, although Izzy kept the store closed in order to care for Sure, I was able to spend time with them. One of the last things I did in South Philadelphia that year was to visit Izzy and his family at home for a shiva call after Sure's death (shiva is the traditional seven-day mourning period following burial). Although several people I knew had died that year, this was the hardest loss for me. Izzy never opened his luncheonette again.

Izzy's Organizations

The most accessible of Izzy's organizations was of course his store, which was open in the daytime Monday, Tuesday, and Thursday through Sat-urday. All kinds of people came through the door, and all were treated to an alert, caring, 75-year-old man who had lived his life in the neighbor-hood. The area was home to many who needed help—the poor, the el-derly, the physically and mentally disabled, and those abandoned by fam-ily and friends. Alongside the needy were people functioning fully in society, working in the neighborhood and Center City, supporting fami-lies and friends, and active in a variety of recreational, social, and chari-table groups. More than anyone else that I met in the neighborhood, Izzy bridged the two groups. He took on more voluntary tasks than others, often in order to provide immediate relief to someone in need, but his main goal was to ensure the continuity of organizations and traditions. This man was an educator in the fullest sense of the word.

Within the local Jewish community, Izzy was the only person actively in contact with children, ensuring them a place in the community. Although elderly, he was doing what he had known how to do his whole life. His shul, in the 1940's, was the only one with a large school and youth group. Back then, together with some formally trained teachers, Izzy ran the Sunday school. The school was housed in the largest Orthodox shul then in the area, Shaari Eliohu. Izzy's synagogue was always organizationally separate from the old shul, but its name, Young People's Congregation Shari Eli, derived from the original shared address. According to Izzy, the Shaari Eliohu old-timers were jealous of what the Young People's Congregation had to offer. Finally, in 1952, the Conservative Y.P.C. shul took their children, then numbering 122, and bought a corner house in the neighborhood that became their new home. In the 1980's, after some years without a Sunday school, Izzy organized a new one to serve the ten or twelve children who participated. The other two functioning shuls provided no special activities for children. Izzy was the only neighborhood Jew who had the energy and vision to look toward the future.

The first time I met Izzy in October 1982, he invited my wife and me to visit the Sunday school. It seemed to me that he wanted the children and parents to see that outsiders and younger people were interested in the school and the Jewish activities of the children. Izzy read Bible stories to the students and taught them prayers in Hebrew and poems in English. His school aide, one of the Jewish mothers, supervised their drawing. And, importantly, the children put money in the *pushke* (charity box), teaching them the necessity of *tsdoke* (charity) in Jewish life. Seeing this, I was again reminded of my preconceptions and the need to vigilantly monitor them. For both here and at the senior center, I expected South Philadelphians to be recipients, not givers, of charity. And I expected Izzy's school to be different from contemporary synagogue schools. But in fact it was not so different. As in other communities, the teacher, Izzy, invited the children and their parents to come to synagogue, especially for Friday-night prayers. Some came regularly, others only when he had prepared them to participate in a special service.

One such occasion was a Purim celebration in February 1983. In the sanctuary, Izzy showed the children the megillah (the scroll containing the Book of Esther). They recited the *shma* (the prayer in each service that declares one's faith in God, that the Lord is one). Then each child came up to the front and recited a poem about Purim in English. The parents and one grandmother seated in the back pews clapped after each child performed, and the children ran back to kiss them after they had finished reciting. After this ritual, we all went up to the social hall, a large room with tables and a kitchen, to eat *homentashn* (Haman's pockets, pastries filled with fruit and poppy seeds). After the parents and children left, Izzy gave me a tour of the building. He was especially proud of the woodwork on the pews, carved by an Italian American neighbor, and he pointed out the burglar alarm system. The building seemed well kept and clean.

In December 1984, when my wife, Hannah, and I attended the children's Hanukkah party, the entire event took place in the social hall. I played games with the children, and at Izzy's request I talked to them a bit about the history of the Jews in South Philadelphia. Then I taught them a few songs in Yiddish. Izzy had been skeptical about their ability to learn the Yiddish songs. But the Yiddish was spelled out in Latin-lettered transcription and they did fine. In February 1985 we visited again, and I decided to teach the children Purim songs. A few months later, Izzy told me that for him it was the most important achievement of the year. In Izzy's school, I witnessed a moment in Jewish time, an attempt to keep the flame burning. I learned about what is vital for nurturance and continuity.

During our visit at Hanukkah, both Hannah and I talked with the parents. I welcomed this opportunity, because I rarely met this younger cohort during my days in the neighborhood, when most of them were at work. Most of the couples were composed of one Jewish and one non-Jewish member. They told us that they appreciated Izzy and the fact that the shul welcomed them. They wished there were more Jewish activities for their children. This comment caused my brain to spin—the Center, I thought, the old Jewish Educational Center for children and youth, which is empty every afternoon, could be turned back into a Jewish youth center. I drew the line at becoming a neighborhood reformer, but I mentioned the idea to Izzy and the Center staff. I had been to intergenerational programs at the Center with local elementary school pupils, had heard about weekend programs with suburban synagogue children, and thought that a visit by the local Sunday school children would be a big hit.

Izzy and the Center staff were enthusiastic about the idea of an intergenerational program, and they planned a Wednesday after-lunch program during Easter vacation. Izzy wanted the children to perform the Yiddish songs I had taught them for Hanukkah and Purim, so on the day of the program, the children, their parents, Izzy, and Sure went to the Center early to practice. Izzy planned an entire program of recitation. Somehow, I ended up mostly leading the adults in song, and the Yiddish songs were not featured. Nonetheless, the Center members and children had a wonderful time doing improvisational theater, an outgrowth of a current Center class.

I had hoped that this get-together would be an opportunity for members of Izzy's shul to come to the Center and that it would lead to increased contact between Jews in the neighborhood. Izzy had started announcing the program at shul in March, but on the day of the program only Izzy and Sure appeared. I still do not understand why the others would not attend and why so few ever attended programs at the Center. Annie, the Center's program director, had invited Izzy and Sure for lunch that day, but Izzy told me they would come after lunch. Eating in such a place was not for them. Like others in the neighborhood, they viewed the senior center as a place for the elderly to receive a handout and did not want any part of it. But both Izzy and Sure enjoyed themselves, and Izzy was treated like a guest of honor, bestowed with the public recognition he rarely received. Izzy told others about the intergenerational event. For him it was a special reward for his quiet labors.

Izzy was intent on maintaining Jewish life in the neighborhood, and the natural institution through which to do that was the shul. Although the congregation hired a rabbi, who came on Saturday, Izzy and his friends kept the institution functioning. He was the one with memories of the flurry of organized religious activity in the 1930's. He listed for me all the catering halls, community centers, and movie theaters that were converted into chapels for the high-holiday services. The orthodox Shaari Eliohu used to be the largest shul in the neighborhood, with a minyan at 5, 6, 7, and 8 o'clock. His Y.P.C. shul attracted three hundred people for holiday services and was forced to look for new quarters. At the end, though, the orthodox shul had only four members. At the Friday-night service at Izzy's Y.P.C. shul, refreshments were served as an inducement for attendees and children. Hannah and I become members of the shul as an expression of our support.

When I suggested to Izzy that the other Conservative shul, Adath Sholem, only a few blocks away, was a competitor, he disagreed. There were no competitors, he claimed. Indeed, when I described their activities, he responded positively, not critically or with animosity. Some members of the other shul, though, scoffed at Y.P.C. Shari Eli, calling it a social club with a rabbi who was not a real rabbi. But Izzy continued his work, oblivious to any derision.

Although the various Masonic groups to which Izzy belonged, all Jewish in membership, seemed somewhat exotic to me, I had heard about them from my father, who had been a mason. The lodge Izzy spoke of most frequently was that of Pruzhan-Shereshov, his parents' hometown in Belorussia, from which they had emigrated as teenagers. My grandparents had belonged to *landsmanshaftn*, but I did not know any American-born activists. Izzy was the secretary of the organization; he and Sure kept the books. How did this fit with his other communal work? Hannah had been researching these groups in New York and Israel and had uncovered a new generation of leaders, following in the footsteps of the immigrant founders. Here I was to know one firsthand. Although a few South Philadelphians were members of a lodge or *farein*, no one I met was a leader like Izzy.

The Prushin-Shershow Beneficial Association was a citywide group that must have had a large South Philadelphia membership in the past. At a meeting of the group in Northeast Philadelphia, I was introduced to members residing in South Philadelphia, and I was surprised to learn that I did not know every Jew in the neighborhood. The organization had about three hundred members and met monthly. They went on occasional excursions and held banquets, and the group still functioned as a mutual aid society, providing burial and death benefits. In fact, when Izzy and Sure went on vacation, they left behind a replacement contact with a list of undertakers and funeral parlors in case a member died while they were away.

Izzy and his brothers joined the organization when they were nineteen. At that time, in 1930, there were about a thousand members. In the 1980's very few young people belonged. Izzy claimed that the Belorussian town was wiped off the map during World War II, and the group had only a few survivors of the war. Actually, several of the members did not even know about the place, were related in no way to other members, and belonged only for the social connections and benefits. Izzy invited me to speak to his lodge, as he called it, and in June 1985 I did. After a dairy buffet meal, Izzy ran the meeting, delivering financial, cemetery, and business reports. The rabbi of Y.P.C. Shari Eli, who lived in Northeast Philadelphia, said some blessings and told some jokes. I sang and explained a funny but intricate Yiddish song, and Izzy's brother, a former Mummer in South Philadelphia, played the mandolin. The two of us constituted the entertainment. Izzy introduced me by telling about my work at the Center and with the children. Virtually everyone at the Pruzhaner meeting claimed to speak Yiddish, but I was the only one who actually did. Izzy insisted later that this was one of the best meetings in two or three years.

Izzy's allegiance to this lodge went back a generation—his parents were among the first members. He belonged to a cousins' club (an organized group of extended-family members that met regularly) as well. What was the meaning of these organizations to their members? For Izzy, in some small way, they preserved ties to his past.

Izzy, Yiddish, and 'A glezl tey'

Izzy's parents spoke only English in their business and at home, although his grandmother had used Yiddish. His parents limited their usage to when they did not want the children to understand, but Izzy managed to learn the language since it was spoken all around the neighborhood. Although I heard Izzy speak Yiddish, it was not until I recorded a conversation with him and Sure that I realized how fluent he was. Sure, who arrived from Ukraine at age ten, spoke her native dialect, but somewhat haltingly. After coming to America, she and her siblings stopped speaking Yiddish except to their mother. In fact, one of Sure's sisters-in-law learned Yiddish specifically to communicate with Sure's mother. In contrast, Izzy spoke Yiddish regularly with his customers. Their children, they say, did not learn Yiddish and did not want to.

Izzy was delighted to be able to speak Yiddish and to have the opportunity to pass it on to another generation. I witnessed the glee with which he reacted to the Sunday school children's renditions of Yiddish songs. He told me of a phone call from a man who could speak only Hebrew and Yiddish (see Chapter 11). The phone conversation ended with an invitation for more talk: "Kum tsu un mir'n hobn a glezl tey un a shtikl keyk un mir veln redn" (Come over and we'll have a glass of tea and a piece of cake, and we'll talk). The glass of tea symbolized the old way of talking and the chance to get to know someone better. Talking was a vital activity in South Philadelphia, and the neighborhood residents savored circumstances that fostered lively conversation, especially in Yiddish.

CHAPTER FOUR

'A Gleyzele Tey' (A Glass of Tea)
A Yiddish Conversation Group

Each Friday morning at 10:30 A.M. the Sunshine Room at the Center was readied for A gleyzele tey, our weekly Yiddish conversation group. The maintenance person at the Center set up three contiguous tables and fourteen folding metal chairs around the table, together with a row of four chairs on the outside of the circle. As the group grew, a few extra chairs were added to the periphery of the circle, and later an additional table that allowed four more participants to sit. During the last three months that the group convened, increased attendance necessitated a move upstairs to the men's lounge. There the same seating format with larger tables and additional chairs at the periphery made room for the growing group, which numbered as many as 37 participants. In addition to setting up the tables and chairs, the maintenance person set an electric urn to boil water and laid out instant coffee, tea bags, cups, napkins, sugar, and powdered creamer.

I made additional arrangements. I supplemented the beverage supplies with concentrated lemon juice and occasionally sugar cubes. Each week I also brought kosher cookies of different varieties, enough so that each participant could have a few. I divided the cookies among five plates, which I spaced evenly around the table. The kosher label was in accordance with the Center's policy of serving only food prepared under kosher supervision. I also connected the flat-shaped microphones and placed them on the table at two points equidistant from the ends. I adjusted the settings on the tape

recorder and placed it on the table in front of my seat. All of these preparations were completed before any participants entered the room.

I designed the physical structure of the meeting with the intention of establishing a warm, inviting atmosphere. Those sitting in the circle had eye
contact with each other and could be seen and heard when they spoke. The
tea and cookies enhanced the informal, social nature of the meeting. For
many elderly people, any food item is treated as a topic of conversation and
is an enticement to participate. In Europe and in American Jewish immigrant life, social conversation and entertaining at home were invariably accompanied by a glass of tea, so the name A gleyzele tey evoked thoughts of
comfort and friends. At the Center, the glass was replaced by a styrofoam
cup, but the custom served as a focal point for the assemblage of people,
most of whom had many other opportunities to talk with each other.

How did these Yiddish conversation sessions fit in with the other activities at the Center? There were not many regularly scheduled groups or
classes. Two social clubs that charged dues met weekly after lunch to hear
a speaker or entertainer and to celebrate special events. During much of
the year a group of single older women was convened by the supervisor of
the social workers to discuss issues of common interest. One member,
Gedalye, taught a small group of members how to read and write Yiddish
every Tuesday morning. In addition, courses in such things as creative writing, improvisational theater, and exotic cultures were offered.

Even though I did not talk much during the sessions, I was recognized
as the convener, especially because I was younger than the participants and
not a Center member. I did not consider the Gleyzele tey a class, but members did refer to it as such and to me as the teacher. I did not want to be
viewed as an expert in Yiddish who could teach people how to talk. My intention was to help create a comfortable atmosphere in which unencum-
bered conversation would be the central activity. My main purpose was to
observe. Part of the reason the participants called our meetings a class was
the lack of other terms for regularly scheduled group activities facilitated
by Center staff. Although they turned to me only seldom for information
about Yiddish, I, like a teacher, was viewed as the authority who initiated
the group and made sure the proceedings were organized and started and
finished on time. At first, I did not do even those things, but later I had to
or too many satellite conversations took place, the noise level rose, and participants stopped attending sessions because of the disorder.

Attendance

From the beginning, the participants said that the Gleyzele tey meetings
were different from other Center activities. They told Center staff members

that they enjoyed the sessions and that they felt at home in them. Poor attendance was a problem in the Center's other morning classes, but not in A gleyzele tey. A core group attended regularly throughout the year. Starting at the end of April, when the weather improved, attendance at the Center increased in general, since illness among the elderly was greater in the winter. In June, the *Jewish Exponent* printed an article about the Gleyzele tey group, and attendance increased again; Center members, other neighborhood Jews, and even a few people from other sections of the city started coming. Some came only occasionally, and others came primarily for the lunch that followed; non-Jewish members who did not understand any Yiddish came a few times for general sociability or for free tea and cookies.

The average size of the group was sixteen during the first seven months and 27 during the last four months. The number of people attending was highest during the last six sessions, an average of 33. Although the dynamics of the discussions were colored by the individuals who attended—by their backgrounds and ways of speaking Yiddish—and by the nature of the long-term relationships among them, the number of people who participated most clearly determined the opportunities for communication. The group functioned best when there were fewer than seventeen participants. During the last few sessions, the number of ongoing conversations peripheral to the main one distracted many of the participants, as did the number of people entering and leaving during the session. The noise level became too great for some, and they left the room. Impaired hearing was the biggest barrier to social interaction in the group; in the smaller room, with fewer participants, members found it easier to hear the speakers. Their ability to hear what was being said was reflected in their degree of participation and the speed of their responses. I had to intervene more often to police unruliness as the size of the group increased.

In many respects, the Gleyzele tey core participants were representative of the Jewish population of South Philadelphia, although only a fraction of the Jewish population was affiliated with the Center. From my investigation of the community it became clear that, in addition to the shut-ins who did not leave their houses, a large group of independent seniors did not join because they viewed Center members as belonging to a lower socioeconomic class, as people who needed social services and a subsidized meal, who did not have a full life at home, and who were dependent on an institution for friendship and activity. I found this perception to be inaccurate.

Who were the group members? Leye fell somewhere between the independents and the members who spent five days a week at the Center. She attended the Gleyzele tey group, the Yiddish class, a social club, and the knitting class. She walked to the Center, though she could have ridden in the Center van. Her husband, Yankl A., still helped people in the neighborhood with their plumbing problems. He participated in only five Gleyzele tey sessions.

Khatshe was an older immigrant who came to the Center daily. Rivke A. and Rivke B., in their mid-seventies, immigrated to America as teenagers; they traveled to the Center on public buses two days a week from neighboring Center City. Rivke A. served as a volunteer hostess in the Center's dining hall. Shmiel-Leyb and Ester-Sosye were among the few Jews remaining in Southwest Philadelphia, and they traveled to the Center daily by public bus, about a one-hour trip. Then in their mid-eighties, they originally came to South Philadelphia as young children from Bessarabia and Ukraine. American-born Menakhem, a retired dentist, and his wife Basye B., also lived in a non-Jewish neighborhood, Germantown, and drove to the Center in their car. Yankl B. had spent his whole life in South Philadelphia and lived alone above his father's former clothing store on the zibete. A kind of lost soul and free spirit who dressed shabbily and disrupted many Center get-togethers, Yankl B. attended most Gleyzele tey sessions and always had something to say. Blumke and Feyge attended religiously, but they mostly just listened. Feyge was generally quiet at the Center, but Blumke was boisterous and constantly joking. Although she hardly ever joined the Yiddish conversations, Blumke constantly remarked that she looked forward to Friday mornings. Rounding out the regular core were lifelong South Philadelphian Yiddish speakers Tsipe-Khashe, Itke, Roze, and Feygl-Asye.

Some spoke Yiddish often, others seldom. Some actively attended synagogue, others not at all. They had held different jobs and ranged from being quite wealthy to needing public assistance. The group consisted mainly of women.

One Day in the Life of A gleyzele tey

Friday, May 26, 1985, 10:00 A.M.

I enter the main door of the Center. Off the foyer to the right is the men's lounge. This is the first time the Yiddish conversation group will be convening at this location. The room provides ample space and adequate air-conditioning for the summer months. The walls are painted blue. The room is dark and cold. The maintenance staff has assembled the tables and chairs, and hot water is boiling in the urn. I quickly take out the microphones and tape recorder and place them in their proper positions. I had discovered that since the table is a rectangle, I should sit at the center of one of the long sides, rather than at the head, in order to be as close as possible to all the participants. I divide up the cookies.

Yankl B. arrives at 10:15. He only has two blocks to walk. When he arrives early I know that he has not eaten breakfast. I pour him a cup of coffee and place a plate of cookies at a seat at the corner of the table nearest the urn. In Yiddish we discuss the young man who administers the activities of Yankl B.'s Orthodox shul. Yankl B. criticizes him for sometimes setting everything up on Saturday for the Sabbath services and then going off to work instead of staying to pray. Yankl B. does not care for the man's nontraditional behavior. I dispute Yankl B., saying he should feel grateful that the young man keeps the shul going. I point out that it is difficult to be observant in South Philadelphia today. Yankl B. does not accept that.

R. P.: Se volt im geven zeyer shver. (It would be very hard for him.)
Y. B.: Gunisht shver. (Not hard at all.)

Itke comes in five minutes later, having walked the two blocks from her house. I greet her, "Gut morgn" (Good morning). Yankl B. had just been in the hospital for a few days because of problems with his feet, and Itke says to him, "How do you feel, Jack?" He answers her, "You want to know?" and proceeds to give her a hard time. I ask her, "Tsi vilt ir epes trinken?" (Do you want to drink something?) and she says, "Coffee." Yankl B. makes an issue of Itke's custom of lighting Sabbath candles. Itke responds that it is nothing special, but that the older women at the Center are surprised and view her as old-fashioned.

Y. B.: Dayne shvester bentshn lekht? (Your sisters bless candles?)
I.: YE. (YEAH.)
Y. B.: Take? (Really?)
I.: Vus aza, vus aza greyse kunst tsu bentshn likht? (What's so, what's such a great trick to bless candles?)
Y. B.: Si nit ken kinst, but e— (It's not a trick, but e—)
I.: Mir zaynen, mir kimen fun azelkhe eltern. Mayn mame hot gebentsht likht un mir bentshn likht. (We are, we come from that kind of parents. My mother blessed candles and we bless candles.)
Y. B.: Bay mirz a greyse zakh bekoz e— (For me it's a big thing because e—)
I.: He always makes an issue of I bentsh likht (bless candles), like it was e—
R. P.: He's impressed, he's impressed.
Y. B.: No, ir farshteyt— (No, you understand—)
R. P.: Vayl er zikht tsvishn di mentshn du o un er gefint az zeyer veynik kenen dos tien. (Because he searches among the people here and he finds that very few can do that.)

I.: Well, a lot of di eltere, ikh bin a sakh yinger fin zey. (Well, a lot of the older, I am a lot younger than them.)

R. P.: No, zey tien, zey fargesn. (No, they do, they forget.)

I.: Ye, but zey zugn tsu mir, di tist dokh (?), ikh halt a peysakh vi mayn mame hot geton (Yeah, but they say to me, you are still doing (?), I keep Passover like my mother did), and they look at me a young woman like you? Oh, you're not modern. I say so—so be it.

But now Yankl B. comes to his main point. It is not that he is not truly impressed by Itke's religiosity. At the Friday afternoon cafe at the Center and at celebrations she is a conspicuous dancer, gyrating at the center of the dance floor. He is perplexed by the contrast of this ostentatious behavior and her observance of traditional customs and says what's on his mind.

Y. B.: Azey vi di tonst, vi ke men bentshn lekht in gontsn mitn pu—mitn mugn in droysn? (The way that you dance, how can you bless candles completely with your p—with your stomach exposed?)

I.: With the WHAT?

Y. B.: Mit de—mit der pipik in droysn. (With yo—, with your bellybutton sticking out.)

I.: Mit der PIPIK? (With my BELLYBUTTON?) You never saw my pipik (bellybutton)!

Y. B.: Well you shake it, don't you baby?

I.: That's it.

Itke then addresses me in English, telling me that Yankl B. only likes to tease her. He has known her since she was eight, when her mother would take her into Yankl B.'s father's store. According to Itke, Yankl B. was in love with her when she was ten. She switches to Yiddish and says that she does what her mother did. But Yankl B. then criticizes her for not having children, and Itke tells him he never even got married because no one wanted him. Her retort to Yankl B. is, "Verst sheyn eyver butl" (You're already becoming senile).

Itke had asked me the day before to identify some Yiddish words that her sister had asked about, and she, Yankl B., and I talk about Yiddish words. Yankl B. remembers the saying, "Er vakst vi ropene" or "kropene" and asks if I know it. He does not know what *ropene* means but knows the saying means "to grow without help, wild, automatically."[1] Then, interestingly, he says that he teaches me and I teach him. I wonder to myself what I teach him.

It is 10:30; more people enter. Leye is first. I go downstairs to remind people that we are meeting upstairs. The first van load arrives, including Khatshe. Itke and Yankl B., who were speaking Yiddish, address Khatshe in English, but he does not hear them. Shmiel-Leyb and Ester-Sosye arrive and she says to him, "Vi geysti zitsn, Saem?" (Where are you going to sit, Sam?) Yankl B. and Itke converse in Yiddish with Khatshe, Yankl B. asking Khatshe for the meaning of *ropene* and explaining that the saying means "Er vakst aleyn" (It grows without aid). Itke recalls a saying about growth, "vakst vi a tsibele mit de kop in drerd" (grows like an onion with its head in the ground).

Roze comes in in her wheelchair and says good morning to Ester-Sosye in English. Ester-Sosye and Leye converse in English. Khatshe does not know the word *ropene*, and Itke pronounces that Yankl B. "makht zayn eygene shprakh" (creates his own language). Itke offers Roze some coffee. Surele arrives and starts talking to Leye in English and sits down next to her. Rivke A. and Rivke B. enter together, speaking to each other sometimes in English, sometimes in Yiddish. Yankl B. has been annoying Itke and touching her. She threatens him, "If you hit me once more, so help me God, you're gonna feel it." I return from downstairs and serve those people that do not yet have tea or coffee. Roze and the two Rivkes are discussing Roze's health. Roze tells them, "Vi se kimt azey geyt es avek" (Just as it comes on, so it goes away). Khatshe tells Rivke A. that the knishes she gave him yesterday were very good. Yankl B. asks where they are. Rivke A. says, "Ikh makh mayn eygene resipi" (I make my own recipe), whereupon Roze comments, "Zi vet ufefenen a restorant, zol zi nor zayn gezint" (She will open up a restaurant, she should only be well).

I ask, "Vos iz gevorn mit Blumke? Vu iz Blumke haynt?" (What happened to Blumke? Where is Blumke today?) "You saw her already? You saw Lilly?" Roze answers, "Lilly will be here. She's on the second shift." Gershon says he wants mild tea. I respond "shvakh" (weak). Leye asks Rivke B., "Vus tien di kinder?" (How are the kids doing?) Noise from conversation emanates from all sides of the table. Itke complains about Yankl B., "Er iz meshuge af teyt" (He is dead crazy). Roze tells the two Rivkes, "You can never plan anything, a mentsh trakht un got lakht" (man proposes and God disposes). Itke finally yells over to Roze that her drink is ready. Roze says to her, "Kim" (Come), whereupon Itke responds, "Kum," and they alternately banter *kim* and *kum* a few times. Itke says, "I'm a Litvak,[2] what can I tell you? Ikh zog kum aher nit kim aher" (I say *kum aher* [come here] not *kim aher*). I ask Shmiel-Leyb if he wants a drink, and he says "kove" (coffee). The buzz of talk and laughter fills the room, English in one corner, the Yiddish of Roze and the two Rivkes in another.

Ezra arrives, and since he usually does not stay long, I ask him, "Ezra, ir vilt zitsn mit undz a bisl?" (Ezra, do you want to sit with us a little?) He answers, "Yes, a *bisl* but don't give me a *file shisl* (whole bowl)," the rhyme from a familiar proverb. I ask Ezra in Yiddish if he wants tea, with or without lemon. He comments, "Zey vus far a tayer yingl" (Look what a dear boy). He takes one look at Yankl B.'s charred and ragged pants and immediately switches to English, "Hey, what happened to your pants?" "I burned it," Yankl B. responds. "You burned it, crazy," says Ezra. Gershon explains, "He backed up on the gas range." And Yankl B. adds, "The chair is burned too." Ezra starts to sing in Yiddish, "A brivele shrab ikh tsi man momen" (I write a little letter to my mother), one of the tunes he remembers from his youth when he acted on the Yiddish stage. Itke pays no attention to Ezra's singing and says to him, pointing to Yankl B., "Nem im avek" (Take him away). She turns to Yankl B. and tells him, "You look like mayne tsures af der linker zayt" (very bad; literally, my troubles on the left side). I announce, "Mir veln bald onheybm" (We will start right away). I remark that Feygl-Asye, who lives across the street, has not yet arrived. Ester A. enters the room, and I ask her, "Ken ikh aykh derlangen epes tsu trinken?" (Can I serve you something to drink?) She answers, "I'll help myself, thank you."

I start the discussions by asking, "Vozhe hert zekh? Tsi hot emetser indz gebrakht epes nayes haynt?" (What's new? Did anyone bring us some news today?) Feygl-Asye comes in out of breath. I ask the group, "Vos makhn indzer(e) kranke layt? Tsi zenen ale gevorn gezint?" (How are our sick people? Has everyone become healthy?) Rivke A. says, "A bisele beser" (A little better). Rivke B. volunteers, "Man zin fort in Israeyel" (My son is traveling to Israel). The discussion takes off from there. Twenty-four people attend the session, twenty around the table and four more in a row of chairs near the door. Seven of the members attending do not participate in the conversation, including Blumke and Feyge.

Rivke B. reports on the visit of her son's in-laws, who are wealthy people who live in Switzerland and Israel. She is glad that they have left already, without having to eat in her apartment, since she does not keep kosher and they are very observant. She recalls that at her son's wedding, the in-laws seemed very dissatisfied but little by little have accepted Rivke's family. "So, ba der khosene hob ikh gezeyn iz zi geveyn epes azoy farzorgt, azoy vi nit a khosene nor bay a fyunere" (So, at the wedding I saw that she was so worried, not like at a wedding, but at a funeral). After describing who had attended the wedding from her family, and how she now reminded her in-laws of their initial displeasure, and they now laugh, Rivke reconsiders how she might have felt if she was in their place, explaining in English, "Maybe I would be the same way." She continues in Yiddish, "Efsher volt ikh ekh azoy gefilt, ven se kimt epes a meydl vus ikh veys nit un vus, plitsling e—hobm zey khosene" (Maybe I would have felt the same way, when some kind of girl I didn't know shows up and that, suddenly e—they get married).

Rivke B.'s son's in-laws are Lubavitcher Hasidim, and Roze asks what that means. I explain what this sect is and something about their history and beliefs. Rivke A. recounts then that some Lubavitcher Hasidim had once come to the Center and behaved very poorly, saying things that were insulting to non-Jews. She felt this was improper because the Center membership consists of both Jews and non-Jews, and that they should have been more sensitive to the situation.

Zey zanen amul du gekimen. In zey hobm zekh nisht sheyn beheyvd, veys dokh, se es iz a gemiks se du e—e—kristlekhe ekh en zeym zekh tseret vus hot zikh nisht gefit, in ze hobm zekh tsetontst. I—bin ikh tse(ge)gan onest tse god Fraeni e tel yuw, zug ikh, Fraeni beter red tsu zey bekoz svet vern du, met zekh unfangen faytn eyns mitn tsveytn. Bekoz siz a gemikst folk, in a di kimst bitvin a gemikst folk darfste visn vus tse redn darfst zekh nit ifheybm oyvn hoykh, in dem ondern aruplozn (?) der erd. Its not rayt.

They came here once. And they didn't behave well, you know, th—it is a mix there are e—e—Christians here also and they said things that were not fitting, and they did dancing. I—so I went honest to God Franny will tell you, and I said, Franny you'd better speak to them because it will develop here, they'll start to fight with one another. Because it's a mixed crowd, and when you come among a mixed crowd you have to know what to say you must not raise yourself up to the heavens, and degrade the other person (?) into the ground. It's not right.

Roze continues with a story about seeing Hasidim in New York and being told that they are loan sharks. Itke says, not just in New York, but they have a center in Northeast Philadelphia. I ask if they remember Hasidim in South Philadelphia. Yankl B. mentions Rabbi Isaacson's name. Rivke A. says she didn't see them in Russia, but she remembers them from Warsaw on her way to America. Rivke B. calls them "greyse ganuvim" (big thieves) and Roze agrees, "Ye, ye" (Yeah, yeah).

Rivke A. then retells a narrative she has told in a previous session, about how Rabbi Isaacson's wife did not want to pay for a printing job that Rivke A.'s son had done for him. The *rebitsin* (rabbi's wife) said, "Got vet batsuln" (God will pay). Rivke A. ends by implying that all Hasidim are dishonest. She goes on to tell about the rabbi's daughter's wedding. I ask about the rabbi's son, about whom I had heard some rumors in the neighborhood. Rivke A. expounds on his character too and tells that her grandchild once went to play baseball at a game organized by the rabbi's son but ran away when he saw the rabbi's garb. While Rivke A. delivers her cluster of narratives, people in the room talk to each other from time to time, and many laugh at her description of the Hasidic rabbi playing baseball in his kapote (long black coat) and *shtrayml* (traditional fur hat with a wide brim). Yankl B. retorts that it's not so bad, "Vus iz aza min geferlekhe manse?" (Why is this such an outlandish story?) He tells of the priests playing base-ball in their official garb at Boys' Town. Rivke A. tries to respond, but Yankl B. interrupts, "Vart, di redst a sakh" (Wait, you talk a lot) and "God damn it." He does not let her speak and tells her to wait a minute. A general commotion arises in the room and Rivke A. tries again to answer Yankl B., but to no avail. I intercede. "Eyn minit, me vil zikh nisht tsekrign" (Wait a minute, we don't want to start a fight).

I tell Yankl B. he may talk, but no yelling. People continue to talk as Yankl B. speaks. He argues that Rivke A. does not know what went on in this neighborhood because she lived on Third Street, out of the area. Yankl B. does, however, agree that Rabbi Isaacson was a "moneyman." Rivke A. tries to talk again, but Yankl B. shuts her up. In the group people continue to talk to each other. I defend Rivke A., telling Yankl B. that al-though she did not live in the neighborhood, she did business with the rabbi, and her parents continued to live in the neighborhood. Yankl B. wants to talk and jokingly tells Rivke A. she should let him talk because he is older than she is. A commotion arises from the side conversations when Yankl B. talks, and goes on during Rivke A.'s next narrative about the rabbi. Yankl B. is surprised by the strong language Rivke used in talking to the rabbi. Rivke A. ends, "Yes I did, bekoz er nisht gevin ken mentsh" (be-cause he wasn't a good human being).

The many private conversations continue while Yankl B. and Rivke A. talk about the rabbi. I declare, "Mir viln tsigeyn tse a nayer teme, vayl ikh meyn az mir hobm oysgeshept Raebay Ayzikson" (Let's go on to a new topic, because I think we've exhausted Rabbi Isaacson). Rivke A. laughs. Ezra asks then, "Who knew Rabbi Pupko?" A few people answer that they did and a buzz starts throughout the room. Itke asks us to change the topic. I remember that we have already heard this story and that it created strife, so I say we don't want to repeat ourselves. Feygl-Asye and Roze agree. Ester A. recalls in Yiddish that years ago at home there was a "*pishke*" (*pushke*, charity box) and Hasidim came to collect the money. Roze retorts in English that they put it in their pocket, whereupon Feygl-Asye objects and says, "No, no, that's, that's how they got Palestine." The noise in the room increases again.

I try to quiet the crowd down by raising my voice. They listen, and I in-troduce a new topic, the holiday Shavuoth (*shvues*), which was to take place that weekend. I ask them to describe what they remember about cele-brating the holiday at home. Several people answer "*milkhiks*" (milchigs, dairy food), which is eaten on the holiday, and many conversations start at once. I recognize Khatshe, but Ezra pleads, "Will you give me a chance to talk, too?" I reply, "No, eyn minit" (one minute). Ezra is dissatisfied, "Eyn minit? Ikh vart she(n) tsen minit" (I'm waiting already ten minutes). Yankl says, "Sha, sha" (Quiet, quiet) to quiet the crowd, and I plead, "Mentshn, mentshn!" (People, people!) I say first Khatshe will speak and then Ezra. Khatshe says something about dairy food. Then Itke, Ester A., Yankl B., and I talk about the meaning of the holiday.

Ezra starts to speak about Moses breaking the tablets, then proceeds to talk about his own belief in the Jewish religion, about the Sabbath being the holiest day, and about being caught by Rabbi Pupko when he was smoking on Yom Kippur on the street. We have heard this story before. Ezra criticizes the neighborhood residents who attend synagogue and then go back to running their businesses on the Sabbath. He questions whether they are Jews. Itke and Feygl-Asye object. From previous experience I know that certain individuals become very angry when statements are made criticizing the Jewish religion and the religiosity of members. People get very passionate about this topic. I say,

Du o kritikern mir nisht ken mentshn, mir zugn zey nisht vi zikh tse firn, mir raysn nisht arop. Iz vil—viln mir mer nisht redn vegn dem. (Here we don't criticize anyone, we don't tell them how to behave, we don't cut people down. So let's not speak about this anymore.)

But Ezra does not heed me and criticizes a man from Snyder Avenue who attends synagogue. He says these are not Jews, and I respond that we do not want to judge. Itke again begs that we change the topic.

I ask if anyone has more to say about *shvues*. Shmiel-Leyb mentions decorating the house with flowers. I make a joke about Blumke, who sits next to me, and *blumen* (flowers), which we should bring into our homes. Ezra starts to explain that he believes in one God, nature. Feygl-Asye is angry, "Here we go again." Ezra tells of the slaughter of Jews that he observed during the pogroms of Petlura in Ukraine after World War I, and declares that that is why he lost his faith. Itke speaks angrily about Jews who ridicule themselves, and she gets up to leave. In English, she asks Feygl-Asye, next to her, if she is staying. Itke walks out, but Feygl-Asye stays. Ezra asks, "Vi iz indzer got?" (Where is our God?) and Yankl B. answers, "Er iz du" (He is here). Ezra continues, but people do not listen, they talk. Ezra, now in animated fashion, tells of the pogroms and their aftermath. Roze tells Rivke B. that Ezra is a wonderful person because he cares for his sick wife.

I try to make peace and recognize both sides, saying that what Ezra told us is true because he lived through it, but that some people reacted by losing their faith and others by becoming more religious. Feygl-Asye interprets such events as a test of God, and Yankl B. agrees. Feygl-Asye says,

"Me tur nit zindikn kign im (We are not allowed to sin against him), no matter what." Feygl-Asye becomes excited and shows her emotional involvement by switching to a high-pitched voice that changes volume abruptly. Her mother recently died, and she views Ezra's declaration as an attack on her own faith. Everyone is silent as she recounts how her mother's survival from age 48 to 91 was a defiance of medical knowledge. She raises her voice when she declares, "Ikh GLEYB in got" (I BELIEVE in God). The group has been spellbound, responding when Feygl-Asye finishes with a buzz of comments, including Roze's "Me darf gleybm" (One has to believe) (see complete text of this narrative in Appendix D).

I then comment that we have spoken earlier about believing in God and that we cannot force anyone to believe; we will no longer talk about who is or is not observant, and we will not insult people, whether they are observant or not. We talk further about *shvues* and yizkor. I then introduce a new topic: how we raise boys differently from girls. Do they remember, I ask, that sons were treated differently from the daughters, and what was expected of them? Roze asks if we can control today's children at all. Rivke A. says that only sons used to be sent to college. Ezra wants to talk and says he has a question. He sings a song in Yiddish, the "Song of Songs," about King Solomon. He asks, "If Solomon had a thousand wives, can we believe in him?" I tell him that I am sorry, but we are not talking about that and that we should get back to the topic. Ezra yells and several people talk. Rivke A. expounds on her contention that girls and boys are treated the same way. She supports this with examples about her daughter's children. Feygl-Asye says that years ago women had to serve their husbands. I recognize Yankl B. He says, "Ven man pap hot gevolt shlugn man shvester hot er mir gegibn dem patsh nit man shvester" (When my pop wanted to hit my sister he slapped me not my sister). Then Yankl B. continues with his standard conservative position, that too much freedom is not good. A woman should stay at home and her husband should go to work.

Rivke A. does not accept that. "That's not true, man tokhter geyt arbetn" (My daughter goes to work). But Yankl does not let her finish, and speaks louder, saying in Yiddish that he is not talking about her daughter, but about people in general. But Rivke A. pursues, explaining that her daughter does not have to work, but wants to; she has two college degrees. Rivke A. then tells that her son-in-law, who was raised in an orphanage, wanted his wife at home when the children were little. Yankl interrupts her, but Rivke A. goes on. In the middle of this exchange, Ezra interrupts to criticize religion. I tell him that is not the topic. I call on Roze, who says that her son worked harder to put himself through college than her daughter did. I then ask if mothers are closer to daughters. Much conversation ensues. Ester-Sosye speaks in English about her family, in which her parents sent the boys to college and the girls to work. I pursue with a question, whether daughters aren't emotionally closer to their mothers than sons. Gershon says yes, but Rivke A. tells of a family incident to illustrate the issue. She suggested to her son that she buy a ring for his wife, since she is leaving a ring for each of her two daughters in her will. He, however, disagreed, arguing that daughters, not sons, care for their mothers when they are ill, and that a daughter-in-law will sooner care for her own mother. The Gleyzele tey group agrees with this judgment (see text of narrative, Appendix D).

When I turn to Rive-Rukhl, she relates that she is the only one in her family to have a son, and he is very special, but her sisters' and brother's daughters are much closer to their parents than her son is to his parents. Shmiel-Leyb then says that he remembers that sons were raised to be "kodish iber hindert in tsvantsik yur" (to say the memorial prayer after the death of a parent [literally, after 120 years]), and daughters were taught to work at home. Then Ezra starts, "Ikh veys nokh a man, ikh veys a man vus er hot dray kinder" (I know another man, I know a man who has three children). He tells that he does everything for his sick wife (Yankl whispers, "Er get gaembling" [He gambles]) and the sons do nothing, but the daughter is wonderful and visits and calls daily. Roze says, "He's a diamond." Ezra says, "Vus ikh gey dirkh in man leybn yetst (What I am going through in my life now), nobody would." He concludes, "A tokhter iz di beste" (A daughter is the best).

Feygl-Asye then says she was close to her mother, but not all daughters are that way. At this opportunity, she wants to correct something she said in the group more than three months earlier. We had been discussing the proliferation of street people, and Feygl-Asye had said the responsibility lies with the mother. She wants to correct herself because she has thought the issue over and decided that sometimes it is the character of the child or the influence of peers that counts; it is not always the fault of the parents. Rivke A. starts talking again about her daughter, who helps disturbed children from wealthy homes in which parents mistreat children. But Feygl-Asye repeats her position again that parents are not always responsible. She takes her own comments very seriously and wants to correct the record of what she had said in the group: "Iz mir gekimen afn gedank, ikh ho(b) gezukt epes, ikh bin nit ken lignerte bot ikh darf oysbesern vus ikh hob gezukt bekoz ikh vil nisht me zol denken ikh bashildik ile mul" (I realized that I said something, I am not a liar but I have to correct that which I said because I don't want people to think that I always blame).

Rivke A. starts to talk, but Yankl B. had wanted to say something and I give him a turn. People on the other side of the room continue to talk while he is speaking. Then Rivke A. speaks up, and I ask who will be closer to the

mother thirty years later, a boy or a girl. Rivke A. says the girl, but it de-
pends on the daughter-in-law. I see that the lunch hour is close and announce that it is time to end the session. Rivke A. does not take the cue
and goes on about the influence of a child's friends at college. Feygl-Asye
agrees that parents "hobm nit di gantse deye" (don't have the whole say in
things). I end by saying, "Est gezinterheyt, un hot a gut, a git shabes aykh
in a git yontif" (Eat well, and have a good, a good Sabbath to you and a
happy holiday). People respond, "Ameyn, umeyn" (Amen). Blumke tells
me that she likes this room very much. Leye discusses a folk song with me
that makes fun of a Hasidic rabbi. Roze and Rivke A. continue a conversation in Yiddish on the last topic. People leave the room. Roze says, "Vi iz
man Bil?" (Where is my Bill?), looking for the staff member who helps her
with her wheelchair down the steps. I tell Leye that I hope her husband
Yankl will receive a good report from the doctor. I stop to talk to Yisrul,
who had sat through the meeting quietly, and to his younger card-playing
partner, a retarded fellow of 60 who says he speaks Yiddish. I leave the
room and go downstairs.

The Flow of Conversation: Topic, Language Choice, Control

An examination of one meeting of the Gleyzele tey group nine months
after its inception revealed characteristics common to all of the sessions
over the course of the year.

Each meeting consisted of a pre-session period, during which the members assembled. At this time, when fewer people were present than during
the meeting itself, concentrated interaction among individuals, including
myself, took place. However, the tape recorder could not always pick up the
multitude of simultaneous discussions that sometimes developed. Since the
recording began before the entrance of the members, and I would leave
the room for periods of time, speech was recorded during my absence.
During the main discussion period, generally one person talked while the
group listened, although satellite conversations did sometimes develop.
Since most participants attended lunch after the session, the recorded
post-session period was usually brief, consisting of leave-taking and occasional conversations between myself and a member.

As I mentioned earlier, the beverage-serving ritual and the idea of sharing conversation over a glass of tea—indeed, the very name of the group—
were designed to facilitate comfortable talk. Ultimately, however, the ritual
took on even more significance than I had anticipated. At the initial meeting, I realized that it would be unwieldy for each member to serve his or

her own beverage. This was mostly due to the space constraints and the physical disabilities of some of the participants. Some people helped themselves, but I ended up waiting on most of them, and most participants seemed to enjoy being catered to. This made me a focus of the program in a way I had not expected.

The proceedings of the May 24 meeting demonstrate the range in attitudes regarding my offer to serve, from Ezra's condescending reference to me as a "nice little boy," to Ester A.'s assertion that she could do it herself. In general, the participants liked the personal attention, something many of them seldom received in their present lives. Similarly, they seemed to appreciate my concern for their well-being, such as when I inquired about the health and whereabouts of members during the session. In fact, I always started the group discussion by asking for news of the members, and I always wished everyone well at the end. Thus, I believe they attended the group not only for conversation in Yiddish but also to be with me, a person who cared about them.

The pre-session period on this date was particularly revealing about the relationship between the residents and myself, as well as about the alliances among the residents. In addition, the proceedings illustrated social constraints on language choice. In my discussion with Yankl B., for example, I disagreed with his criticism of Hal, the young man who organized the operation of the Orthodox synagogue. At the beginning of the year, I might have worried that this type of disagreement would jeopardize my relationship with a potential neighborhood contact. But as time progressed, it became clear to me that expressing opinions only led to mutual respect.

A person's degree of religious observance was always a controversial topic among the residents. Debates on this topic resulted in disruptive altercations, people leaving sessions, and a residual atmosphere of disorder that prevented further interactions. Before the meeting under discussion, we had not broached the issue for four months.

The issue of language choice and the constraints impinging on it were evident immediately. When Itke entered, I greeted her in Yiddish. She, however, approached Yankl B. in English, and he responded in English, despite the fact that he had just been talking to me in Yiddish. The initial, immediate, and most emotionally charged language is English. Consequently, although Ezra and Yankl B. are fluent Yiddish speakers, Ezra, upon noticing Yankl B.'s charred pants, made his exclamation in English, and Yankl B. responded similarly. I greeted the participants and conversed with them almost entirely in Yiddish, but occasionally I matched their English with English and maintained the same level of formality, as when I responded to Itke, "He's impressed." Most of them can also maintain a Yiddish conversation, although, for example, Itke could rarely sustain Yiddish speech for very long. During the pre-session, Itke used the two languages to express single thoughts, unlike Yankl B., who maintained long stretches of Yiddish. Itke turned to English speech for her emotional outburst, "You never saw my pipik!" This was an inducement for Yankl B. to respond in English. Following this interchange, Itke addressed me in English, although we had previously been talking in Yiddish. Thus, the introduction of English initiates a chain reaction. Sometimes, the members continued their conversations in Yiddish after the formal end of the session, as Roze and Rivke A. did after our conversation about whether girls or boys have closer relationships with their mothers.

In the group, Rivke A. and Rivke B. might have been the only ones who naturally shared Yiddish talk outside of the sessions. They entered the room speaking Yiddish, although at other times they spoke English together. For the other members, Yiddish conversation was sparked by the Gleyzele tey sessions. It was a rare occurrence for Shmiel-Leyb and Ester-Sosye to speak Yiddish together; they told me that they did not speak Yiddish at home and that their son did not understand Yiddish. Thus, the Gleyzele tey sessions served as an impetus and opportunity to speak Yiddish, but they did not necessarily mirror the existing sociolinguistic condition in the neighborhood.

Generally, we did not discuss the meaning of specific Yiddish words during the meetings. Once during a pre-session, though, because Itke had been discussing particular words with her sister, she had come to me with specific questions. The two people approached as experts were Khatshe, the 100-year-old, European-born, senior member, and myself. I tried not to pose as a Yiddish expert, because many of the neighborhood residents had a much better command of the language than I did, and especially because I wanted them to feel comfortable with their Yiddish in my presence. I was, nevertheless, viewed as an authority.

The kind of conversations that took place at the Center were possible only among neighbors who had known each other and talked to each other over a lifetime. The preliminary bantering between Yankl B. and Itke, who had known each other for 60 years, continued familiar patterns of interaction. The residents saw themselves and others as having fixed roles and images, and their talk reinforced those positions. Itke, on this occasion and on many others, viewed herself as the self-righteous upholder of Jewish tradition and observance. She thought of herself as traditional like her mother, and at any opportunity she broadcast this self-image. Yankl B., who had known her for a long time and watched her behavior, was not afraid to question her words and actions, expressing doubt about her chasteness and religious devotion. Yankl B., on the other hand, was viewed by his neighbors and fellow Gleyzele tey members as "meshuge af teyt" (dead crazy). They, therefore, did not really listen to him and went on with their own conversations whenever he talked. His ideas were quite insightful, but because he had been pegged as crazy, he was largely ignored.

This one session illustrates the characteristic aspects of Yiddish speech in the neighborhood. Certain individuals, such as Itke, switched back and forth from Yiddish to English. English was also sometimes used to conclude a narrative, as in Rivke A.'s story about the Hasidim visiting the Center, which she ended with, "It's not right." Feygl-Asye switched to English to speak about her mother's longevity, saying, "She surpassed medical science and medical knowledge" (see text of narrative in Appendix D). But it was also clear from Feygl-Asye's behavior that she could keep up a long stretch of Yiddish speech about a very intimate and emotional issue, her mother's recent death and their closeness.

Other features that indicated variation in Yiddish ways of talking came up when Itke made a point of stressing her identity as a speaker of the northeast European Yiddish dialect when Roze said "kim" (come) to her. Then several members took part in a short discussion on dialectal variation in pronunciation. Itke demonstrated phonological forms that do not usually co-occur in dialects of Eastern Yiddish; Feygl-Asye, although to a lesser extent, similarly exhibited such variation. Rivke B. and Ezra, both European-born, used the verb *visn* (to know facts, not a person, in standard Yiddish) to apply to people. In addition, the residents demonstrated their facility with several Yiddish speech genres. Proverbs were very much alive in South Philadelphia Yiddish, as was illustrated by Roze, Ezra, and Itke. Itke applied a humorous *glaykhvertl*, or aphorism in the form of a simile, to describe Yankl's appearance. Roze utilized a saying of bonopetition regarding Rivke A.'s health.[3] Furthermore, Ezra sang Yiddish songs on two occasions. In short, Yiddish speech is enriched by a variety of folklore genres. During the main discussion period, group members exhibited a range of speech behavior from Rivke A.'s fluency to silence, demonstrated by Feyge, Blumke, and Moyshe. These speech behaviors and their implications are discussed in greater detail later on.

Despite my initial inclinations, I became the participant who most dominantly structured the flow of conversation during the main discussion period. By the end of May, the time of the meeting noted above, attendance at the Gleyzele tey session had increased to such an extent that the sheer maintenance of order required my leadership and guidance. In fact, the members turned to me for such intervention. I did my best to discern the level of disorder and struggle, and when necessary to reroute the path of events and interaction. Thus I sometimes changed the topic if for no other reason than to involve different participants. With too many noisy participants, it sometimes became impossible for the quieter members to talk when they so desired.

Perhaps my most important role was to signal the start of the discussion period. On rare occasions, in a smaller group, a member would say something that caught the attention of most listeners, influenced them to cease their private conversations, and involved them sufficiently to continue as a group with the new topic. During the May 24 session, I signaled the start of the session, as I had done at other meetings, by raising my voice, addressing the entire group, and inquiring about the health of the members who were not present, as well as asking for news from those at the meeting. In this session, Rivke B. responded by talking about her son's trip to Israel. This led to a change in topic, to her in-laws, who happen to be Hasidim. The topic then changed to Hasidim in general, which subsequently evolved into a discussion of the immoral behavior of the Hasidim and a criticism of all observant Jews. Throughout, I was involved in recognizing the speakers and in stopping arguments. The Gleyzele tey sessions evolved on their own, thanks to the institutional setting and members' participation, but their development also responded to my personality and conscious intervention.

The flow of conversation cannot be viewed in an isolated manner for a given session. Individuals have histories, and so do groups. I have alluded to the known behavior of such participants as Itke and Yankl B., and the way that such familiarity and stereotyping colored all of the members' reactions to them in the sessions, and indeed in the neighborhood. On May 24, the Gleyzele tey sessions had a history of more than nine months. The liveliest and testiest arguments had centered on the issue of religious observance. Some, such as Rivke A. and Ezra, were consistently distrustful and excoriating in their references to Orthodox Jews. Yankl B., Itke, and Feygl-Asye took the opposite position, defending belief in God and often criticizing those who were not observant.

No middle ground could be reached on such issues, as was evident from the several attempts we had made at group discussions the previous fall. For the sake of peace, friendship, and group continuity, I had placed a ban on the criticism of either freethinkers or observant Jews. No one objected to such a ban, primarily, I believe, because the participants wanted the group to continue. The participants, including the strongest advocates of the two positions, preferred to see the group treat other issues rather than disintegrate in strife. But on May 24 these divisive subjects, which had not been raised in the Gleyzele tey group for the preceding four months, resurfaced. An examination of the flow of topics during this session may reveal why it was so difficult to keep the discussion away from the issues we had shunned. The discussions about Rabbi Isaacson followed the earlier flow of conversation.

1. Rivke A. and Yankl B. discuss Rabbi Isaacson.
2. I declare that we should start a new topic.
3. Ezra raises Rabbi Pupko's name.
4. Itke begs that we change the topic.
5. I tell Ezra that we have heard that story already; Feygl-Asye and Roze agree.
6. Discussion of the *pishke* (charity box) by Ester A., Roze, and Feygl-Asye.
7. I try to quiet the group, introduce the topic of the holiday *shvues*, but it does not catch on or generate narratives or active conversation.
8. Ezra discusses his antireligion stance.
9. Itke and Feygl-Asye object.
10. I say we will not criticize people because of their religiosity.
11. Ezra criticizes observant neighborhood Jews.
12. The topic of *shvues* again does not yield a good response.
13. Ezra declares his lack of belief in God, tying it to his having lived through pogroms as a child.
14. Itke leaves.
15. I attempt to make peace and recognize both points of view.
16. Feygl-Asye declares her faith, based on the story of her mother's life being lengthened by 40 years.
17. I declare that we will no longer discuss belief in God.
18. Again I introduce *shvues* as a topic, and it goes nowhere.
19. I introduce a new topic, differences in raising girls and boys.
20. Ezra again raises the topic of antireligion.
21. I tell him sorry, no more.

In this list of the major interactions, it is clear that one man, Ezra, continued to advance his position long after other supporters of his stance had lost interest in furthering it, and at a time when the group as a whole had moved on to another topic. In analyzing the situation, I realized that although Ezra had come to several group sessions he had never stayed for more than a few minutes. A group grows organically as a whole, just as an individual does. Standards of proper and improper behavior are set over time. Ezra had not been through the growing pains of the group, and he had not been trained in its practices: in his absence the group had agreed that personal attack of neighbors about their religious practices should be avoided for the welfare of the group. Five of the twenty-one major speech turns in the above list involved Ezra's assertion of a topic the group had agreed to shun. During this series of interchanges, only one other event (number 16), Feygl-Asye's narrative, which asserted her faith in God, represented a member's attempt to bring the issue back into the discussion. However, seven of the twenty-one events were attempts by me to avert the topic. This series of exchanges shows how one person who does not abide by the rules can disrupt a whole group, and how much intervention a group leader must make to maintain order under those circumstances.

A different example from another session underscores that it is no simple matter for a newcomer or outsider to enter a discussion group that has established its own acceptable ways of talking. The purpose of the Gleyzele tey, as a forum for speaking Yiddish together, became clear to the participants during the first meetings. Later, Yitskhok came to a group discussion and became interested in the topic of President Reagan's visit to the Nazi graves in Bitburg. When Yitskhok started to speak English, Itke admonished him, "Talk Jewish!"[4] This self-controlling device to maintain a Yiddish discussion, along with the equivalent order in Yiddish, "Red yidish," had become a common cry in the group. Yitskhok, however, thinking the main purpose of the group was to analyze topics, answered innocently, "What is the difference? These people understand."

The group's members took their participation in the Yiddish discussion group seriously. Feygl-Asye's desire to correct the record regarding an opinion she had expressed more than three months earlier, and Yankl B.'s disclosure that his father used to hit him when his sister misbehaved reflects the participants' willingness to share deeply personal convictions and memories with the group. Ezra's parable about a man, a sick wife, and three children was evident to most of his neighbors as an expression of despair about his own situation. Even boisterous scolding, such as when Yankl B. told Rivke A. to shut up, showed that participants were able to tell their fellow members what they felt about them. The Gleyzele tey group setting, in short, provided an atmosphere in which unself-conscious talk in Yiddish could proceed.

Negotiating Issues in Yiddish

Do the recordings of the Gleyzele tey sessions reveal the verbal techniques participants used to communicate ideas and emotions that were significant to them? Knowing that many of the residents enjoyed talking, do we have evidence to indicate that these sessions were more than an opportunity to deliver a monologue on subjects dear to them? How did participants react to one another's words?

Research in social psychology has long demonstrated that the size of the group influences the nature of social interaction and the behavior of individual members (Hare, Borgatta, and Bales 1955). Much of that research was based on small groups of strangers in test situations. Much of the work on conversational analysis has also involved small groups (e.g., Tannen 1984). Stubbs has pointed out the difficulty of tape recording large groups, such as students in a classroom. Instead, he taped discussions of small groups of students with their teachers, observed larger classes, and took written notes for comparison with the recorded speech (1983: 222).

Social psychologists would not consider the Gleyzele tey group, nine participants at its smallest, to be a small group. The group was open to all members; participants could not be turned away. Gleyzele tey members often had known one another for many years, interacting on a regular basis, and thus they brought shared knowledge into each Friday-morning session. As the group grew, it became more difficult to maintain the rule that only one speaker should talk at a time. In addition, some participants were only listeners in Yiddish, not speakers. Over a year's time, the group interacted in enough circumstances to provide me with numerous opportunities to compare and contrast their use of Yiddish.

The participants were able and willing to talk about a variety of topics, including sex and the senior citizen, how to improve the quality of life in the neighborhood, intermarriage, and the interaction of Jews and non-Jews. The last topic was a particularly emotional one for the members, calling to mind vivid memories of anti-Semitic incidents in America and the pogroms that some had lived through in Ukraine after World War I. Interestingly, both sets of narratives derived from the speakers' youth.

Although our discussions covered general topics, such as the effect of the changing economy on marriages, children without parents, and artificial insemination, the preponderant subject matter was Jewish in nature. It is not clear that the participants, protected from the non-Jewish world by a language that only they could understand, viewed the Gleyzele tey as an in-group, a place to discuss Jewish problems only for Jewish ears. I tend not to accept this interpretation. Non-Jews attended sessions, and the members did not exhibit any discomfort at their presence. On the contrary, on one occasion Ester-Sosye interrupted the proceedings several times to request that we translate for the benefit of a non-Jewish woman sitting next to her. Another time, a non-Jewish Center member, Fred, attended a session and was able to take part in the conversation by speaking English, since he understood Yiddish perfectly. What seems more likely is that (1) the members of the group appreciated having a time to discuss Jewish issues, and (2) they knew that the Jewish focus matched my preference. Taking advantage of my interest in these topics, participants ably discussed subjects that did not particularly relate to Jews, but they favored Jewish topics.

The flow of topics followed from members' narratives and responses. Usually when a member shared a personal story, the rest of the group paid attention and peripheral conversations subsided. During the session described above, for example, when Feygl-Asye began to tell dramatically the story of her mother's life, the room immediately quieted down. It was only later in her narrative that participants began talking to each other about what she said.

Any personalized account or a shift in that direction was sure to garner the greatest level of attention and ensure increased participation. In one session, the group discussed the black Jews from Ethiopia who settled in Israel, and the conversation moved from the exotic to the personal. In the middle of the discussion, Ester A. said: "Ikh vil aykh freygn a frage" (I want to ask you a question). The question was not simple, nor did it deal directly with Ethiopian Jews. Ester A. told the story of her adopted black grandson and the ritual ceremonies he went through as a child in order to be declared Jewish by an Orthodox rabbi. Her question came at the end of the narrative: "Is he Jewish?" Roze replied that she thought he was Jewish, because the mother "hot im ifgekhovet idishkayt" (raised him with Jewishness). On the other hand, Roze said, other people would not consider him Jewish. Leye, who had proposed the topic of Ethiopian Jewry, started to say something. Roze, however, continued with her main contribution, her concern about her own grandchildren. Her son-in-law was not Jewish and insisted that his children were also not Jewish, even though Roze went to the synagogue after they were born, gave them Jewish names, and considered them Jewish. Thus, the group quickly moved from a discussion of the Ethiopian Jews to a discussion of the Jewishness of their own offspring, which ultimately struck at the precariousness of Jewish heritage and identity.

In this same session, about 25 minutes later, the discussion turned back to Ester A.'s grandson. She concluded in English that "the situation stinks," since the couple had divorced and the boy was having problems. Roze at this point consoled Ester and told her that the boy would be accepted, that Americans were used to similarly unconventional families. Thus, to some degree, the interaction in these sessions was aimed at giving reassurance to fellow participants, helping them to feel better about their lives.

The effects of verbal interaction cannot be judged simply by a dyadic relationship. We cannot leave it as: Ester said something, Roze responded to Ester, Ester felt better. The meaning of communication in a group setting cannot be gleaned from a conversation between two individuals. An emotion or opinion that is expressed and shared by a whole group has a strong effect on an individual. A communicator who transmits such a shared emotion through speech, and raises the consciousness of the group by identifying a common value, may be called a conversational star. In addition to demonstrating his or her skills of rhetoric, the conversational star identifies the values shared by a group by eliciting an appreciation of those values.

In the Gleyzele tey group, Rivke A. was a conversational star. She always stressed the moral to be learned from the narrative, and group members remembered her lessons long afterwards. In one discussion of relations between Jews and non-Jews, her narrative raised the group to an emotional height. Rivke asked in English, "Can I say something?" and then proceeded, "Ikh veys nit tsi se rekhtik, bot azoy hob ikh gereyst mane kinder; akhits riligiyez tse zan darfn ze(y) zan mentshn" (I don't know if it's right, but this is the way I raised my children; besides being religious they have to be good human beings). What followed was her description of her daughter's desire to use her allowance to buy a corsage for a poor African American girl in her class to wear at graduation (see text in Appendix D). Rivke commended and rewarded her daughter, stating how important it is to help all those in need, not only members of your own religious or ethnic group. After Rivke's presentation, three participants responded. Leye said, "Dus iz mentshlekhkayt" (This is being humane). Itke said, "Di blut iz di zelbe" (The blood is the same). Basye B. remarked, "Me denkt nit nor fun zikh me denkt fun ale mentshn" (You don't think only about yourself you think about everyone). Rivke A.'s style of talk and her message had electrified the audience. Her morality lesson, illustrated by way of personal example, had elevated the group's discussion from expressing their daily concerns to recognizing their shared humane ideals. Very few other people in the group were ever able to have such an effect.

The process of communication in a group may also include short pronouncements such as "I am here," "I wish to speak," or "I am bored." These and many other small interchanges occurred during the meetings. Let us examine one 45-second sequence.

Khone is hard of hearing and is usually only able to understand the person next to her. She enters the room after the meeting has been in session for a while and sits down next to Leye. Unconcerned with the proceedings because she is deaf, and also because it is Yankl B. who is speaking, Khone starts talking to Leye because she wants Leye's husband, Yankl A., to do some plumbing work at her house. Itke, on the other hand, wants people to pay attention to Yankl B. during this discussion of current synagogue life. Menakhem, the vice-president of one of the neighborhood Conservative synagogues, Congregation Adath Shalom, and Yankl B. are sparring. Since Menakhem rarely speaks Yiddish in a session, Yankl. B. assumes that he does not know what the word *yerishe* (heritage) means, and he uses his Yiddish in an undeniably condescending manner. In the 45 seconds of dialogue, he manages to tell Khone three times that she should be quiet. But the last time he loses his temper and shouts in English. Rivke A. does not understand why Yankl B. is upset, and she claims that Khone is not talking, even though it is clear that she is.

> *Yankl B.* [to Khone]: Di vilst geyn redn oder di vilst geyn aheym? (You want to speak, or you want to go home?)
> *Itke*: Please, there's a speaker here.
> *Rivke A.*: Zol zi zikh avekzetsn. (Let her sit down.)
> [general uproar]
> *Menakhem*: Er veyst fun gornisht, er veyst fun gornisht. (He knows nothing, he knows nothing.)
> *Yankl B.* [to Khone]: Hey, grager, grager! (Hey, noisemaker, noisemaker!)
> *Itke*: Er veyst, er veyst. (He knows, he knows.)
> *Yankl B.*: Mit a kaymelon fin a—fin fiftsik yur tserik, a shil iz far dray zakhn, toyre, lernen, dovenen, in lernen vus i—i—i—indzere eltern hobm ge—i—ibergelozt fa—far a yerishe. Veyst vu— vus a yerishe iz? (No less than fifty years ago, a synagogue was for three things, torah, studying, praying, and learning that which ou—ou—ou—our ancestors left us a—as a heritage. You know what a *yerishe* is?)
> *Menakhem*: Yeah, I know yerishe, yeah, heritage, heritage.
> *Yankl B.*: Hayntike tsaytn iz a tropele ondersh, me geyt in shil zen a klob. (Nowadays it's a little bit different, you go to synagogue to see a club.) [Khone is carrying on a conversation at the other end of the table.] Me geyt arayn in shil, haynt iz a freylekher shobes. Far vus a freylekher shobes? Er hot a barmitsve, hot yener hot hot— (You go into the synagogue, today it's a merry shabbos. Why a merry shabbos? This one has a bar-mitzvah, the other one has, has—)
> *Itke*: Please!
> *Yankl B.*: [screaming] What's a matter with you, can't you hear?
> *R. P.*: Eyn minit. (One minute.)
> *Rivke A.*: Zi redt nit. (She's not talking.)

Any interpretation of these proceedings requires knowing who the participants are and how they have related in the past. Otherwise, it would be impossible to understand why Yankl B. is given little attention and why Khone continues to talk. This group sequence is a mixture of Yiddish and

English. People are told to sit down and to shut up in Yiddish. However, Itke, and finally Yankl B., express their strongest emotions in English.

Recordings of the pre-sessions, including the periods when I was not present, confirm the general pattern in the neighborhood that most talk was in English. Yiddish was reserved for special circumstances, such as when one of the older immigrant men was present, or for singing a song. The people who spoke Yiddish at these times were also the ones most likely to do so at other times, such as Rivke A., Rivke B., Khatshe, and to a lesser extent, Yankl B. and Leye. During the more formal main part of the session, however, people clearly assumed that if they wanted to talk, they should do so in Yiddish. Thus, there was general acceptance of this special allotment of time at the Center only for Yiddish talk. Speaking Yiddish was one of the main reasons for attending the session. Therefore, a member, such as Basye B., who never spoke Yiddish at other times, forced herself to talk because she delighted in having an audience. Blumke, on the other hand, who hardly ever spoke Yiddish but was a talkative person, was content to attend for the entire year and just listen. She was one of the most enthusiastic members.

If members who normally did not speak Yiddish to each other were willing to congregate weekly to do so, there must have been special motivating factors. I examine these shortly. The enthusiasm with which the members accepted the rule of speaking only Yiddish during the proceedings was indicated by the order "Red yidish" (Speak Yiddish), volunteered at certain times when the rule was broken. Neither I nor the residents made a point of correcting someone's Yiddish; rarely did we do so. In other words, almost any level of language was accepted. Of the twelve corrections I recorded during the year nine of them were initiated by Yankl B., perhaps another indicator of why the residents generally resented his behavior.

The Participants' Reactions

The Gleyzele tey was one of the Center's most successful programs in recent years, in terms of the attendance and enthusiasm of the participants. To understand why, one must examine the needs of the participants, including my own, and the ways in which the program satisfied those needs.

The name itself was both symbolic and real. When I suggested the name I had no idea that the image it conveyed was already part of the reality of Jewish South Philadelphia. One day when I was sitting in the home of Yisrul, one of the Center's oldest members, he served tea in a glass with lump sugar. The Gleyzele tey still lived in South Philadelphia. Dveyre told me that her brother, who had recently died, frequently requested a *gleyzl tey* and lump sugar when he came to visit. But for most of the participants it was a custom that came alive in a new form on Friday mornings.

The use of their Yiddish names was also a resurrection of things past, since very often only their parents had addressed these South Philadelphians by those names. After the year of meetings had concluded, Leye published a note in the Center's September 1985 issue of the *Beacon*, saying that the participants were "encouraged . . . to use *mame loshen* (mother tongue) and [were] called . . . by names our parents called us, [which enabled] our present . . . [to be] enriched by a link with our past."

Only one participant expressed the view that the Gleyzele tey program could be interpreted as a mission for rescuing Yiddish. During the sessions, we rarely, if ever, discussed the future of the language. But Yankl B. was prescient. At the first meeting of the group, he said, out of context: "Ikh veys nit vus di vilst du roteven, indz o di vilst roteven dem yingern folk. Mir zenen arup finem mark" (I do not know who you want to save, us or you want to save the younger generation. We are all washed up).

Yankl B. put the issue on the agenda once again in a January 1985 *Beacon* report on the Gleyzele tey: "Even now when the Yiddish language is in jeopardy the Almighty sent us Rakhmiel to teach and restore the language, over a gleyzele tey." Although only Yankl B. defined the purpose of the group as an attempt to restore the language, perhaps this was also an underlying purpose of some participants.

On many occasions, members expressed their enjoyment at hearing Yiddish spoken and having the opportunity to speak Yiddish. After one of the meetings, when I left the room, two participants who did not speak Yiddish told each other that they loved hearing it spoken. A reporter for the Jewish Community Centers interviewed members for an article that appeared in two local Jewish newspapers, *Jewish Exponent* and *JCC Impact*, in June and July 1985. One member reinforced Yankl B.'s theme of the renewal of a "dying language," which had not been aired in our group meetings or during my extensive contact with members outside the group meetings.

Yiddish is a dying language. It is wonderful to get together and speak it. As a child I spoke Yiddish fluently, but with the passing of my parents, I stopped. Now I'm speaking it again. The group has really kept together. We talk about things in our childhood and what happened in our lives. It's really nostalgic.

The seemingly incongruous juxtaposition of dying and joy points to underlying feelings that were seldom expressed but were definitely associated with this extraordinary group experience in South Philadelphia. Although most of the neighborhood Jews were elderly, death and dying were not subjects for discussion. The numerous possibilities for termination or revitalization of a language (Dorian, ed. 1989) were hardly broached. As the Yiddish speaker above implied, simply speaking a dying language helps keep it alive, unites past and present, and is more powerful than nostalgia alone, especially within the shared group context. For that member, as well as for others, the activity of the group induced feelings and memories associated with childhood. A second member who was interviewed for the newspaper articles also stressed the place of Yiddish in her early biography and then emphasized my catalytic role in the group. It became clear that the element of joy associated with speaking Yiddish and with congregating for this purpose ensured the group's existence and development. The success of the group also reflected the members' realization that the activity was significant for me. In my own comments for the articles about the Center I said: "The people here have given me a great deal of strength because they are so strong. I have learned from them and gained personal strength and satisfaction that will stay with me as long as I live."

Social interaction meant more to the members than just a chance to hear and speak Yiddish. One participant, in a farewell letter to me that was printed in the October 1985 *Beacon*, spoke for others when she expressed appreciation for the respect and attention they received from me and thanks that I cared about their personal lives and showed concern for their welfare. This was especially important for the elderly residents who lived far from family. The Friday-morning meetings were also a time devoted to a Jewish activity, using a Jewish language, and usually focusing on a Jewish topic. For the shrinking Jewish community, each Jewish activity was valued, and a new activity was especially welcome. My relative youth symbolized for these elderly Jews the continuity of their customs and values. It was refreshing for them to see that a language they associated with their own youth and their parents was alive.

Perhaps the strongest link between the Yiddish Gleyzele tey group and the participants' lives was in terms of their Jewish identity. Although I did not raise the issue of the purpose of the session and the members' responses, one member, Reyzl, mentioned it on several occasions:

"Iz derfar iz dayn kles gevorn azoy groys, bekos di host zey dermant, az siz take du dus yidishkayt." (Therefore your class became so big, because you reminded them, that yiddishkeit is really present.)

Ikh gey krik tse dir. Di host getun a byutiful zakh. Di host gebrenkt dus yidishkayt tsu di mentshn. (I return to you. You did a beautiful thing. You brought yiddishkeit to the people.)

Ikhn akh zugn de reyne emes e—Rakhmiel, a, ir (h)ot gebrenkt, aza vunder af idishkayt tse de mentshn vus gekimen tsim senter vus (h)ot, fa- fargesn dos idishkayt iz nokh du. (I'll tell you the pure truth e—Rakhmiel, th[at], you brought, such a fascination with yiddishkeit to the people that came to the Center who have, forgotten that yiddishkeit is still around.)

By the end of my year in South Philadelphia, it was clear to me that the residents and I had retrieved many of the connections between Yiddish language, yiddishkeit, and the personal and group identity of the South Philadelphia Jews.

PART II

Identities

CHAPTER FIVE

A Jewish Place

The Jews in South Philadelphia experienced overlapping identities based on gender, religion, occupation, class, age, region, and ethnicity. On the issue of identity, I was curious about how they would answer the question, "Who am I?" and how they may have seen themselves differently at different times (Yuval-Davis 1994: 409).[1] For reasons that had as much to do with me as with them, I discovered a considerable amount about certain arenas and little about others. For example, I explored questions of occupational identity in some depth, because I was fascinated by the extent to which work and business associations shaped the lives of the residents. Khatshe, the eldest neighborhood resident, who celebrated his one hundredth birthday during my year in South Philadelphia, had retired from work 35 years earlier; yet, in an interview, he was most animated when talking about his baking career. Others who had been retired from active employment for many years did not dwell at all on the past.

The residents' almost exclusive affiliation with Jewish religious, cultural, and fraternal organizations became evident, but my blinders almost prevented me from knowing how varied these affiliations could be. An experience from my early group fieldwork project has remained a constant reminder to me about my limitations. My student partner and I were doing an interview with the owner of the local smoked fish store, a Jewish shopkeeper in his late sixties. I was jolted by my partner's question: "Do you bowl?" she asked. To my surprise, this question opened up a rich and useful discussion of his favorite pastime and longtime involvement in a Jewish bowling league. Left to my own ideas of what was Jewish and what was appropriate for old people, I might never have learned that Jewish bowling leagues flourished in South Philadelphia. As I developed close associations with the residents over time, I became aware of many facets of their lives that would have eluded me on a shorter visit.[2]

Identity formation and change, for both individuals and groups, has to do with how an individual relates to others. Although during this study I was concerned with feelings about a particular neighborhood, maintaining a historical perspective has helped me to understand that "spaces have always been hierarchically interconnected" (Gupta and Ferguson 1992: 8). Social change is accompanied by modification of this hierarchy and often involves the alteration of identities. South Philadelphia Jews are linked to their non-Jewish neighbors, to other parts of the city and world, and to previous generations in distant places and times. The process of self-identification involves seeing oneself as belonging to a particular group and seeing others as different, as belonging to another group. Such acts of identification are very real for the individuals involved and have repercussions for the ways that groups see themselves. In fact, these acts are sufficient for defining groups and identities (Le Page and Tabouret-Keller 1985: 2, 247–48). As individuals establish the identities that are important to them, seemingly objective dividers, such as history, race, and gender, can fall by the wayside. Acts of identification establish social realities, linking past, present, and future for individuals and groups (see P. Weinreich 1989a: 224).

Leye

Leye's life experience illustrates the complex ways in which South Philadelphians' acts of identification gave meaning to their lives. Asked to think about the most interesting period of her life, Leye recalled the 1930's, when she was single and active in what she calls the progressive cultural movement. A devotee of the theater of the Left, a member of the John Reed Club, an activist for the Office Workers Union and later the International Labor Defense, she was engaged in the struggle for a just world. After marriage, Leye stayed at home, managing the household and doing the bookkeeping for her husband, Yankl A., a plumber. She views her own life story as dull in comparison with that of Yankl A., who arrived in Philadelphia at age sixteen from Stavistsh, in *Kiver gubernye* (the government or province in the Russian empire with Kiev as its capital). Stavistsh was near Belotserkve, a town also known by its Yiddish names *Shvartse time* or *Sde lovon*, the birthplace of many South Philadelphia Jews. A landsmanshaft and a neighborhood synagogue carrying this town name functioned until the 1970's. Yankl A. was a Communist Party member, volunteering his time as a hardworking union organizer while earning his living as a plumber.

At the age of 77, Leye could look back on a life centered in South Philadelphia but inspired by global political and cultural interests. She was born in New York City, the eldest child of parents who had arrived from Kovl, *Voliner gubernye* (Volin province). By the time she was five her family had settled in South Philadelphia in an area of new houses at Third and Gladstone Streets, which is still home to South Philadelphia Jews.

Leye's father was the first person in New York to put ice cream on a hot waffle, and he eventually sold the treat from twenty pushcarts. Later on, in Philadelphia, he had difficulty earning a living and moved the family to West Philadelphia for a few years, where Leye graduated from high school. Back in South Philadelphia, she lived at home with her parents until her marriage, working as a bookkeeper in a department store. Leye and Yankl A. moved into their house in 1940. Leye's mother lived with them in their South Philadelphia home until the end of her life.

Yankl A. had lived in this house with his family for more than fifteen years before his wedding, the downstairs having served as the family tailor shop. There Yankl A. and Leye raised their daughter, their only child after the death of a young son from Tay-Sachs disease. Leye's mother and Yankl A.'s sister and husband lived on the second and third floors. Leye's daughter went to the same elementary school that her mother had attended, and she graduated from college. She became a teacher and lived with her husband and children in Maryland.

A lover of music, theater, and literature, Leye had become actively involved in Center programs, but on principle refrained from partaking in the subsidized lunch program. One day a week, she and Yankl A. drove to New Jersey to volunteer at a Jewish Center attended by friends who had moved away from South Philadelphia. But they preferred the unpretentious local Center to the New Jersey one frequented by the "petty bourgeois." Even though few other South Philadelphia Jews shared Leye and Yankl A.'s cultural and political commitments, both still felt at home in the neighborhood.

Not surprisingly, given her allegiances and interests over the years, Leye had overlapping areas of self-identification. As a youngster and throughout life, Leye viewed herself as an American-born child of immigrants. She always was interested in the arts, especially theater, and vividly recalled the details of her European-born uncle's involvement in Yiddish theater performance. He took her, a little girl, along to the get-togethers of his colleagues, where Leye would recite dramatic Yiddish poetry prepared under his tutelage.

But a stronger, more pervasive tie for this American-born daughter of immigrants and for the man she married was to the neighborhood and the house of the parental generation. Leye and Yankl A. remained all their married years in the house that Yankl A.'s immigrant parents had occupied, and the immediate physical setting served as a constant reminder of the immigrants and their culture. Most of their peers moved away and lost those daily cues of a way of life where three and sometimes four generations lived together.

Their political consciousness and their support of leftist activism distinguished Leye and Yankl A. from most of their neighbors, although some of the older immigrants had been socialist-leaning in their youth and still belonged to labor unions. Leye's interest in the arts and cultural expression, including her participation in a course on exotic cultures offered at the Center, stemmed from her concern for oppressed peoples. For Leye, culture had special value when tied to the struggle for a better world. She and her husband were the only neighborhood residents who belonged to Philadelphia's Sholem Aleichem Club, a secular organization that supported liberal political efforts and Jewish cultural expression. My wife and I were also members, although we did not know Leye and Yankl before meeting them in South Philadelphia. We discovered that we had some friends in common, and I talked about those people with Yankl A. and Leye. In general, Leye and Yankl A. aspired to a different level of political and cultural knowledge from most neighborhood people, but the working-class background of the residents represented a forthrightness and nobility that attracted them.

Like some of the other wives in the neighborhood, such as Libe and Sure, Leye always assumed that I would rather speak with her husband than with her. Although she was articulate, well read, politically astute, and involved in many activities, she saw herself as secondary to her husband. As the woman of the house, she kept the household organized, had primary responsibility for raising their daughter, kept all the records for the plumbing business, and was the center of an extended family living under one roof, but she still did not consider herself an interesting woman. This may have been false modesty, but she repeatedly referred me to Yankl A. for compelling stories and information.

Characteristics of the Population

Out of a total Jewish neighborhood population of three to four thousand, I had contact with only a few hundred Jewish residents, most of whom were older than 60.[3] A few had children and grandchildren living in the neighborhood, and many had relatives in other parts of greater Philadelphia. The Jewish Sunday school was attended by ten pupils, only one of whom had two parents who were born Jewish. Jewish residents intermarried and had close personal friendships with many of their neighbors of Italian background. Jews and Jewish institutions were more concentrated on the western side of the neighborhood, near the section inhabited by Italian Americans (see map, Appendix A).

American-born Jews, most of them natives of South Philadelphia, composed approximately three-quarters of the neighborhood Jewish population. Immigrants included those who came to America in the first years of the century as well as those who arrived in the post–World War II years. I met two residents who came from the Soviet Union in the 1970's, one of whom welcomed her daughter and son-in-law to South Philadelphia in 1985. Almost all residents owned the houses in which they lived, and many had inhabited the same house for more than 60 years. Very few had settled in the neighborhood during the previous 30 years. Some of the subjects of this study had moved out of the neighborhood but returned daily or a few days a week to work, to participate in the activities of the Center, or just to be close to familiar surroundings and friendly faces. The 30 participants whose conversations with me I taped had a mean age of 74.6 (see Appendix B). There were nine males and 21 females, eleven born in Eastern Europe and nineteen in the United States or Great Britain. Appendix B provides some additional information about these 30 individuals.[4] They had worked in a variety of retail enterprises and in factories, government service, and teaching. Some of the women had worked at home, but most had held jobs outside the home, including several who provided the only financial support for their children and parents. I met only a few college graduates; most of the American-born residents had graduated from high school. Those with children reported that their offspring lived in different parts of the United States and had achieved a range of education levels and occupations. Many of the neighborhood residents had lived with or near their parents for most of their lives and were often the siblings who provided the most care for them during their last years.

A survey by Rotman of some of the characteristics of the South Philadelphia Jewish population yielded statistics that agree with most of my findings: in general, the neighborhood was 60 percent female; 65 percent of the residents had lived in South Philadelphia for 50 years or more; 76 percent were older than 62, and an additional 14 percent were older than 50; 34 percent had completed twelfth grade; 81 percent were well enough to get out of the house, and 55 percent traveled outside the neighborhood regularly; 40 percent kept kosher (followed the Jewish dietary laws); 37 percent belonged to a synagogue; 31 percent belonged to a Jewish benevolent association (lodge, landsmanshaft, *farein*); 70 percent claimed to speak Yiddish, and 34 percent claimed to read or write Yiddish; 24 percent claimed to read or write Hebrew (1980: 27–47).

Neighborhood and Community

One of my goals was to get better acquainted with the neighborhood of South Philadelphia. The residents' connection to their pasts, to those who lived there before, and to their neighbors interested me most of all. I see the Jews as part of the neighborhood and stress their residence there, though I hope not to the exclusion of other addresses that are vital to their identities.

Sociologists have interpreted the terms "neighborhood" and "community" in many ways, but the term "neighborhood" always implies geographic boundaries (see M. R. Williams 1985: 29–50; Wireman 1984: 29–50). As noted earlier, the residential pattern of Jews within South Philadelphia has changed over the past century. South Philadelphia, for the Jewish residents I met, meant the southeast corner of the region where they were concentrated. But views differed. Basye A. said, for example, "They call South Philadelphia from Market Street south. I don't. I call South Philadelphia from Snyder Avenue south." When the Jews talked about a feeling for neighborhood, they were referring to a synthesis of the South Philadelphia streets they lived on and the Jewish community in South Philadelphia.

The relationship of ethnic group to neighborhood is far from simple. Suttles notes that neighborhoods identified with single ethnic groups may actually be the home of several ethnic groups, and that these neighborhoods can maintain their identities and boundaries despite shifts in ethnic composition (1972: 27). This may have been the case for the Jews of South Philadelphia, who were once a majority in an area of South Philadelphia and had become a small minority, even though the rest of Philadelphia does not perceive the area as Jewish. Suttles points out that today's concept of community symbolizes a collectivity or place of shared hopes and feelings (1972: 265). Bender's survey (1978: 7) of the history of the scholarly and popular definition of community concludes that the best definition is "a network of social relations marked by mutuality and emotional bonds . . . and it may or may not be coterminous with a specific, contiguous territory" (1978: 7). I use the term "community" in agreement with three traditions. First, in Jewish history, the word *kehile* (Yiddish, community; Hebrew, *kehila*) describes local, organized Jewish communal structures and their constituent associations and institutions. Second, sociologists and historians who study American Jewry apply the term "community" to regional aggregates of Jews and their organizations. Third, I use "community" to connote shared emotional bonds, independent of geographic commonality. I also heed the warning of the anthropologist Varenne (1986) who has analyzed the symbolic power of community in American culture. He argues against the loose and widespread American use of "community," especially to apply to situations in which a shared inner psychological state cannot be demonstrated for a social group.

Jews have remained on almost every street of the southeastern corner of South Philadelphia, as a dispersed minority on streets where they once constituted a concentrated majority (see map, Appendix A). The Jewish residents identified with both their South Philadelphia neighborhood and their South Philadelphia Jewish community. I understand their feelings of neighborhood identity to be a mixture of both allegiances. Their preoccupation with their relations with non-Jews in the neighborhood further illustrates that, for these Jews, it was impossible to identify as neighborhood residents independently from being Jewish.

The Residents' Feeling for Neighborhood

Narratives of everyday life experience can provide evidence of the shared values that group members hold (Labov and Waletzky 1967; Labov 1972b: 354–96; Polanyi 1989; Linde 1993). The narratives I recorded during my conversations with South Philadelphians strongly reflected neighborhood life and underscored the residents' feelings about place and Jewish community. Saying that "questions about where one lives become queries about who one is," Hummon has argued that community ideology and identity are central to American culture. Indeed, he has found that community imagery translates into self-imagery (Hummon 1990: xiv, 148).

Beyle recounted the following narrative to me in the presence of her sister, Elke. The two lived together in the house where their parents had lived and where they themselves grew up. Elke's husband had died recently and Beyle's second husband had died a few years earlier. The conversation took place around the kitchen table in their house. It was a spring afternoon, the door to the back yard from the kitchen was open, and the barking of a neighbor's dog could be heard from time to time. The three of us sipped iced tea. Conversation had turned to the sensitive topic of how former South Philadelphians looked down on the residents who remained. In Yiddish, speaking practically without a pause, Beyle told dramatically of a reunion of the *zekste* (Sixth Street). I had read about high-school class reunions, but this was the first time I had heard of South Philadelphia block alumni associations. The high level of excitement accompanying Beyle's delivery was a sign of the great emotional meaning she ascribed to the topic. She was one of the few participants still living on the street.

So, we assembled together, they recognized me right away, they recognized her, but I had to look at them and I still didn't know, who is who, someone came in decked out in high leather boots, and made up as though she was an actress at the very least, her face tanned, very well dressed, she says, "And who are you?" Right off I recognized from the voice that she's from high high society. So I told her, I say, "And who are you?" When she told me who she is, I didn't believe that was she. She says, "You know, it was very very good that they called me, but I was on the Riviera," that's where she was . . . She just arrived from the Riviera for that bit of a luncheon over there . . .

But she sat herself down alone right away, she shouldn't have to sit with us, I say to her, "Where do you live?" She says, "Penn Valley." She says, "And where do you live," I say, "I am still on Sixth Street." She jumped away in case I was carrying lice on my body and they might crawl on her. She says to her [Beyle's sister] because she's, after all, she's, she was the eldest. She says (?), "Where do you live?" She says, "I don't live in the city, I live in Saint Thomas." "This is how you allow your sister to live in South Philadelphia?" Didn't she? [Beyle turns and addresses this last question to Elke.] (See Yiddish original of this narrative in Appendix D.)

Beyle's delivery and the account itself indicate that the issues here speak to deep, core ideas of who she is. Beyle reveals here the pain and anger she feels at being considered inferior by the Jews of her generation who left the neighborhood. The siblings and friends who had moved away frequently labeled the South Philadelphia Jews as poor, old-fashioned, lacking in sophistication, and living in filth and fear. The neighborhood Jews had internalized these stereotypes and often fought to free themselves from identifying with them. In my experience, no one ever mentioned any former residents who were envious that the remaining Jews were close to their parents, had friendly neighbors, and were comfortable in their familiar surroundings.

Beyle's incessant talk is noteworthy. She is animated and emotionally involved in the telling and seems to be reenacting the encounter with her childhood neighbor at the reunion. There is practically no faltering, pausing, or stuttering.[5] She conveys sarcasm and irony by manipulating her voice quality and using qualifying statements such as "at the very least" (in the Yiddish original: *khotsh*), the extra "very" in "very very good" (in the Yiddish original: *zeyer zeyer git*), and the extra "high" in "high, high society" (in the Yiddish original: *hekhe, hekhe fentster*). With artistry, Beyle contrasts the Riviera with the reunion luncheon, which she belittles by calling it a *shtikl lontshn dortn* ("that bit of a luncheon over there"). By these linguistic means she contrasts the fanciful world of the condescending childhood friend with her and her and her sister's normal, everyday existence. Beyle achieves this further by addressing the woman with the lengthened and emphasized [u] of the prestigious Yiddish standard and northeastern European dialect: *Vi voynstu:?* (Where do you live?), in contrast to the [i] she otherwise uses consistently in her dialect of northern Ukraine. The language she uses to describe the woman's reaction to being told that Beyle still lives in the old neighborhood is an effective and original use of a metaphor appropriate to the culture of a Yiddish speaker, recoiling from someone who may be infested with lice.

Beyle, the youngest of the Yiddish speakers whose speech I recorded, was a master of Yiddish speech, a most fluent and colorful raconteur. Her story was full of the raw emotion that characterized the feelings of those who stayed on. Among this group, those who were critical of aspects of South Philadelphia life still identified with the neighborhood. No one expressed shame or embarrassment or an unwillingness to call themselves South Philadelphians. For most, the attachment to this place was all they knew. Itke expressed this clearly: "Fun di munit ikh ho geefnt mayn eygn iz geven porter strit. Ikh veys nit ken andere heym, . . . dus iz geven mayn gas." (From the minute I opened my eyes it was Porter Street. I don't know another home, . . . this was my street.)

The links binding people to neighborhood and community are clearly illustrated by the life of Feygl-Asye. The storefront entrance to Feygl-Asye's house told a story of family and neighborhood change. After some neighborhood hooligans broke the front window on Christmas Eve, half of it was boarded over and covered with graffiti. She did not have enough money to pay to replace the glass. Inside, the signs of past and present mingled. Feygl-Asye had a penchant for growing things and had dozens of plants and cuttings that responded to the sunlight coming through the functioning half of the window. Several built-in clothes racks, a mannequin, and a mangle were evidence of the family's former tailor and dry-cleaning shop. At one point the room held a hospital bed for Feygl-Asye's ailing mother. In railroad-car fashion, the next room was a rather dark living room full of old furniture and family photos, from which steps led upstairs. Behind the living room was an eat-in kitchen that opened onto a cement-covered yard.

Feygl-Asye, born in the neighborhood 66 years ago, had lived in this house for 38 years when I knew her. She went to school in the neighborhood, graduating from Southern High School for Girls. She also finished the local Talmud Torah in the present Center building across from her house. The youngest of three children, she had nieces and nephews in Philadelphia and other eastern cities, but she never married.

Both her parents were young when they came from the area of Smile in Ukraine to settle in South Philadelphia. They married in Philadelphia and raised a family, the father starting out as a garment worker and eventually opening his own small business after losing his job. Feygl-Asye worked in a variety of factory, office, and sales positions, until she was laid off at age 52, ten years before she was eligible for social security. The next years were difficult because her mother wanted her to help run the house and store rather than go back to work. After her mother died, Itke, a Center member, convinced Feyge-Asye to come to the Center twice weekly. With breathing troubles and a high-pitched voice, Feygl-Asye conveyed an agitated demeanor to those around her. She was an intelligent person who read and had an interest in the issues of the day. The chance to socialize at the Center was the mark of a new phase of life in her native neighborhood, now that her role as caretaker was over.

Studies of factors that promote attachment to place have shown that "residing in a neighborhood a long time is not, by itself, enough to create affective attachment," but that voluntary ties and local friends are most effective in promoting such feelings (Gerson, Stueve, and Fischer 1977: 156). Feygl-Asye and her neighbors still viewed their neighborhood as warm and friendly. "It's heymish" (It's homey), said Izzy. "Ven di voynst in South Filadelfya, yeyder eyner iz bakentlekh mit dir" (When you live in South Philadelphia, you know everyone), Roze agreed. Feygl-Asye recalled, "Du iz gevin heymishe mentshn vus hobm mir gekont in ikh ho(b) zey gekent, in ikh ho(b) zey geglakht, in zey mir" (Here were familiar people who knew me and I knew them, and I liked them, and they me). It was this neighborly concern that made the residents feel at home in the area, and that indeed defined its uniqueness for them. Basye asserted, "We are warm and that's the difference between South Philadelphia and the rest of the city."

One of the oldest residents, Yisrul, interpreted the flight of the Jews as a striving to outdo their neighbors, to be like the *hekhe fentster* (the fancy crowd). Basye said emphatically, "When they moved away to the Northeast [Philadelphia], they went into their own little houses, they closed the door, turned on the air conditioner and forgot the rest of the world." Tsipe-Khashe recalled how devastated she had felt in the 1930's when her boyfriend's parents disapproved of his going out with a South Philadelphia girl.

The main advantage of the neighborhood, the residents said, was that people knew you and cared about you. In one speech, Feygl-Asye recalled an encounter she had with Izzy's sister, who had moved away from South Philadelphia.

Zug ikh, how do you like it? Zukt zi, see it's like this way. Du, zukt zi, az ikh ken gey—ibergeyn tsvey skveyr ken ikh zey ken zugn halo tsu fuftsik mentshn. Zey kenen mikh, ikh ken zey i—, dort iz pinkt farkert . . . Dort ken ikh ibergeyn fuftsik stritlakh, in eyber tsvey mentshn zugn halo oder derkenen dir iz men gliklekh. Siz ondersh.

I say, how do you like it? She says, see it's like this way. Here, she says, I can go— cross two squares; I can see can say hello to fifty people. They know me, I know them and, there it's the exact opposite . . . There I can cross fifty streets, and you're lucky if two people say hello or recognize you. It's different.

Those kinds of tales, comparing friends and relatives who had moved to the Northeast with the South Philadelphia crowd, are part of a genre that was used often in the storytelling repertoire of most South Philadelphians. The contrast of one community as symbolizing the good life and another as inferior is typical in popular ideologies of towns, cities, and suburbs in contemporary America (Hummon 1990: 180). Many South Philadelphia Jews developed a retort to the derision of their family members and former neighbors, as Itke illustrated:

See I'm always up at the Northeast and I see people that e—I thought, God forbid, you know they're not here or sumpthin? . . . And I see them I said to my sister, oh I know her. She says she lives here, you know. One of them came over to me. Itke! I says yeah. Oh you finally moved up here. I say I beg your pardon. I'm visiting here, I do not live here. How do you live downtown? I says how do I live downtown? Do you look better than me? I say do I have any horns here. I say I wouldn't trade with you or anybody. I say I'm comfortable. She says, oh the neighborhood. I says, do you have nice neighbors? I have wonderful neighbors, I have no complaints.

Contrasted with Itke's low-keyed sarcasm was Reyzl's feisty, more insulting response. I asked her how she answered people who criticized her for staying in South Philadelphia. "Ir veyst vus ikh zug? Ole shmuts vus hot aroysgemuft fin Sowth Filadelfya voynt vi di voynst, thaets awl. Ikh ker nit." (You know what I say? All the dirt that moved out of South Philadelphia is living where you live, that's all. I don't care.)

The distinct Jewish nature of the neighborhood loomed high in the consciousness of the residents, particularly when they recalled the past. Some of the people realized that the responsibility of maintaining the neighborhood's rich Jewish tradition rested on them, limited as their resources may have been. "[We're] like old-fashioned, old-time Jews, we're proud of it, not ashamed of it, we're holding on to what's left of us." Despite their conviction that South Philadelphia was perceived as inferior by the rest of the city, residents took seriously the responsibility of upholding the long-standing Jewish presence in the neighborhood.

Most of the local Jews commented about the diminished Jewish nature of the neighborhood, but they rarely complained about it. Their grievances were not that their new neighbors were not Jewish, but rather that some of them were vandals, drug pushers, addicts, and anti-Semites. What bothered many of the Jewish residents were the threats to person and property. Youngsters put wood in the keyhole of one synagogue, drew swastikas on another, and attached a chain from a car to its pillars, trying to pull it down. They also broke into houses and vandalized the Center, eventually destroying the building by arson in December 1985. The synagogue near the neighborhood's western perimeter, however, did not experience such acts of malice. While some of the elderly felt especially vulnerable, Yisrul lived alone at age 95, left his door unlocked, and claimed that the local children were his good friends. When I visited him, I brought along my fears of the group of teenagers who sat on Yisrul's stoop and caught myself locking his front door.

Some expressed negative sentiments about the neighborhood. Dveyre, for example, felt that her non-Jewish neighbors had persistently persecuted her. Masha, on the other hand, lived two blocks away and reported that her neighbors were helpful and friendly. Itke felt safe in South Philadelphia and said no one bothered her, whereas Rive-Rukhl and Moyshe B., who lived on the same block, were frightened by the drug traffic and violence brought there by new residents. A Jewish barber said that he lived in a good neighborhood, unlike the unsafe area near the Center, which was only two streets from him. Certain neighborhood characteristics varied block by block and were perceived uniquely by the residents.

Even within one household, family members related to the neighborhood in diverse ways. Leye was ready to move. Her house had been broken into three times while she was home, and she had been knocked down and held at knifepoint. But Yankl A., her husband, was attached to the house in which he had lived with his parents, and he was not ready to leave. Ester-Beyle was content in the house she had lived in for 38 years. She was slightly handicapped, knew many people nearby, and took advantage of the Center down the street. Her husband, Shmuel-Arn, was "one hundred percent dissatisfied where we live," especially because of the young vandals.

As the participant-observer, I frequently expressed opinions that were diametrically opposed to those of the local people, despite their more intimate knowledge of how things used to be and how they had changed. In one conversation, I praised the neighborhood to Leye, who thought it had become extremely dangerous. If a resident complained about the condition of the streets, I emphasized the positive aspects of the area. My responses were intended to make them feel good about themselves. Yet I also had sentimental reasons for responding as I did to their complaints. Wishing to see the local Jewish community remain and thrive, I expressed dismay that agencies did not help settle recent Soviet Jewish immigrants in

South Philadelphia. Izhak, however, realized that settlement in South Philadelphia would have been counterproductive. After all, "Zay hot men aribergebrenkt aher me zol zay tsaygn az Amerike iz beser vi Rusnland" (They were brought over here to show them that America is superior to Russia).

Although many agreed with me about the advantages of living in the neighborhood, such as having children exposed to their grandparents' generation while growing up, my positive outlook did not generally sway their opinions about their surroundings. Although I felt sad and helpless about the abandoned stores, with time I came to understand the residents' perspectives better. I had, after all, never lived in such an old and unfashionable area, and initially I had shared some of their negative views. I had been surprised when well-dressed people attended the Center, when the synagogue Hanukkah party was well organized, and when the Sunday school children were intelligent and alert. I was challenged to confront my own preconceptions, and then to try to resolve them.

In general, the Jewish residents were proud of their traditions, appreciated the image of friendly, closely interacting neighbors, and did not yearn for the way of life of those who had left the neighborhood. Still, it is difficult to explain with certainty why they had stayed, some of them for almost a century, while most of their family members, friends, and neighbors had left. The factors that held the South Philadelphia Jews in place were complex. Leye was ready to leave in her old age, when it is hardest, yet pointed to employment and family ties, as well as the institutional anchor in her life, the Center, as reasons to stay:

I have great respect for a livelihood. Here we had a livelihood so we had to stay. I didn't want to go because e—I saw that the man e—was bringing in more money, than I even need and e—I am comfortable, and e—my mother was here, and my sister, and all around us, and now it's a little i—a—e—the Center keeps me going a little. (My translation)

My enthusiasm for communal continuity seemed a mere abstraction in the presence of the fierce reality of being in South Philadelphia for a lifetime. The long-standing ambivalence that the residents felt as they continued to identify with the neighborhood was the way they dealt best with their way of life, their age, and their relationship to place and community.

Jews and Non-Jews

The relationships that South Philadelphia Jews maintained with non-Jews comprised an intricate montage of separation and amalgamation. On a community level distances were maintained, even though on an individual level friendships and intermarriages were abundant. Attitudes and behaviors followed from those in previous generations. In the third generation, the children of the group of residents constituting the focus of this study, the permeability of barriers between Jews and other ethnic groups had increased greatly. This tendency was evident in the second generation. In my research, I did not extensively examine the relation of the non-Jewish residents to Jews in the community. However, it did become clear that the Jewish residents were similar to their white non-Jewish neighbors in many ways. Both groups supported the mayoral candidacy of conservative former mayor Rizzo. Few residents, Jewish or non-Jewish, were professionals or executives in large businesses; rather, most ran small businesses and were engaged in blue-collar work. The South Philadelphians, Jewish and non-Jewish, shared the same socioeconomic status and did not seem intent on changing their social position.

All of the Jews lived on streets where the majority of their neighbors were not Jewish. Even if they would have preferred to live in a heavily Jewish neighborhood, as they did in the past, most of the Jewish residents did not complain about their neighbors. Some were very close friends; some of the elderly Jews depended on their neighbors for help. Both Jews and non-Jews participated in most Center activities. Most married young Jews in the neighborhood had non-Jewish spouses. And many of the residents' children not living in the area were married to non-Jews. Despite these close contacts, paradoxically, the organizational affiliations for the older residents were exclusively Jewish.

Reyzl recalled that all 52 families living on her street were Jewish many years earlier. During my study, there were only six Jewish households there, all of them made up of single people. She claimed that this had been true for the past ten to fifteen years. Yisrul lived on her street, and Dveyre's daughter and granddaughter lived near the corner. This was the typical residence pattern in the neighborhood.

A few of the older Jewish women had been married to non-Jews, including two who attended the Gleyzele tey group. In addition, some of the older residents grew up on the fringes of the neighborhood, where the streets were inhabited largely by non-Jews, and therefore they had mostly non-Jewish friends. Yet all of the elderly Jewish subjects seemed to have received the message that Jews had been persecuted by non-Jews and that even today one should be wary of antisemitism. They learned this lesson whether they were born in Europe or America.

Just as the Ukrainian immigrants most often repeated stories of the pogroms, most of the American-born residents recalled being called "dirty Jew" and being beaten up by non-Jewish children. The conflicts they reported occurred largely with Irish-American children near Second and

Front Streets, blocks where Orthodox Jews with beards were subjected to physical abuse.

The Jews were not comfortable talking about certain ethnic groups. At the mention of blacks, Puerto Ricans, or Koreans, their voices might suddenly lower to a whisper, even if I was the only one present and had no tape recorder. I was sometimes disappointed in myself for not protesting their racist remarks; but as the ethnographer, I chose to avoid unnecessary conflict and remained silent, an uncomfortable position for me at these times.

The racist comments notwithstanding, their day-to-day relations with non-Jews were cordial at least. One non-Jewish senior volunteer at the Center was born in South Philadelphia, a child of Christian Russian Orthodox immigrants from Kiev, and had attended the Yiddish class led by a Center member. The Center had one devoted African American member who attended all of its activities. The members also developed close relations with several African American staff. Non-Jewish participants in the art class created Jewish ritual objects, and all members participated in the Oneg Shabbat (*oyneg shabes*) celebration, the Passover seder (*seyder*), and other Jewish holiday get-togethers. Administered under Jewish auspices, the Center did not officially celebrate non-Jewish religious holidays, but Italian songs were sometimes sung along with Yiddish and Hebrew ones. Jewish members had collected money for a new school planned by the nuns at one member's church. One active Jewish member was proud of a famous artist nun to whom she was related through a child's marriage. Two Jewish sisters, Elke and Beyle, maintained close friendships with a nun and with black families who lived on the Caribbean island where the sisters had lived.

The chief arena for intimate contact with non-Jews was within the family, for in most Jewish families in South Philadelphia there had been instances of intermarriage. Interfaith marriages between those over age 50 were not common. Of the twelve such marriages I knew about, in only two did the Jewish partner cease to identify as a Jew. Many of the children, nieces, and nephews of Jewish South Philadelphians had married non-Jews, though most of them no longer lived in the neighborhood. I was familiar with ten intermarried third-generation South Philadelphia Jews who lived in the neighborhood, seven of whom sent their children to the Sunday school. Second-generation parents were satisfied with their children's marriages only if the non-Jewish partner had converted. Since most had not, the residents usually reported tension and anguish in the family. When intermarriage was discussed, either in private or in public, the Jews generally expressed the belief that it diminished Jewish continuity and tradition.[6]

My own response to discovering examples of intermarriage in the neighborhood reflected my preconceived images of the generations. When one of the Center staff members told me that she grew up bilingual, her Italian surname clearly suggested to me that she spoke Italian and English. In fact, Yiddish was her first language. I was equally surprised when a Center member, Carmen, brought her mother into the Gleyzele tey session and her mother, who also had an Italian family name, told me that her own name was Leyke, a loving Yiddish diminutive. I expected the older residents to be traditional and old-worldly, even though I was aware that some of the older social conventions had disappeared from the neighborhood. Yet I expected almost anything from the younger people. Itzik, at the age of 26 the youngest proprietor on the zibete, was a child of Holocaust survivors and received an Orthodox Jewish day-school education while he was growing up in the neighborhood; but I was not surprised to meet his Asian girlfriend, who lived with him and worked in his designer jeans store. Although the older residents did not openly welcome neighborhood newcomers from Southeast Asia, I did not hear them criticize Itzik, perhaps because they gave him credit for being a good businessman and making improvements to his parents' store after they retired to Arizona. So, as I did, the older residents, too, had different standards and expectations for the younger generation.

Perhaps the ideal situation for the elderly Jews in South Philadelphia today is best illustrated by the case of Basye A. The residents with family nearby did not usually suffer from isolation and familial neglect. With so few young Jews in the neighborhood, it was unlikely that a Jewish child or grandchild would meet a Jewish mate in the neighborhood or even settle in the area. Basye's son Moyshe, 33, ran the upholstering business with her and shared her penchant for local politics; both of them served as Democratic committee representatives. Moyshe's political connection landed him an additional job in City Hall. The previous summer, some of the local Jewish residents had attended Moyshe's wedding to a recent convert to Judaism, whose family lived and worked on the zibete. She had gone through training and conversion under the direction of the rabbi at Izzy's shul. The family, including her ten-year-old son from a previous marriage, attended services every Friday evening. The boy, although not Jewish, identified to such an extent with the Judaism of his mother and stepfather that he insisted on attending Izzy's Sunday school and was the first one to show up each week. This atypical path of Jewish continuity in South Philadelphia brought the Jewish and non-Jewish communities together.

Acts of vandalism in the neighborhood were mostly limited to the mischief of gangs of youngsters. Some, like Shmuel-Arn, president of Adath Shalom synagogue, thought that all of the vandalism directed at Jewish institutions was motivated by antisemitism. Feygl-Asye, on the other hand, whose front window was broken by vandals, stressed that in general the non-Jewish residents who had moved to the neighborhood were not the problem. Rather she felt that the increase in crime was caused by only a few individuals.

In general, although South Philadelphia Jews did not dislike non-Jews, their overt ethnic pride and affinity for Jews took precedence. For example, Blumke had had only non-Jewish friends as a child, and she stated, "I love Jewish people. Your own is your own, but I get along with everyone." Itke accepted non-Jews who were similar to Jews: "Few goyim (non-Jewish) friends I have, they have like idish harts (a Jewish heart), you know, they're nice." Dveyre's credo was to remain true to Jewish traditions: "So dos tsaygt dir, az ven me hot respekt far zikh aleyn, in vos mir zayn geboyrn gevorn this is the most important thing" (So this shows you, that when you have respect for yourself, for that with which you were born, this is the most important thing).

In searching for patterns in the relationships of Jewish South Philadelphians with their non-Jewish neighbors, I found almost no affiliation with non-Jews in organizational life. They had day-to-day contacts with neighbors, but closeness resulted more from intermarriage than because of friendship ties. The older residents, ever aware of the history of antisemitism in Europe and America, identified strongly as Jews in the face of this legacy. Even though most no longer experienced antisemitism, the growth of the non-Jewish population intensified their isolation in the neighborhood and their loyalty to their Jewishness. Oddly, the main hope for intergenerational continuity in the neighborhood was provided by the non-Jews who converted and married young Jews. Some Jewish residents thought highly of their non-Jewish neighbors; others resented them. Whatever their stance, the Jews of South Philadelphia could not neglect the non-Jews in their midst.

Observance of Jewish Traditions

The neighborhood Jews referred to the overall sense of being Jewish by the term "yiddishkeit," which pervaded their existence. This state of being, as they defined it, included growing up with Jewish family and neighbors, believing in God, observing the dietary laws, preparing traditional dishes, speaking Yiddish, celebrating holidays, and trusting in Jewish folk belief. In my sample, in which the age of the bulk of informants ranged from 60 to 100, variation in observance and sense of yiddishkeit did not relate directly to age or place of birth. All of the elderly residents had strong Jewish identities.

Yiddishkeit was part of their uncontested birthright. As Dveyre, 83, who arrived in South Philadelphia from England at six months of age, remarked,

"Ikh denk az (I think that) it's not your religion, it's your roots that are instilled." She did not consider herself fanatic but prayed to God for help, observed kashrus (the dietary laws), and lit candles on Friday night. She noted the difficulty of obtaining kosher meat without a kosher butcher in the neighborhood.

Because when my daughter was almost dying I prayed to God day and night God should bring her home to her little orphan, and he answered me. But I'm not a fanatic Jew, you know what I mean? But I am—my daughter came in Friday. She brought me a *khale* (challah) for shabes. So e—she takes a look, the candles are on the table. She says, Mother, it's kinda early. I say, no it's not too early. I says I don't wanna forget. But you know life here is very hard for me. I have such troubles with meat. You have to call and sometimes when he wants he sends an order, sometimes he doesn't want to he—. (My translation)

Several of the people vividly remembered going with a mother or grandmother to see Leybele *opshprekher* (the exorcist), a neighborhood figure known for his ability to ward off the evil eye. Mothers also tried on their own to ensure the health of sickly children by giving them an additional name like Khaye or Khayim (life) or by reviving the folk custom of buying back sick children from the devil. Rivke A. recalled her mother placing a knife under her pillow when she was giving birth so that it should be "sheydik tsi sheydim" (harmful to the evil spirits). Although the residents did not typically engage in such folk practices, they wanted to believe in their powers and enjoyed recalling times when such traditions were part of daily life.

Beyle, who rarely attended synagogue, went to a Reform Jewish wedding and complained that the rabbi reminded her of a priest. With the synagogue near her house closed, Tsipe-Khashe did not see the Jews pass by her door on their way to services, so the Jewish holidays did not have as much meaning for her as before. Shmuel-Arn, president of one of the Conservative synagogues, remarked to me, "Ours is not a synagogue; this is a shul" (Yiddish word for synagogue). He liked to think that in his place of worship they were doing things traditionally, although he told of increased participation of women and the leadership of a female rabbi. Members like Dvoyre felt uncomfortable, however, about the expanding women's roles in ritual ("Religion News," *South Philadelphia Review East*, November 1, 1984, p. E35).

Nostalgia is a complicated sentiment. Blumke, 74, had cared for her mother until her recent death at the age of 101. She did not keep a kosher home; in fact, she savored a good ham and cheese sandwich. Yet, she missed the religious elderly Jews who used to live on her block. The strictly Orthodox behavior of her nephew and his wife, who dressed in traditional garb and would not eat at his mother's house because it was not kosher, was characterized by Blumke as "fanatic." In other words, for her, religious observance was important as a link to memories of the past, but not as a living tradition.

Jewish customs of the past were vividly preserved as selective memories of childhood. Ester-Beyle, 66, for example, recreated the smells and tastes upon coming home from school on Friday afternoon:

> *E.-B.:* She was a good housekeeper and a really good cook, e—she
> could bake very well. I came from school every Friday, I, there
> was only one brother. Only I went to high school. Uh—so I
> came from school on Friday. When she heard me come in. She
> had already removed the liver from the chicken, and she put it
> into the soup. And she had a kaiser roll and when I came Friday,
> this is the first thing that she gave me from school, a chicken
> liver freshly cooked, just well cooked, he, he, he [laughs], that
> was delicious.
>
> *R. P.:* A delicacy, wow.
>
> *E.-B.:* And the dining room table from end to end was full of baked
> things, all sorts of coffee cakes and rolls. And my brothers
> came and took things home.
>
> *R. P.:* Home.
>
> *E.-B.:* To their wives.
>
> *R. P.:* They were able to come Friday.
>
> *E.-B.:* Each Friday. Oh yes. They didn't eat dinner there, but they
> took home what my mother baked. (See Yiddish original of
> narrative in Appendix D.)

The excitement in Ester-Beyle's voice was clear, as if she were entering her mother's house today. That time, Friday afternoon, divided the week and set the stage for the most festive time at home, Friday evening, *erev shabbos*. Time and again the residents indulged in romantic reminiscences of the delicious dishes their mothers prepared for the Sabbath.

Although many synagogues existed in the neighborhood, residents reported that their parents were not strictly observant. Most of them worked on shabbos. Yet they knew when shabbos began and were aware of its requirements. On the zibete, after the shabbos candles were lit in the kitchen behind the store, the kitchen door was closed so that the shopkeeper would not have to walk past the candles while he was working. Beyle reported that her father, a baker, would work all of Friday night and go to shul early Saturday morning when he came home from work. During my stay in South Philadelphia, Izzy went to shul on Saturdays while his wife minded the store. These people were traditional Jews, albeit discriminating in the traditions they observed. Other South Philadelphia Jews never went to the synagogue and did not observe kashrus or shabbos but whole-heartedly perceived themselves as committed and caring Jews.

Their varying patterns of religious observance over the years reflected the intersection of modified personal priorities, changing communal institutions, transitional neighborhood composition, and the desire to maintain authentic traditions. Izhak, in the first years in his store on the zibete, donned talis (prayer shawl) and tfillin (phylacteries) every morning. But as he worked longer hours, he searched for something to eliminate from his schedule and decided to curtail his daily prayers. Although he was still a synagogue member, he had lost the ability to read a prayer book with ease.

In contrast, when her children were in junior high school, Ester-Beyle felt a need to practice Judaism more intensely and started attending synagogue alone on Friday night. She had not given her daughter a Jewish education, although she herself had studied at the Talmud Torah on the high-school level. Her renewed religious activity appealed to her husband Shmuel-Arn, and both became very involved in synagogue life.

A third resident, Shmiel-Leyb, 86, confessed that he was not as observant as before, primarily because there were no longer any active, functioning synagogues in his neighborhood. Ironically, years earlier he had moved there from Camden, N.J., which was close to his work, precisely because he wanted to be near a daily minyan in order to say kaddish (the prayer for the dead) for his father. His wife, Ester-Sosye, emphasized that their home was still kosher and that their son and daughter-in-law living in New York State were strictly Orthodox.

Kashrus was the main characteristic of Jewish home life according to the South Philadelphia Jews. When Itke compared her mother-in-law and mother, the difference in kashrus was the major difference in their yiddishkeit: "May shvigerz geven mer moderner vi ma mame. Zhit nit gegleybt tsi fil in yidishkayt. . . . The, shvigerz nit geven vi ma mame, mit di kosherkayt in alesdi—" (My mother-in-law was more modern than my mother. She didn't believe too much in yiddishkeit. . . . My, mother-in-law was not like my mother, with being kosher and everythin—).

As with the Sabbath, awareness of the mandate of kashrus was greater than the actual observance of the laws. European-born Rivke A., who went to the Center and the neighborhood to remember her childhood and the world of her deceased parents, discussed the delicious shrimp rolls that she bought. In contrast, Dveyre's fourteen-year-old granddaughter, one of the few Jewish teenagers living in the neighborhood, was intent on keeping kosher. Similar discontinuities were evident in earlier generations, too. Basye A., whose father strayed from his original Orthodoxy, recalled that he would declare as kosher only those food items that he enjoyed. His home was strictly kosher, but fried oysters were deemed kosher when eaten in the restaurant. Having been exposed to such mixed messages, Basye insisted that her own children's observance be more uniform. When they were babies, a meal consisting of chicken and baby food vegetables was accompanied by juice. They would have to wait a few hours for their milk bottle. She would tell them, "This is the yiddishkeit."

Even people who did not keep kosher, did not attend synagogue, and did not observe shabbos or yom tov (*yontif*, holiday) still allied themselves with the concept of yiddishkeit. To them, it meant being Jewish. Referring to her daughter, Roze said, "bekoz ikh hob azoy gevalt az zi zol zan yidishkeyt" (because I really wanted her to be yiddishkeit). She lamented the fact that the daughter might have lost that yiddishkeit by marrying a non-Jew and taking her children to church. When I asked Feygl-Asye if her parents were *frim* (observant), she avoided that label and opted for the more inclusive "mir zenen yidish" (we are Jewish). Obviously the strong ethnic identity of South Philadelphia Jews has deep roots that still permeate contemporary life.

Belonging

Jewish personal and group identification was reinforced by almost exclusive participation in organizations with a Jewish membership and a Jewish program of activities. Nevertheless, the Jews in South Philadelphia exhibited a variety of interests that were not limited to Jewish concerns, including charity work, the creative arts, sports, politics, gambling, drinking, dancing, reading, and social action. One might have expected them to affiliate with groups—and not specifically Jewish groups—that would help them pursue their interests. The only such nonsectarian voluntary associations, however, were those of a few individuals involved in political work in the neighborhood and of the president of the Congress Mummers Club, who also attended synagogue.

Not only was organizational affiliation almost exclusively Jewish in nature, but most of the Jews I met had only Jewish friends. Despite the fact that many of the Jews in the neighborhood were old and sick, the barriers between ethnic and religious groups remained.[7] Of course, since this project was an ethnographic study of a community by one investigator, it is possible that I overlooked certain sectors—for example, the shut-ins who did not leave home for socializing or shopping, or people living on peripheral streets with no other Jewish residents nearby.

The three synagogues, or shuls, attracted a unique clientele. The Orthodox Congregation Shivtei Yeshuron–Heysiner–Ezras Israel was different from the other two in several ways: proportionately more European-born men participated here; management of the shul was concentrated in the hands of young Hal and his mother; four of the men who went to daven (pray) had a reputation for looking for free food handouts (consequently, they appreciated the platters served at the kiddush [*kidish*, blessing over the wine]); two of them got paid for attending a minyan in town (an irregular procedure, since attendance at services was normally voluntary); and the rabbi and hazan (*khazn*, cantor) lived in the neighborhood. Both of the Conservative shuls had more people involved in planning and implementing activities, particularly Congregation Adath Shalom. Many of its members were active at the Center, unlike the members of Y.P.C. Shari Eli. Both institutions hired a rabbi and a hazan, who lived in other areas of the city. The Orthodox shul held services on holidays, each Saturday morning, and also on Friday and Saturday evenings for the part of the year with long daylight hours. Adath Shalom had services on Friday evenings and Saturday mornings and was open for the men's club on Sunday mornings. Shari Eli met for services and kiddush on Friday evenings and Saturday mornings; the Sunday school met there each week. Both Adath Shalom and Shari Eli had a sisterhood, and members also got together on business and social occasions.

Although the Jewish community was small, there was little communication among the three shuls. Shivtei Yeshuron–Heysiner–Ezras Israel did not advertise its activities. Most South Philadelphia Jews did not even know there was a functioning Orthodox shul in the neighborhood. Although Shari Eli had participated in negotiations with the two groups that ultimately merged to form Adath Shalom 25 years earlier, there was virtually no communication between the members of the two Conservative shuls during my stay there; they seemed to have independent social networks. There were, however, members who ventured a critical opinion of a rival shul. Shmuel-Arn commented that at Adath Shalom they did not view Shari Eli as a shul but as a social club. Yisrul, at 95, had attended several shuls until they closed, one by one. Two years earlier he had voted for the expansion of women's participation in ritual at his shul, Adath Shalom. He vied for the honor of making kiddush at the Center with the other venerable member, 100-year-old Khatshe, who had been a member of the Orthodox shul for 65 years. Yisrul was proud to know all the possible versions of the kiddush by heart and claimed that Khatshe, whom he referred to as "der beker" (the baker), was unlettered and not as adept as he in matters of ritual. This was Yisrul's opinion of Shivtei Yeshuron–Heysiner–Ezras Israel:

Siz azey ortodoksish vi e—azey vi goyish, e—e—an ortodoksishe shil meyn ikh zi darf zayn andersh, ugehit ale dinim, but e—du halt men of a shil e—bloyz azey— az me kimt unesn. Se kimn dray layter fin danet zakh unesn. . . . Kent zikh for-shteln vus aza min grobe yingn zey zenen ale, az eyner a gantser tier dortn in yener shil, a gantse, no, a gantser knaker, freykt er mir, in der shil vus ikh gey, iz shabes meyg men makhn a bal-mitsve?

It's so Orthodox, almost as if it were Christian, e—e—I think an Orthodox shul must be different, all laws must be observed, but here they keep a shul going e— just like that—to come and fill yourself with food. Three people from here go to gorge themselves. . . . You can just imagine what kind of uncouth bunch they all are, that one of the big activists there in that shul, a big, no, a big shot, asks me, if at the shul I attend you're allowed to have a bar-mitzvah on shabbos.

The presence of these independently functioning synagogues in South Philadelphia revealed much about the structure of this small Jewish community. It did not function like other small communities in which members knew each other. Rather, in many ways, the community operated as it had 30 or 40 years earlier when it counted a much larger population. Jews remained scattered over different streets, aware of only their own organizations and synagogues, with little increased opportunity to meet the small numbers that constituted their compatriots. Often, I brought Jewish news into the neighborhood and was in the rare position of linking, however superficially, autonomous social networks and institutions.

The one institution whose membership represented the intersection of a variety of socioeconomic classes, ages, and personal interests was the Center. In contrast with the shul, which largely functioned on the weekend, the Center was the neighborhood's Monday-through-Friday Jewish institution. For people who did not wish to affiliate with a shul, the Center was the only outlet for organized activities with Jewish content. Jews and non-Jews, who otherwise would not socialize, could meet there. In a way, by the establishment of a Jewish senior center, the Jewish community was given a new route for forming social bonds. Some people made new friends; others renewed old acquaintances. Blumke, Roze, and Itke, for example, had worked together in a pocketbook factory about fifty years earlier. Although they all remained in South Philadelphia, their lives had taken different directions. When they began going to the Center, they rekindled their former friendship. For the people who attended daily the Center provided a unique opportunity for repeated close interaction. In the life of the aged, who are not very mobile, this chance was rare.

Many Jewish South Philadelphians were more involved in Jewish life during their youth than in adulthood, and in later life they turned to the Center to become reattached. Blumke, for one, began to feel the special need to be with Jews when her mother died. Other elderly Jews were lonely and went to the Center for companionship. Eighty-six year-old Surele, who had lost all her siblings, asserted that the Center kept her alive. Roze echoed this sentiment; since becoming wheelchair-bound, the Center had been her main outlet for fighting depression, getting physical exercise, and broadening her mental horizon.

Because the Center attracted about two hundred people to its programs and only 70 percent were Jewish, it is clear that most South Philadelphia Jews were not members. Presumably, the nonmembers did not feel the need to receive the social services the Center provided; they preferred to manage their lives without the aid of communal institutions.

It is interesting that many of Adath Shalom's members belonged to the Center, while Shari Eli's did not. I do not understand the make-up of the membership rolls well enough to account for this difference, but there seemed to be other correlations in their patterns of affiliation. Members of Adath Shalom tended to affiliate with the local post of the Jewish War Veterans; many of the male members of Shari Eli belonged to the Masons. These diverse group affiliations may have been a means for a small community to maintain its identity and attract various kinds of members, allowing them to feel comfortable within the community. The separate affiliation networks may also have been a relic of the past, when the Jewish community was much larger.

Both the Jewish War Veterans and the Masons had their headquarters in South Philadelphia and were part of the American Jewish experience rather than offshoots of old-world or immigrant bodies. The popular image of South Philadelphia as old-fashioned and a home for immigrants tended to overlook such groups. The Masons are not thought of as a Jewish fraternal organization, though many children of Jewish immigrants joined the order, establishing units with a totally Jewish membership. Such was the case for the Square Club, a social and charitable Masonic organization, and the Blue Lodge, a business organization. The Square Club met "downtown," the term residents used to refer to South Philadelphia. The other Masonic groups met at the Masonic Temple "in town," the residents' term for Center City. Izzy, for example, belonged to two additional Masonic units, the Keystone Chapter and Council.

When the Jewish War Veterans sold their local building, the men's post tried meeting in the Northeast, but returned to South Philadelphia because attendance was better. The Ladies Auxiliary, the only group to attract members from outside the neighborhood, always met in South Philadelphia. Of its 60 members, almost half attended meetings regularly. The Ladies Auxiliary was a social club but also did charity work, especially for soldiers (mostly non-Jewish) in the veterans' hospitals.

Thus, within the neighborhood, South Philadelphia Jews could affiliate with a variety of Jewish groups and institutions: three synagogues, the Center, the veterans' post and its women's affiliate, and the Masonic Square Club. In addition, the Social Service Department at Albert Einstein Hospital's Daroff Division organized a group of Jewish volunteers who met at the hospital, ate together, and performed volunteer services. I visited the hospital once to determine whether Jewish patients were living in the environs of the hospital, which was north of the core neighborhood on which I was concentrating. The staff could not identify many such residents but introduced me to a group of seven Jewish volunteers, two from the hospital area and the rest from the region with which I was familiar. Once again, I met residents I did not know and was reminded that my study brought me in contact with only a fraction, perhaps 15 to 20 percent, of the neighborhood's Jewish residents.

Several of the Jewish organizations with which the residents were affiliated did meet in the Northeast, about ten miles from the neighborhood and difficult to reach by public transportation. One could understand the South Philadelphia residents' disappointment when a Philadelphia Jewish group that had met "in town" in order to be central to Jews from all parts of the city moved to the Northeast. Older residents without cars could not travel that far at night. The organizations were generally oriented toward fraternal socialization and mutual aid. Residents reported affiliation with several such groups: Pannonia Beneficial Association, B'nai Chaim Social, Judaic Union, Sholem Aleichem Club, United Jewish Organization, Prushin-Shershow Beneficial Association, and the Rovner Society. These were all Philadelphia-based groups. There were almost no reports of membership in branches of large national organizations such as Hadassah, Pioneer Women, B'nai B'rith, the American Jewish Congress, or the American Jewish Committee. However, Khatshe belonged to the Workmen's Circle, and Libe was an inactive member of ORT.

Social Networks

The organized groups provided one opportunity for socializing. Of these, only the Center provided for frequent (almost daily) contact and unstructured time to share news and emotions. These interactions met the social needs of some; for others, particularly those without many Jewish neighbors, the telephone was a major conduit for communicating with friends. This method of communication was not available for study, except when I was directly involved in telephone conversations, so it was difficult to gain a picture of the variety and frequency of telephone contacts. The telephone was certainly the most frequently used means of communicating with friends and family members in other neighborhoods and cities. For example, Khatshe talked to some of his children on the phone during the week, but on Sundays he spoke with all seven of them. In general, visits with family occurred much less frequently than phone conversations. Some residents hardly ever received a visitor or left the neighborhood to call on someone. In contrast, Izzy and Sure and Itke traveled to the Northeast weekly to visit family members. Likewise, Yisrul's son spent Mondays in South Philadelphia with his father.

In the South Philadelphia sample for which I maintained files according to name (120 individuals), slightly more than one-third of the residents lived alone. Those living with others included husbands and wives, one pair of sisters, and extended families. It is important to examine the segment of the population that lived alone and was confined to home, the shut-ins. According to Rotman's survey (1980: 46) this sector may have represented as many as 19 percent of South Philadelphia's Jews. The Center arranged social, medical, and nutrition services for more than four hundred clients, most of whom were homebound. A large proportion of them were not Jewish, as contrasted with the Jewish majority of members who went to the building to participate in activities. The reasons for the disparity may have related to differences in the socioeconomic level of local Jews and non-Jews or in traditions of accepting social welfare aid. Most likely it reflected the ease with which the non-Jewish majority in the neighborhood could avail itself of social services from the largest neighborhood provider. Yet the non-Jewish population was generally not interested in attending social and cultural activities in this Jewish institution. My impression of the Jewish population and its social networks was that the shut-in residents did not predominate. And I emphasize that my research design was concerned with active social networks for communication and therefore omitted these residents.

Friends, besides talking on the telephone, also met on the zibete and at the shopping center; they played cards at each other's houses, took inexpensive bus trips to Atlantic City, and went into town together. Members of Adath Shalom organized frequent bus trips to Atlantic City, for example, where members and other neighborhood residents went for the evening to walk on the boardwalk, take in a show, play the tables or the machines, have a meal, and be home early enough to get enough sleep for their next day's activities. Itke and Dvoyre, who had both lost their husbands, went with the group; the two were also officers of the South Philadelphia Social Club at the Center. Izhak and Libe, also members of the synagogue, occasionally closed their store early to catch an independent bus to Atlantic City. They sometimes met family and friends on the boardwalk but had no desire to socialize with synagogue or Center members.

Yankl C. was an old friend of Blumke and Roze's. He stopped by Roze's house every evening to talk. He and Reyzl also went out together; they both lived alone, away from their children and grandchildren. Blumke and Roze, besides seeing each other daily at the Center and playing cards together, talked each night on the telephone. They also kept in touch on the phone with Surele, Tsipe-Khashe, and Tillie, all Center members. Blumke's sister, who lived with her husband three blocks away, brought Blumke a freshly cooked dinner platter almost every evening. Roze lived with her brother and around the corner from her daughter and grandchildren. Thus, both had frequent contact with family and friends.

At the Center, one small group played cards sequestered in the upstairs lounge away from most other activity. They were the men's club members, who included Berl, whose wife was the eloquent spokeswoman for the Center's Advisory Council, Ezra, who kept house for his mentally disturbed wife, Radio, who was too young to be a Center member and was slow in gait and speech, and Yisrul. At first I thought Yisrul's interest was playing cards, but as I got to know him better I learned that this card-playing men's club member stayed up nights reading Yiddish literature; and in numerous discussions in his house he revealed to me his astute observations of culture and society. He received the Yiddish paper at home and was the only active reader of the Center's Yiddish book collection. He told me that he read Sholem Aleykhem three or four hours a night and that it inspired him.

Also at the Center, Rivke A. and Rivke B. sat and talked together. Both came from Ukraine as girls, and although one was well-to-do and the other of modest income, one having left South Philadelphia at an early age and the other having left the neighborhood for Center City in her seventies, they found a lot to talk about: children and grandchildren, sickness and health, food and clothing, neighbors and other Center members. Rivke A. enjoyed speaking with people who remembered her parents. Rivke B. stopped in at her brother-in-law and sister-in-law's house in the neighborhood and walked from the bus to the Center along the zibete to see the storekeepers and her former neighbors, including Libe and Izhak, who had a chair waiting for her.

When Feygl-Asye went to the Center, she sat with Itke. At the large supermarket in the local shopping center I met the two of them in the aisles. Feygl-Asye knew that Itke had many friends and a large family in the Northeast but that she only spoke on the phone with a few neighbors. From this helping relationship in which Itke guided Feygl-Asye out into the world, both derived benefits.

At Izzy's on the zibete some of the same folks went every day for their morning coffee or lunch, and Izzy's friends from Shari Eli and the Masons stopped by the window to chat. At Malke and Avrum's doorstep, people said hello, and some regulars, such as Sure B., were there often. I had met her at Libe and Izhak's and at the Center's Extension Club. Sure B. was a Holocaust survivor and her family was in Israel; she had difficulty reading and writing English and stayed in the neighborhood most of the time, not knowing how to travel to different parts of the city. Leye, when she was on the zibete, greeted Malke at her store step. Malke referred to Leye as *di plumberke* (the plumber's wife). Yankl A. and Leye, who had an auto-mobile, drove Malke home from the Northeast after meetings of the B'nai Chaim Social organization. At Libe and Izhak's linoleum store, Frume-Basye was a regular; she sat and complained about life with her husband, who was a rabbi and also an Orthodox shochet (*shoykhet*, a person licensed by rabbinical authority to slaughter animals and poultry for use as food). She preferred dancing and singing to the proper role of a rebbitzin (rabbi's wife), a role she had taken on ten years earlier. She was a public figure in the neighborhood, but Libe and Izhak remained her most dependable confidants.

Some people were well known throughout the community, whereas others associated with only one or two neighbors. Some residents belonged to several organizations and nurtured diverse friendships; others restricted their interactions to the family. Some relationships went back more than half a century; neighborhood and life cycle changes, however, caused some of the elderly to forge new social links. As in any community, some people disapproved of others, and such aversions ensured that social networks did not overlap. In my attempts to draw sociometric network diagrams, Izzy appeared as a network star, linked to a variety of individuals. However, even Izzy was not a part of certain independent networks, which reflected the segregation of institutional and social connections one might expect in a much larger community (see Moreno 1953; L. Milroy 1980; Labov 1984). I was continually reminded of the depth of historical experience living on in South Philadelphia.

CHAPTER SIX

Coming Home to
South Philadelphia

Community Continuity: Young Jews and Newcomers

The old Jews of South Philadelphia dominated the neighborhood, and it was among this cohort that the Yiddish speakers were to be found. However, to understand the concerns of the community, the presence or absence of younger Jews and new Jewish residents must be addressed, albeit briefly. This matter is essential to a discussion of the residents' awareness of the question of community continuity and the transmission of Jewish culture to future generations.

Rotman reported that only 11 percent of the neighborhood population was younger than 50 (1980:33). This figure was probably low, because her initial sample was based on Jewish family names and on records of hospitals and communal institutions that served more older people than youngsters. In my qualitative research project, I identified 66 Jews younger than 50, including converts and children of Jewish mothers and non-Jewish fathers. I met only 24 of these people personally; the others were described to me by relatives, neighbors, and friends. The group consisted of eighteen single individuals without children, three single mothers, four Jewish couples, eleven Jewish members of intermarried couples (only two of whom were Jewish males), two converted Jews, and 24 children under twenty. Virtually all of the Jews under 50 were born in South Philadelphia and lived near or with their parents and grandparents.

A description of one scene illustrates the simultaneous continuities and discontinuities of ethnic custom and language. At Shari Eli's Sunday School, Izzy had taught the children to recite the *shma* (the Jewish credo of belief in one God) by heart, in Hebrew. The children were welcome to participate in Friday-night services. But most of what they learned on Sunday involved the declamation in English of poems about the Jewish holidays. One Sunday before Purim, a boy recited a poem that contained a word pronounced like the English "moon." The reference was to the Yiddish *mun* or *mon* (poppyseeds), a filling used in the special baked goods of Purim, *homentashn*. None of the children knew the word *mun* or the food it referred to. Later, the boy's mother told me that she remembered clearly learning to make *mun* cookies from her mother's neighbor. She grew up in an Orthodox Jewish home and heard Yiddish spoken there; her husband is a converted Jew. I described Libe's delicious *mun-kikhelekh* (poppyseed cookies). Libe had given me a big bag on my last visit to her linoleum store, part of our newly acquired habit of exchanging food. When I asked the mother whether she knew Libe, she thought a minute and finally exclaimed yes, but that she had not seen her in years. Here was another example of the lack of connectedness in this small Jewish community.

'A farshterter peysakh' (A Ruined Passover)

April 10, 1985, twelve noon, the third seder at the Center is about to begin. This is the biggest event of the year in Jewish South Philadelphia. Almost two hundred people congregate at decorated tables for a service and meal. Right before the program is to start, the receptionist tells me that the police have come to the Center and need a person who can speak Yiddish. In the hallway a female police officer explains to me that an elderly neighborhood woman will not release the body of her husband, who has just died. She speaks no English, but neighbors say she speaks Yiddish. Would I come to help the police in this case? The police did not want to leave the woman alone with the body. Reluctantly I decide to leave the seder and my wife, Hannah, who had accompanied me. Before I leave I push the "record" button on my tape recorder so that I will have a record of the spoken events and rituals.

I am intrigued to find out who this woman is. Riding in the police car with the officer, I confidently tell her that something in the story makes no sense. There are no Jews in South Philadelphia who speak no English. I have never had occasion to be on the little street where the woman lives, one block in length between Fourth and Fifth Streets. The sun shines in through the two front windows as I enter the house. Several colored rugs are on the floor and pieces of fabric are on the sofas in the bright living room. A short woman in her seventies with brownish-gray hair, a cast on one arm and a hearing aid in one ear, wearing a print dress, comes down the stairs across from the entrance door. Her name is Marye. She is crying, and I address her in Yiddish, saying that I heard about her misfortune and came to help her, from the Jewish Center. She responds calmly, but expresses surprise that her husband has died so suddenly; she and her husband were out together shopping at the Italian market only that morning.

I was prepared to meet a resistant, noncommunicative person. But the problem is that she does not, in fact, speak English, the police cannot speak Yiddish with her, and neither could they find someone nearby to do so. Three other officers are in the house, one of whom is Jewish. The dead body is in the upstairs bathroom. The police need some information, a doctor to sign the death certificate, and arrangements to be made by the next of kin for removal of the body to a funeral parlor. My task is difficult because I want to comfort the woman, yet I understand the situation and the need to help expedite the arrangements. All that we have in common at the moment is Yiddish speech.

I can tell from Marye's accent, gold-filled teeth, and general appearance that she is a recent immigrant from the Soviet Union. When I ask, she says that she has been here eight years and that she lived in Kiev but was born in Chernobyl. I tell her that I know of the famous Hasidic rebbe from Chernobyl. She says her grandfather worked in the rebbe's court. I try to get Marye to sit down, but she paces the room and is very confused. Her husband was not sick. When the police find nitroglycerine pills, she says they are hers. The name of the physician on the prescription sounds familiar to me. He is an old Jewish doctor who lives in the neighborhood and is just retiring because his wife is ill. Many of the residents are upset about losing their trusted physician. In fact, Marye says that she and her husband began to go to a younger doctor. The police, however, call the old doctor, who knows Marye's husband and agrees to sign the death certificate.

When I asked about relatives, Marye says she has no one in Philadelphia, only a grandson in New York City. Her daughter lives in Belgium and her son is in the Soviet Union. She married Arn when she came to Philadelphia, not knowing him from before. It was an arranged marriage of convenience. She had no place to stay, and he wanted someone to manage the household. He was a widower with no children; he had come from Russia more than 60 years earlier. Marye and he communicated in Yiddish and Russian. I try to find out about his next of kin. Marye says there is a sister and brother-in-law. Although the police and I are able to locate the telephone numbers, we cannot reach them. I find a dues notice from a fraternal organization that arrived in the mail, the Judaic Union. I phone the secretary, who informs me that they take care of burial preparations but not funeral arrangements, and recommends two funeral parlors. I arrange for the body to be taken to the funeral parlor. Marye does not know what a funeral parlor is, since they do not function in the Soviet Union and are also not traditional Jewish institutions.

Meanwhile, Marye becomes a little more at ease. She insists on covering the mirrors in the living and dining rooms with sheets of white cotton, which she pulls out from under couch cushions. This is a Jewish custom for a house in mourning, and she remembers it. I am able to leave a message for her grandson on the phone. When he calls, Marye speaks to him in Russian and Yiddish. He comes later that day. She calls her daughter in Belgium, crying and screaming over the phone, also in Yiddish and Russian.

After two hours, a social worker from the Center comes to relieve me but cannot communicate with Marye. After almost ten years in the neighborhood, Marye is unaware that a Jewish center, or "klub," as she calls it, functions in the area and that people there would help her. The police officer stays the whole time, despite the fact that her superiors think she is taking too long. When she takes me back to the Center, the seder is over. Later I am able to listen to the proceedings on my tape. Some residents do know Arn, the husband, who lived in the neighborhood so many years. He was an officer of a shul that closed recently, and the building was razed. No one knows Marye, who was in a state of isolation in the neighborhood. People saw her over the years, and several sources of gossip ventured opinions about how bad the marriage was. A few women report that Arn wanted to marry them.

In these odd circumstances, I had located a Yiddish speaker who knew no English. Her one English word was "star" (store). After that, I visited her many times, met her family, and welcomed her daughter and son-in-law, a couple in their fifties, who settled in the neighborhood later that summer. They too were Yiddish speakers. I recorded several conversations with Marye, and she became a Center member. Although Marye did, in fact, have a few Jewish neighbors, it still is not clear to me who told the police that Marye spoke Yiddish.

In the neighborhood, Marye was the person most dependent on the spoken and printed Yiddish word. Only Yisrul, the 95-year-old immigrant, read the Yiddish newspaper religiously. He, of course, was used to hearing English speech after almost 80 years in America. But Marye's isolation from the world of English put her closer to the immigrant generation. She went to the Center regularly after Arn's death but still clung to the news of the weekly Yiddish press to teach her about the contemporary world. At the Center, although so many members could speak Yiddish, only a few communicated with her. Beyle, the most fluent of the American-born Yiddish speakers, complained that she could not understand Marye because her Yiddish was full of Russian words. Their Yiddish world was tied to their parents and their own ways of thinking. They did not view Marye as someone who shared their own European heritage who had been miraculously placed in their everyday midst in South Philadelphia, but as someone foreign who should learn to be American. And Marye could not understand why there was so much talk about Yiddish at the Center but so few people for her to speak to there.

I often dreamed of a revived Jewish community in South Philadelphia that would be fed by the incoming wave of Soviet Jewish immigrants. In my dream, the Center would go back to being a Hebrew school and teen center; merchants in the area would speak English with a Russian accent. When I mentioned my ideas to others, I was told that the neighborhood did not have sufficient housing available for an influx of new residents. Throughout the 1970's and 1980's, the organized Philadelphia Jewish community helped to resettle most Soviet immigrants in the Northeast and greater Northeast sections of the city. The immigrants were searching for quick economic, educational, and social mobility. I was told that the welcoming Philadelphia Jews would not want to stigmatize the newcomers by making them live in a neighborhood that symbolized everything old and traditional. But looking at the boarded-up brownstones and abandoned synagogues, I could not help but dream of continuity in a new form. Somehow my stay in the neighborhood symbolized for me as well as for the elderly Jews a hope that Jewish life could once again ignite the drab, bare streets lined with small row houses.

The newcomer Russian Jews in the neighborhood were not to be seen. During my first year in the neighborhood, I met a young Russian who bought an old corner grocery near the Center. Somehow or other he was steered into this area of failing small businesses. Within a few months he was gone from the neighborhood. That same year I met an elderly immigrant woman at the Center who had come from Russia a few years back. She had left her family in Brooklyn, New York, to marry an older Jewish man in South Philadelphia, an immigrant from the early years of the century. She was treated like an indentured servant. It took much effort to convince her husband to allow her to leave the house to attend programs at the Center. When he died the following year, she returned to her family in Brooklyn.

My search for Jewish newcomers was largely unsuccessful. My own dream of a renewed Jewish culture in the neighborhood was illusory.

The Young Lead the Old

I wanted to become more familiar with the Orthodox shul and was intrigued by stories of the younger man who served as president and organizer of the institution. Because the shul was open primarily on shabbos, and since, in observance of shabbos, I do not travel, I put off a visit until the weather improved and I could walk there. One summer Saturday morning I set out on the almost three-mile walk.

The Orthodox shul seemed much more private than the two Conservative shuls. Since it did not list its activities in the local press and I knew only four men who davened there, my portrait of Jewish life in the neighborhood seemed incomplete. I did not even know the name of this shul, only its physical location. At this address, I planned to search for a confluence of many of the questions of identity and continuity that intrigued me. If, indeed, part of the attractiveness of the neighborhood, the compelling bond to place, is to be found in the durability of the familiar and the traditional, would not the oldest existing Jewish institution provide a key to the longevity of the community?

Wearing a white shirt, I drape my brown sports jacket over my talis bag, which also holds my tie and yarmulke. My walk takes me by the outdoor stands of the Italian market on Ninth Street. One hour and five minutes later I am in front of the small pillars of the shul, tucked between row houses. I do not have time to cool off. I put on my tie, yarmulke, and jacket and walk in. There is no vestibule; I enter directly into the sanctuary. The bima (raised platform from which the Torah is read and prayers are led) is in the middle of the room, with only seven rows between it and the door. A man of about 70 asks me if I want to see the president. Obviously, strangers do not often come to daven. I say, "No, I'll just sit down." They are reading from the Torah, much further along in the service than I had expected. I put on my talis and wait for the *aliye* (Torah reading) to be over, in order to go up to the edge of the bima to get a siddur (prayer book). A man in the second row, wearing a hat, asks me if I want a *khimesh* (bible). I do not want to take away his, but he says he has another.

From my seat in the back row near the door I can observe the entire group, and I am surprised by what I see. A man from the Center who had been caught using the Center's phone to make obscene calls is here to pray, along with a tall man with a thin moustache whom I had assumed was not Jewish. At one Gleyzele tey session, he had put his cap over an entire plate of cookies and taken them home. Here he is transformed in an elegant-looking suit, and he can say the prayers with the traditional lilt when called up to the Torah. The shul is an equalizer. Those who are shunned in other social settings have a place in the minyan here. Yankl B., the nemesis of many at the Center because of his brash behavior, looks like a prince in his shiny new talis.

Yankl B. notices that I am present, saying, "Oy, he goes to shul, too." I realize that neighborhood Jews view me differently, according to the activities and settings in which we interact. They do not know much about my life, and the Center members largely associate me only with Center activities. Now some of them see the religious, spiritual side. I had not considered this expansion of my image in advance. I was more interested in finding out about the neighborhood than in having the neighborhood find out about me.

Khatshe, the 100-year-old Center member who, in 1922, had moved into a house in back of the then five-year-old shul, waves to me and smiles, and I wave back. Avrum, who runs the notions store on the zibete with his wife, Malke, comes back to say hello after seeing me go up to get a siddur. The shochet, whose wife is known as the rebbitzin, is reading aloud on the bima. He recognizes me too. I overhear Yiddish speech from the pews in the front. Looking at the men in shul, I see seven I know from before, seven I have never seen before, and two others who look familiar. My first reaction is surprise that there always seem to be Jewish South Philadelphians I have not met. Second, I am astonished by the transformations I behold: the shul environment has produced elegant and pious men. I remind myself that congregants are motivated, according to some remarks I have heard, by the food that is served after the service.

A young man in his thirties, wearing an open-collared shirt and a short zippered jacket, is up at the bima. Someone says something to him, and he comes over to my pew. I have surmised correctly that he is the young man responsible for keeping the shul alive. I introduce myself, tell Hal I have heard about him and have met his mother, who works in the Jewish bakery up the street. He asks my name and my father's name, and I am called for the next *aliye*. The gabbai (the organizer of the service) greets me after the Torah portion is read and shows me where to read along. When I step down from the bima, Khatshe is waiting; he shakes my hand and shows me pictures from his party in the shul in January.

People are curious about why I am there. Several ask me if I have *yortsayt* (yahrzeit), a time when occasional visitors appear to mark the year anniversary of a relative's death. The service is ending, and I notice Hal bringing in drinks and food platters from the alley. Khatshe insists that I sit next to him and introduces me as the one who runs the Gleyzele tey at the Center. We drink schnapps. Some of the men grab for the food, but others do not partake at all.

Hal comes over to pour soda and starts talking about the shul. He guides me around the sanctuary, and I see plaques and certificates on the walls,

reminders of the once independent existences of the shuls that now constitute the combined Congregation Shivtei Yeshuron–Heysiner–Ezras Israel.
Hal leads me upstairs to the women's section, which also is the room used
for celebrations, like Khatshe's 100th birthday party. Through two trap
doors, one over the bima, the other over the ark holding the Torahs at the
front, the women can glimpse the service. When I ask Hal if women attend shul, he responds that many come on holidays and sometimes for
yahrzeit. He himself had attended the Dudley Street shul until it closed.
That was his grandfather's shul. When they moved here, his grandfather became the *shames*, and Hal is continuing the job. When I ask Hal his name,
he hesitates at the last name and then gives me his grandfather's name, his
mother's maiden name. All the congregants refer to him that way.

His concerns are mainly about upkeep of the building. He had replaced
two windows that year at a cost of $600. Every year he puts down a new
runner from the door to the bima. Members of four families in the neighborhood provide financially for the shul, but one of them died this year.
The congregation once tried to raise money by renting the building out
to neighborhood people. The members, however, did not approve of the
nonkosher food that was brought in. I tell Hal about the synagogue in
Elkins Park that is willing to help Jews in the neighborhood and has worked
with the Social Service Department at Einstein Southern Hospital. I say
they might be willing to adopt the shul and cover the costs of building
maintenance. I usually do not take an activist stance, but I am especially
touched by his efforts.

I tell Hal that I want to make a donation to the shul. He asks me where I
live and says he has just sold a house in my neighborhood. Yankl B. had
told me Hal was a pharmacist, but now I see that he is also a real estate
agent. Hal talks very matter-of-factly about the shul, as though his work is
no great sacrifice, only a task to be done.

When we come back downstairs, a couple of men are still present, including the talkative one who first greeted me. He says that his street near
the shul is an attractive place for young people to live and tells me to bring
young people to the shul. He is the only one to broach the issue of continuity. I thank Hal and tell him that he is performing a true mitsvah (charitable act). The walk back home is quick and easier than the way down. I
am elated.

The next shabbos, I retrace my steps. Things are the same, except that
Hal is not present. Outside the shul I notice two men. One, the same man
who greeted me the previous week, goes into a grocery store to buy a bag
of potato chips. Yankl B. criticizes him for not buying a kosher brand, but
the man does not seem to understand the significance of his error. Once
again I realize that a person's attendance at the Orthodox shul does not

necessarily mean that he is observant. This is a ritualized Jewish meeting place that reminds the congregants of how their parents prayed. The second man I see outside the shul is a former member who has bought a challah at the bakery for the kiddush. He sits in the pew behind me. He has come from the Northeast to name his new grandchild at the shul. He gets the first *aliye*.

Later during the service I learn from the visitor that this was his shul until he moved away eight years ago. Although he looks younger than the rest of the congregants, he tells me that he is 75. He loved this shul but thinks it is a mess now. He recalls the old days in the shul and would give anything to have them back, he says. There was then a group of young guys who used to daven together. He seems to be referring to American-born men and points to the only one from that group who still comes to shul. They would enjoy themselves, daven together every night, and sit and discuss matters with the rabbi, a "regular guy." I see from his example that the shul still draws some former residents who return to mark an important life event.

My experience at shul today is similar to last week's. The congregants are delighted to see me again. After the service, I talk with Khatshe and the shochet, who complains about the men who only come to eat. There is much excitement around the preparation of the kiddush, since Hal is away. The food lacks the lavish vegetable, egg, fish, and fruit salads of last week, consisting only of sardines, potato chips, challah, coffee cake, ginger ale, club soda, and schnapps. The visitor tells me that Hal has not always been so active. Sometimes he would only come to daven Friday night. I realize that people take over roles as they are vacated, as they feel they are needed.

For my part, I enjoy coming here. I can envision myself coming every week. Here I feel that I am helping to keep an institution and a way of life alive.

Coming Home to South Philadelphia: Jewish Identities

Coming home means going back to our beginnings. Our memories of past associations are sometimes triggered by ideas, events, places, and persons in the present day. I had never before attended services in a small, intimate congregation of old men in an old shul, but it felt like a homecoming for me. The visitor returning to his South Philadelphia shul was drawn back for a moment of special meaning, to mark the continuity of generations, the birth of a grandchild. The shul was his private and communal address for Jewish history.

I was in awe of Hal's hard work, which ensured that the traditional place of Jewish prayer, the site of his own grandfather's dedication, would continue to function as long as he and the other congregants could maintain it. After several years of reflection, I began to understand how fervent my hope was that Jewish life would remain alive, in place, in the face of adversity in South Philadelphia. This dream grew during the time I spent in the neighborhood. During my fieldwork, I encouraged and fostered the Jewish cultural expression of older Jewish residents. My visits to the shul, however, convinced me that I, too, was searching for a spiritual and emotional center within myself, within my past. Although the elderly residents in the neighborhood were my parents' age, I imagined them as my grandparents. I associated old age with my grandparents, not with my elderly parents. My grandparents were all born in Europe and spoke English with a strong accent, unlike most South Philadelphians, but that did not weaken the association. I rarely went to shul with my grandparents; when I did, the shuls were large, Americanized, Orthodox places. But in the South Philadelphia shul, I was drawn to the traditional drone of the davening, to the Yiddish speech that is less common elsewhere in the neighborhood. I constructed a home there for the memories of my grandparents long dead, whom I had been very close to and loved very much. I used the shul as a place to come home to.

People who voluntarily spent every day in the neighborhood became fused in my mind with the neighborhood residents. I did not realize then how many individuals came home to South Philadelphia in one way or other. The elderly woman from Atlantic City who returned for a day to hold court in Izzy's luncheonette was not isolated as a returning pilgrim. There were many in this category: Yankl D., a retired restaurateur, volunteered in the kitchen and as a case worker; he grew up in South Philadelphia, and his mother died there in 1985. Rivke A. lived in the neighborhood for a few years before her marriage, but her parents continued to live there; she was an active Center member, a participant in the Gleyzele tey group, and a dining hall volunteer. One man volunteered to come from his Northeast home to videotape events during the year. As soon as publicity about the Gleyzele tey group appeared in the citywide press, several more people converged on the Center. The members best appreciated Yankl E., a young man in his thirties, a child of Holocaust survivors who attended Hebrew school in the Center building and who returned to hear and speak Yiddish after his parents passed away. The list of daily visitors to South Philadelphia included women and men of all ages.

For these former South Philadelphians, a visit to the new old neighborhood was in some cases a nostalgic escapade, in others a quest for memory and meaning. Since the home and neighborhood of my youth in New York

City are not available to me in the same way, having been reconstructed and repopulated, South Philadelphia can serve me as a surrogate. The special qualities of the neighborhood supported the unfolding of strong Jewish identities. Leye, for example, had dedicated herself to progressive culture for most of her life. She cared for her extended family in the neighborhood and kept the books for her husband's business. As a secular Jew who did not participate in religious life, she walked to the Center to take courses and attend cultural programs and performances. The neighborhood nurtured her, and she identified with its nonpretentious Jews. Her Jewish identity developed from birth and overlapped with her neighborhood identity.

Izzy never left the neighborhood. His perch on the zibete provided an open door for Jewish and non-Jewish neighborhood people. Everyone knew him, and he had a kind word for every pedestrian that passed by his luncheonette's open window. But what drove him were the religious affairs of his shul and the activities of his landsmanshaft and Masonic groups. His affiliations were exclusively Jewish. His concerns were for his ethnic community at a time when its size had diminished to a shadow of its former self. Not a social or political mover, he derived his charisma from an inner strength that defied the mobility of the larger society around him. His creativity and dedication grew together with the isolation and dogged staying in place of the South Philadelphia Jews. Thus, Izzy's Jewish identity was nurtured by an assured historical constancy that flew in the face of change. Izzy's concern for his non-Jewish neighbors and Jewish life and culture outside the neighborhood stemmed from his grounding in South Philadelphia. He was not on the move in any sense of the word, for he had found his place.

Within the diverse community of South Philadelphia Jews, everyone that I met shared a strong neighborhood identity (almost all had lived exclusively in South Philadelphia) and a strong Jewish identity. Their Jewish identity related to family history that included immigration from Eastern Europe and continuous settlement in one of the largest urban centers in the United States. Most Americans were seeking better jobs and different places of residence while the South Philadelphia Jews stayed in one place. Any changes they made were fostered by the constant support of a familiar physical and human environment. Their identification as Jews and South Philadelphians overlapped. They reveled in the face of scorn heaped upon them by siblings who had moved on to greener pastures and by residents of the ever-growing suburbs. The Jewish identity that developed in this shared context recognized the strong communal force of yesteryear without resting solely on this past, and rejoiced in the task of maintaining its institutions and customs.

The paradox of effecting change while staying put (Sanders 1993) reflected the reality of South Philadelphia Jewish life. As the Jewish community shrank, leaving only a few Jewish residents on many streets in the neighborhood, the Jews came into more contact with non-Jews but continued their largely Jewish social networks and their exclusively Jewish organizational affiliations. As most of their children, and the youth in general, disappeared from the neighborhood, the growing elderly population began to adopt the ways of their own parents. Thus, American-born children of immigrants went to synagogue, although they may not have done so when they were younger, as a way of fraternizing with Jews. They viewed their behavior as traditional, and their choices as similar to those of their parents. In actuality, the shul they attended was open only for Sabbath services, not daily, it supported full participation by women, and it was led by a woman rabbi. Such details were different, but in those Jewish environments, viable shared memories were created and Jewish identification was strengthened.

Top: 1. Durfor Street, one of
the many streets in the
neighborhood lined with
row houses. Urban
Archives, Temple University,
Philadelphia, Pa.

Right: 2. The corner of
Sixth and Mercy Streets.
The onetime synagogue
Megidey Tehilim, which
closed in the late 1970's, is
nestled between the row
houses. Courtesy of the
Philadelphia Jewish Archives
Center, Marc Toplin's study
of Ward 1.

Top: 3. The Orthodox shul Shaari Eliohu, built in 1912 at Porter and Eighth Streets. Ornate cupolas cap its corners. Its members had difficulty finding a minyan in 1982. In August 1985, while getting a haircut across the street, I witnessed its demolition by a wrecking ball.

Bottom: 4. Izzy's hotdog stand on the zibete (Seventh Street).

Right: 5. JCC Multi-Service Center South, 1983. (Originally, this was the Jewish Educational Center no. 2; since 1987, it has been called the Stiffel Senior Center of the Jewish Community Centers of Philadelphia.)

Below: 6. Members speak out at a Gleyzele tey session.

Above: 7. On my last day in South Philadelphia before moving to Massachusetts, I posed with senior center members and staff.

Below: 8. The cake served at the farewell party at the senior center says, "Tayerer Rakhmiel Gei Gezunter Hait" (Dear Rakhmiel Go in Good Health).

PART III

Language and Culture

CHAPTER SEVEN

Cycles of Using Yiddish

During my initial visits to the neighborhood in 1982–83, I became aware that many of the local Jews knew Yiddish. But it was only after conversations with a variety of residents, and especially after I grasped the excitement and invigorating response to the Gleyzele tey group, that I saw Yiddish as a vital component of these people's identities. At first, I was fearful that I had artificially injected Yiddish speech into the community. Later, I came to realize that I had simply cleared a path for the resurfacing of skills and emotions that linked those American Jews to their own deep family and neighborhood histories as well as to a long-standing culture that hearkened back to a millennium of European Jewish life.

The South Philadelphia Jews displayed virtuoso talents in their Yiddish usage far too great for their speech to have been mere accommodation to my use of the language. Moreover, the range of emotions—sometimes joyous, other times pensive and even forlorn, but in all instances sincere—pointed to the fact that Yiddish had great meaning in the lives of these Jews. Their use of the language disclosed vital signs relating to culture and identity. Only in later years, after speaking Yiddish with Jews in other communities, did I begin to understand the context of their Yiddish behavior in terms of a broader panorama—the changes in identity over the life course, the meaning of ethnicity in American history, the development of Jewish culture on the local and personal level.

Yiddish speech can show us what is new and what is shared with our parents, just as attitudes about the language point out how we develop new cultural forms and yet remain the children of our parents. The culture of the kitchen, as it were, and the inner self are seldom under the microscope of the cultural historian. I am concerned here with internal states, ideas, experiences, and feelings, as well as public behaviors. As the anthropologist Hannerz states clearly: "Culture . . . is the meanings which people create, and which create people, as members of societies. Culture is in some way collective" (1992: 3). In their evolving identifications, contemporary people have more to integrate than their ancestors. They are more aware of themselves. Yet they have no coherent culture with which to identify (see Hewitt 1989: 42, 169). By "culture" I mean the social knowledge and understanding that are negotiated by people as they make sense of their lives, rather than the more narrow artistic expressions and institutions, such as theater and belles lettres (Ochs 1988; Rosaldo 1989: 26). I feel that the effort at cultural construction undertaken by myself and the South Philadelphians, a collective effort, brought forward emotions and behaviors that help clarify the meaning of language in the development of ethnic identity and culture. We were trying to make sense of the disruptions and challenges to meaning that had taken place in our lifetimes, for us as individuals and as group members (see Hewitt 1989: 244).

Who Speaks Yiddish, When, and to Whom?

This study focuses on the behavior of individuals and not on the description of discrete abstract systems or languages. The conceptual framework for studying speech is based on a theory of linguistic repertoire. Le Page and Tabouret-Keller describe the language of speakers in all societies as a "repertoire of socially-marked systems" (1985: 116). Speakers identify and perceive each system, which may be fragmentary and overlapping, as belonging to a specific group. Language systems and groups of people do not exist outside the perception of individuals. To the definition of linguistic repertoire, Milroy and Milroy add that it is "the totality of styles available to a community" (1985: 119). What they mean by "community" is elusive, but there is agreement that "speakers learn to select from this repertoire in order to fill various communicative needs."

Since, in this study, Yiddish speakers are recognized for their multilingual, multistylistic repertoire, they do not match the description of what Dorian calls "semi-speakers"—that is, people who exhibit speech deviations that are labeled mistakes by fluent speakers but who can nonetheless use words in sentences (1981: 107). Kroskrity (1985), who studied the language Western Mono, has criticized such a categorization on several grounds: (1) it neglects the language the speakers understand but do not speak; (2) it represents the linguist's and not the community's perception; (3) it does not consider the speaker's entire linguistic repertoire; and (4) "semi-speakers" do not represent a single category. Kroskrity's call for an examination of the speaker's linguistic history and his critique of the concept of semi-speaker served as my guidelines for examining how Yiddish fit into individual biographies in South Philadelphia, for viewing the English used during Yiddish conversation as additive aspects of communicative ability, and for generally not approaching Yiddish speech in this neighborhood as a disintegrating system.

I do not believe that Yiddish in South Philadelphia has reached the state of "language death" described by Dorian (1981 and 1982a) and Schmidt (1985); South Philadelphia has too many Yiddish speakers who manipulate their Yiddish in an innovative fashion to consider this a case of language death. A statement by Le Page and Tabouret-Keller closely pertains to Yiddish language use in South Philadelphia: "Languages do not do things; people do things, languages are abstractions from what people do" (1985: 188).

I first overheard Yiddish being spoken at the doorstep of Malke and Avrum's variety store on the zibete. After that, however, I rarely heard Yiddish spoken spontaneously in public. At a Hanukkah (*khanike*) party at Adath Shalom both Shmuel-Arn, the president, and Menakhem, the vice-president, playfully said the Yiddish "antshuldikt mir" (excuse me), when they forgot to make an announcement during their English-language speeches. At the Center birthday party for 95-year-old Yisrul, Sure C., a younger member, got up to address the birthday boy in Yiddish because she had become accustomed to speaking Yiddish to him in her childhood. But these instances were exceptional.

The South Philadelphians used Yiddish in few circumstances, and the number of individuals who could be found speaking Yiddish in public was small. Residents did, however, enjoy Yiddish as a language of formal performance, and the staff at the Center, accordingly, scheduled occasional Yiddish entertainers. The Center director was herself a Yiddish folk singer who often led the members in song. One program featured a singer of patriotic American songs accompanied on an electronic synthesizer. The members, who generally enjoyed music, sang along that afternoon. But not until near the program's end, when they requested Yiddish tunes such as "Sheyn vi di levune" (Beautiful as the Moon), did the crowd became enthusiastic; Itke, Surele, and Pole drew their friends onto the dance floor for lively singing and dancing. Likewise, at Adath Shalom, the audience participated fully and became animated only when a singer's repertoire included a few Yiddish songs.

Publicity about the Gleyzele tey group attracted an actress who had recently emigrated from the Soviet Union. She had performed with the Moscow State Yiddish Theater. During two of her recitations of literary selections in Yiddish, the members sat spellbound. The language and style of Yiddish high culture were different from the Yiddish of their parents' homes, but they savored such performances.

Some Center members themselves excelled at reciting in Yiddish. For example, Dvoyre occasionally told a favorite Yiddish joke at a club meeting. Tsipe-Khashe read her own Yiddish poetry or a translation she had prepared of an English poem. Menakhem presented a humorous *khanike* poem replete with Yiddish terms. At an intergenerational program with the local Sunday School children after the Purim holiday, Ester A. volunteered the traditional Yiddish slogan of itinerant Purim *shpilers* (players), who go from house to house telling the holiday story. Khone sang a song she remembered from her childhood for the *sukes* celebration. At the Center seder a member read a Yiddish rendition of the Four Questions normally recited in Hebrew at the Passover seder. But these performances in Yiddish were the exception; Jewish public events in South Philadelphia were predominantly in English, with traditional prayers chanted in Hebrew. Most Center staff members and local rabbis did not know Yiddish and did not feature it in the programs and services they organized. Most residents, for their part, preferred to perform in English, although they delighted in viewing a Yiddish-language production or singing along to a popular Yiddish melody.

In informal, private exchanges, I found many more instances of communication in Yiddish. Some of the older immigrant men living alone, such as Khatshe, Yisrul, and Moyshe A., chose to converse with each other in Yiddish. In addition to Malke, Avrum, and Marye, some of the younger American-born residents felt that it was appropriate to address these men in Yiddish. At the Orthodox shul, attended by a number of European-born Jewish males, more Yiddish was heard than was usually the case in the neighborhood. At Izzy's luncheonette, one heard a joke in Yiddish or frivolous bantering back and forth. On occasion, even non-Jewish customers showed off their knowledge of Yiddish. More frequently, exchanges in Yiddish took place between Rivke A. and Rivke B., friends at the Center, and the sisters Beyle and Elke, who lived together. Even for them, though, conversation in English was at least as common and as comfortable. That talking in Yiddish took place in the neighborhood when I was not present was demonstrated when a new participant appeared at a Gleyzele tey session. While riding the bus, she had overheard Beyle and Dvoyre talking Yiddish. Intrigued, she spoke with them and was told that if she enjoyed hearing Yiddish spoken, she should come to the Center on Friday mornings.

If lengthy conversations in Yiddish were rare, the use of isolated words and phrases was quite common. For example, Yankl B. used such words as "*momele*" (little mother) and "*kobtsn*" (poor man) when addressing the Sunday School children, who understood no Yiddish at all. And, I found, there were occasions when only Yiddish speech would do. For example, Ester B., who attended the Gleyzele tey sessions but never spoke, found Yiddish words to share with Marye, who spoke no English, as they sat at the same lunch table. Similarly, Berl, whom I had never heard speak Yiddish, claimed that he did not speak Yiddish and that this prompted his mother-in-law to call him the "goyisher yid" (non-Jewish Jew). When Marye and her daughter visited the Center, however, he spoke Yiddish to them. In addition to Marye, the actress from the Soviet Union required attention in Yiddish. Beyle was assigned to fill out Center membership forms for her by interviewing her in Yiddish. Those few individuals who knew no English reminded the neighborhood elderly of previous generations of South Philadelphia Jews with whom they lived and interacted.

Only once did I observe an occasion when Yiddish was purposely used when English might well have sufficed. Yankl D., a senior aide at the Center who grew up in South Philadelphia, requested a special favor for one of his clients from a local Jewish doctor, in Yiddish. Later, he confided that Jewish professionals in the area are more sympathetic when they are addressed in Yiddish. Yankl D. believed that Yiddish was still a signal of group solidarity.

Yiddish over the Life Course

As I became better acquainted with the Jewish residents of South Philadelphia, the history of their language behavior became a natural topic for discussion. When we chatted about their lives, at first I avoided focusing on language because I did not want them to alter their speech to accommodate me. I was following the methodological guidelines of sociolinguists, who prefer to observe informal, unself-conscious speech styles rather than analyze questionnaires and word lists or make language a conscious topic of discussion with informants (Wolfson 1976; Labov 1972a). But as my investigation progressed and most residents freely spoke Yiddish with me, talking about speaking Yiddish became more natural.

Retrospective reports can be questionable but become more reliable as they are confirmed by others. Many South Philadelphia residents grew up knowing one another, and their experiences were comparable or were corroborated by their neighbors. In addition, information about the social context of the neighborhood over time, which I learned about from independent sources, enabled me to validate the residents' autobiographical reports. From their descriptions of events and of the place of Yiddish over the course of their lives, I was able to trace the roots of their present attitudes toward and attachments to language and better understand their current linguistic behavior. I learned that living in South Philadelphia had required mastering the Yiddish language in order to be a full participant. Following are two illustrations.

On occasion, non-Jews attended the Yiddish conversation group at the Center. Fred, an Italian American, disagreed with an opinion expressed during one session and described his feelings in English, obviously having understood the Yiddish conversation. He later explained that he was married to a Jewish woman and had consequently learned a lot of Yiddish. Moyshe B. was the only Sephardic Jew in the group;[1] his parents came from Greece and Turkey and spoke and read Judezmo (Ladino) at home. He attended the Yiddish discussion group with his wife, Rive-Rukhl, an Ashkenazic woman, responded to questions in Yiddish, and could maintain a conversation. Growing up in South Philadelphia, he learned Yiddish not from his peers, but from his friends' parents and grandparents. He acquired more Yiddish from his customers when he peddled neckties and aprons in the neighborhood. No doubt marrying into the Yiddish-speaking family of Rive-Rukhl was also an important factor.

Moyshe's experience points to an overall trend: Yiddish was reserved for interaction with the older generations. The children and grandchildren of immigrants conversed in English among themselves. "Mir hobm geret Yiddish meynli mit mayn miter," says Sure, "bot, e—tsvishn zekh hobm mir geret Inglish" (We mainly spoke Yiddish with my mother, but between ourselves we spoke English). Feygl-Asye referred to English as "Amerikanish" and recalled that she spoke Amerikanish with her brother and sister but Yiddish with her parents, her aunt, their friends, and neighbors. At home at the dinner table they spoke Yiddish, but she and her siblings did not hide Amerikanish from their parents. In other families, such as Ester-Sosye's, speaking English at home was strictly prohibited. Her parents believed that Yiddish was the only language of discourse befitting a Jewish household and punished their children with a slap in the face if they broke the rule.

Immigrants spoke Yiddish at home with their children, whether they could speak English or not. Dveyre and Surele, who both came from England to South Philadelphia as infants, reported that although their parents spoke English very well, they always conversed with their parents in Yiddish. Yet within the family, the younger brother and sister spoke Yiddish only occasionally. Similarly, Leye and her brother, the two older siblings, spoke Yiddish with their parents; the younger children understood but did not speak the language.

Tsipe-Khashe, also the eldest child, recalled how her mother forced her brother to speak Yiddish:

Fleg mayn mame ze e—em zogn, "Eyb du vilst geyn in de mu:viz . . . zolste kumen tsurik un mir zogn vos dust gezen in idish." Er fleg zikh mutshenen. That's how he learned to speak. He didn't speak much later but he understood.

My mother used to say to him, "If you want to go to the movies . . . you'd better come back and tell me what you saw in Yiddish." He used to struggle.

At the same time, there were families in which even the youngest siblings spoke Yiddish exclusively with their parents, according to Ester-Beyle, 66, Itke, 62, and Beyle, 60, each of whom was the youngest child.

Rive-Rukhl clearly remembered the domains of Yiddish usage. All of her friends spoke Yiddish with their parents. Public school, even if most of the students and teachers were Jewish, was viewed as a non-Jewish environment. Playing on the street was part and parcel of the children's own world of activity and, hence, English was the language of choice. School and street required English discourse, whereas the home signaled Yiddish. It is worth noting that Rive-Rukhl associated Yiddish fluency between children and their parents with obligatory attendance at religious school. She recalled:

R. P.: Ir meynt az ir hot upgehit yidish meyn vi di andere kinder in gegnt, oder ale—ale kinder hobm gekent demolt?

R.-R.: Bot ye si di inglish, geyn in skuwl, zayn a kind in geyn in skuwl, hot men geven tsvishn goyim, tsvishn aler e—ley mentshn hot men gedarft redn e—inglish aend in de—di strit az men ge-shpilt in de strit mit di kinder iz geven inglish, mit di kinder, az me fleg arayngeyn ba zey in shtib, iz z—zeyer eltern hobm ekhet geret yidish, hobm mir geret yidish tsi zeyere eltern.

R. P.: Yo, ober a sakh kinder hobm nit gevolt redn yidish mit zeyere eltern, zey hobm nor gevolt redn english.

R.-R.: Ni—nisht nisht in may tsayt, nisht in may tsayt. Mir hobm gedarft geyn in kheyder, ale.

R. P.: Do you think that you kept Yiddish up more than the other neighborhood children, or all children knew how then?

R.-R.: But you see the English, going to school, to be a child and go to school, you were among non-Jews, among all kinds of people you had to speak English and in the street when you played in the street with the children it was English, with the children, when you used to go to their house, their parents also spoke Yiddish, so we spoke Yiddish to their parents.

R. P.: Yes, but many children didn't want to speak Yiddish to their parents, they only wanted to speak English.

R.-R.: Not in my time, not in my time. We had to go to religious school—all of us.

Some of the residents' clearest memories were of arriving at school and not comprehending English. Itke, for example, explained that even though her elder siblings knew English, they could not convince her ahead of time that in school English was obligatory:

I don't know if I told you this story, when I started first grade, fortunately ikh ho gehat a titsher vos ken idish (I had a teacher who knew Yiddish), and there was a little boy he pinched me. So I says, "Gey avek fun mir" (Leave me alone). And the teacher says, "what's the ma—vus iz (what's the matter) What's the matter Ella?" I se—, "Titsher, ert mir geknaypt," (Teacher, he pinched me). She got hysterical. She says, "Me zukt nit knayp, me zukt pintsh" (You don't say *knayp*, you say pinch). I se—, "Pintsh, shmintsh, tut mir vey, ert mir vey, ert mir gibn a gitn knip" (Pinch, shminch, it hurts me, he hurt me, he gave me a good pinch). I didn't know a word. My mother said, "You gotta learn Jewish." She said, "Dist oyslernen english" (You'll learn English). We spoke only Jewish.

The trauma of entering a new and unfamiliar setting for second-language acquisition lingered in the painful remembrance of the jolting encounter with a new name. Elke recalled:

I didn't speak English, I only spoke Yiddish. She calls, Ellen, Ellen, Ellen and I don't answer. I didn't know that that was my name. They used to send papers home with me every day. I brought the papers home. My mother took the papers to my grandfather, "What can be the matter?" Until my uncle, my mother's brother, he said, it's already, first it was from the teacher, then from the principal, "I don't answer to my name, I can't learn anything." They understood by now. My uncle answered in a letter that I can't speak English and I don't understand, therefore I don't answer. At home they started banging it into my head, this is your name, this is your name, this is your name, until it entered my little head. And I am attending school again. And for some reason, in the second or third I went—I was promoted. I go from one class to the next. Anyhow, I started to learn, and I studied well. (See Yiddish original of narrative in Appendix D.)

During my stay in South Philadelphia, very few siblings spoke Yiddish with each other. Itke claimed to always speak Yiddish with her sister, who was twenty years her senior and lived in the Northeast section of Philadelphia. Only Beyle and Elke saw each other daily and spoke Yiddish together. When their parents became ill, these sisters returned to the house in which they grew up and remained together after their husbands died. What distinguished them from their contemporaries was that they spoke both English and Yiddish to each other throughout their lives. What they had in common with many of the other elderly American-born Jews who maintained Yiddish was their proximity to the parent and grandparent generation, with whom they spoke only Yiddish. As children, they lived near, and sometimes with, their grandparents; and even their parents, who had come to America as children, knew very little English.

When the residents I interviewed were children, Yiddish was spoken throughout the neighborhood, on the street and in the stores, and by family members and friends. Therefore, even the American-born residents, who used English with their parents, had ample opportunity to hear and speak Yiddish. As the eldest child, Reyzl spoke Yiddish with her grandfather, her mother's friends, her father's sister who lived with the family, and in general to older people in the neighborhood. When she worked as a clerk in a liquor store on the zibete and in a bank, many of the customers were Yiddish speakers, and Reyzl spoke Yiddish when she was addressed in the language.

Roze's case was different. Since her parents were deaf and did not speak, she learned Yiddish from her grandmother. It was her first language, and her second was sign language. Later in life she used Yiddish with the clientele of the local bar where she was a waitress, and in her own restaurant.

Even though the children of immigrants rarely used Yiddish with their peers, the Yiddish culture of their parents and grandparents was present in their homes. A parallel case involving similar issues is seen nowadays in the lives of Native American youth of the Southwest, who finish their secondary education at boarding schools, removed from the language and culture of older community members. This is coupled with a changing economy that separates them later on from working with members of the older generation at subsistence agriculture, as in years gone by. In South Philadelphia, residents such as Izzy, Shmuel-Arn, Roze, Reyzl, and Yankl B. worked closely with the older generation in retail enterprises. Opportunities for such contacts are seldom available today (see Kroskrity 1993: 103).

The majority of the South Philadelphia Jewish elderly did not use Yiddish with their spouses. Only Malke and Avrum were more comfortable with Yiddish than with English. The older immigrants, Khatshe and Yisrul, spoke Yiddish with their wives, but Libe and Izhak, both European-born, had spoken only English since their marriage. Dveyre, whose second husband was Russian-born, spoke with him in Yiddish. Her granddaughter, who lived in the neighborhood, remembered hearing the language.

Of all the American-born couples, only Basye A. reported speaking Yiddish with her husband, primarily because his mother lived with them and they wanted the children to learn from hearing Yiddish spoken. Basye A.

herself heard no Yiddish while growing up; her mother was born in the United States and spoke Hungarian and English, but no Yiddish. Basye A. learned Yiddish when she worked as a secretary in a synagogue. "I used to think in Jewish," she claimed.

The children of these elderly Jews understood Yiddish but generally did not speak it. Basye A.'s son, who was 34 years old, lived across the street from her. He tried to speak Yiddish to his grandmother and to the rabbi, but he "murders the language," according to Basye. Her daughter understood the language, "but she wouldn't begin to answer anybody in Yiddish." Rivke B. is proud that she taught her children Yiddish at home even though her husband mostly spoke English: "Ikh ho(b) gezukt az yidish iz e—zeyer a gite zakh a(z) me ken" (I said that it is a very good thing to know Yiddish). Her younger son, in his thirties, worked in a furniture store, where the boss spoke to him in Yiddish when he did not want the customers to understand. Rivke was impressed: "Dus hot a sakh tse zugn, er farshteyt in er ret" (That counts a lot, he understands and he speaks).

Yisrul's children, in their sixties, did not speak Yiddish, according to their father. "Bot ven me darf reydn a yidish vort, zey redn a yidish vort" (But when they have to speak Yiddish, they speak). Only three children of neighborhood residents were sent to Yiddish schools. Ester A. spoke fluently as a child and remembered, "Ale mentshn hobm gezokt, zey hobm gemeynt ikh bin ersht gekimen" (Everyone said they thought I had just arrived); she did not speak Yiddish to her children, but her grown daughter in California had started taking a Yiddish course at the Workmen's Circle.

Though most of the Jewish elderly did not transmit Yiddish to their children, they made some attempts. Libe wanted to speak Yiddish to her daughter, but her husband, Izhak, said that she would not know English when she went to school. Their daughter understood more Yiddish than their younger son, however, who as an adult reproached his mother for not speaking Yiddish with him. Libe switched the blame back to her son for having answered in English when she did use Yiddish. "Nu me ken zikh nit lernen azey" (That is no way to learn). The third generation encountered more difficulty learning Yiddish than the children of immigrants who had come at the beginning of the century, since by the 1950's the number of Jews and Jewish institutions in South Philadelphia had diminished.

Very few South Philadelphia Jews in their twenties and thirties were active Yiddish speakers. Itzik, 26, grew up in South Philadelphia and was the youngest entrepreneur on the zibete, having inherited his designer jeans shop from his parents, who were Holocaust survivors. He understood my Yiddish but claimed he could not speak. Only Yankl E., 36, who lived in

South Philadelphia until 1979 and whose younger sister still lived in the area, was a fluent Yiddish speaker of the younger generation. Also a child of Holocaust survivors, he grew up speaking Yiddish at home. He had decided to teach a Yiddish course at his local synagogue and was committed to preserving Yiddish. Publicity about the Gleyzele tey group attracted him back to South Philadelphia.

The isolation that Yankl felt was echoed by the elderly South Philadelphia Jews. With their parents no longer alive, they often had no outlet for their Yiddish. Feygl-Asye told of her friend who said, "Ikh bin aleyn in hoyz. Ikh ken nit ken yidish, se fargest zakh. Bo—so, mir dermonen eyns dos onders" (I am alone in the house. I don't know Yiddish, one forgets. Bu—so, we remind each other). Feygl-Asye joined the Center and appreciated the opportunity to speak Yiddish there.

Marye was more dependent on Yiddish discourse than the other Center members, since she spoke no English. She complained that no one spoke Yiddish at the Center. In the cities where she had lived in the Soviet Union, Chernobyl and Kiev, the older Jews had known Russian, Ukrainian, and Yiddish. "Yo—iz, do, iz a maynse, yidish, yidish, yidish, yidish, yidish, yidish, (v)en se kimt tsu epes iz ken eyn mentsh ken nit ken yidish. Vos iz dos far a maynse?" (Yes—, here, there is a situation, Yiddish, Yiddish, Yiddish, Yiddish, Yiddish, Yiddish, and when something happens not one person knows Yiddish. What kind of situation is that?)

When I asked Tsipe-Khashe, a retired teacher, with whom she spoke Yiddish, she pointed a finger at me:

R. P.: Ober haynt mit veymen ret—ret ir yidish?

Ts.-Kh.: Ikh red tsu zhikh aleyn un mit dikh. [We laugh.] Ikh reyd tsu mayn ketsele.

R. P.: But today to whom do you speak Yiddish?

Ts.-Kh.: I speak to myself and to you. [We laugh.] I speak to my little cat.

I was, in fact, the primary Yiddish interlocutor for many of the elderly Jewish South Philadelphians. Some were quite adept at the language but refused to speak with others. Yisrul understood this as snobbery and mocked those who could speak Yiddish but felt it was beneath them to do so.

Y: Ot kimt ir tse geyn aher tsi, zey ikh az ir—a yid, a emeser yid, me ken mit aykh dirkhreydn zakh(n). Ikh glaykh a me ret yidish ekhet.

R. P.: Yo.

Y: Ikh glaykh di yidish shprakh. Ikh farshtey zi beser.

R. P.: Ikh veys.

ϒ: But veyt. Haynt i(z) du yidn, a(z) ir vilt tsin em reydn a pur verter azoy yidish kikt er aykh un. Er aleyn ken oykh nit ken english, but er makht dem unshtel az er k—, az—er—mdarf tsin em reydn english! Vus hart dir a(z) me vet reydn yidish?

ϒ: You come over here and I see that you—a Jew, a real Jew, one can have a talk with you. I also like it when one speaks Yiddish.

R. P.: Yes.

ϒ: I like the Yiddish language. I understand it better.

R. P.: I know.

ϒ: But wait. Today there are Jews, if you want to speak a few Yiddish words to him, he stares at you. He himself also doesn't know English, but he pretends that he kn—, that—he—you have to speak English to him! What does it bother you that we'll speak Yiddish?

The Persistence of Proverbs

Common ways of talking linked community members to their parents and grandparents in South Philadelphia and to generations of Yiddish speakers around the world. What follows is a description of a facet of language, the use of proverbs, that was widespread in South Philadelphia. From the speakers' point of view, proverbs were a significant means of expressing strong feelings in Yiddish. Matisoff (1979) has discussed the use of "psycho-ostensive expressions" in Yiddish, formulaic phrases that are used parenthetically to convey the emotions of the speaker. Although the variety of the shorter fixed-phrase forms is of interest when exploring the emotive skills of the Yiddish speakers, I was especially impressed by the versatility with which the South Philadelphia Jews used Yiddish proverbs. I focus on the circumstances in which the speakers used proverbs and relate this use to their life experience and their communicative speech strategies. I was surprised to discover that both fluent and nonfluent speakers depended on Yiddish proverbs for expressing many strong emotions and opinions. The extensive maintenance of this genre is one of the most striking demonstrations of the active role of Yiddish in the cultural legacy of this Jewish community.

Research has shown that speakers use proverbs because they can be adapted to shape the course of action (White 1987: 151). Although people may share knowledge of a proverb, they may interpret its meaning in different ways (Kirshenblatt-Gimblett 1973). The hearer of a proverb, knowing the rule expressed in the proverb, will link the rule to the context in which it is being used (Silverman-Weinreich 1978: 6). Thus, the use of proverbs requires interpretation by both the speaker and the listener. It is the power of the proverb to initiate the evaluation of a social situation in a way that implies age-old wisdom, even if the context of application is new and unique.

The futility of searching for a society-specific rule or axiom that corresponds directly to a proverb has been astutely demonstrated by Fabian (1990: 37). It is the identification and use of this means of cultural performance that tells about culture and social relations within the group, within the community. But the relationship between group values and cultural expression is usually not linear and direct. Rather, as Fabian underscores, cultural expression tends to be devious, artistic, and diffuse. "One may use proverbs to change the course of an argument, but one does not argue to change a proverb" (Fabian 1990: 38–39). The use of proverbs creates an aura of dogma and authority that allows the speaker to take control of an argument, even in circumstances that seem to defy reality or logic. In South Philadelphia, the use of proverbs symbolizes the power of ethnic language to the residents, even to those who are not Yiddish speakers.

Researchers are aware of the role that context of performance and social interaction play in coloring the interpretation of a proverb (Seitel 1976; Kirshenblatt-Gimblett 1973; Briggs 1985). The widespread and repeated use of proverbs in South Philadelphia emphasized the importance of their role in the transmission of cultural values and language forms. The retention of the proverb format does not simply signify that which is learned by rote and requires no elaboration or alteration. South Philadelphia Jews used proverbs to convey strong emotional states and adherence to moral positions. The uniformly appropriate use of proverbs, even by the least fluent Yiddish speakers, was noteworthy, and unlike the use of any other linguistic structure within this population.

Shmuel-Arn seldom spoke Yiddish, leaving that to his wife, Ester-Beyle. When he did speak Yiddish, he was inarticulate. He could be classified as one of the least fluent Yiddish speakers in South Philadelphia (see Chapter 8). However, when the opportunity arose to use a Yiddish proverb, Shmuel-Arn knew the appropriate one to select and delivered it without hesitation, clearly pronouncing each word. For example, Ester-Beyle was sometimes too sick to leave the house and stayed there under doctor's orders for months on end. One day during such a period, Shmuel-Arn had come alone to the Center and was eating lunch in the dining hall. We were discussing Ester-Beyle's health, and Shmuel-Arn exclaimed, "Me vert krank shnel ober pameylekh gezint" (You become sick quickly but get healthy slowly). On another occasion, I had telephoned one evening at their home to make an appointment with them for a get-together. They had been sitting on the stoop of their row house that summer evening, and we discussed the neighborhood and their feelings of personal safety. Shmuel-Arn, having previously expressed his negative feelings about the neighborhood quite regularly, told me on the phone that evening about an article on antisemitism he had recently read. I was not particularly interested and wondered if he thought that any topic related to Jews would engage me. But he connected antisemitism to delinquency in the area and expressed his judgment that "se darf vern git fintster, biz se vert lekhtik" (it has to get very dark before it becomes light).

His ability to quote an appropriate Yiddish proverb impressed me on a third occasion. We had a breakfast meeting in town at which oral presentations were made about different Jewish institutions. Shmuel-Arn represented his synagogue, Adath Shalom. We sat together speaking English, our usual language of discourse, and he mentioned that he and Ester-Beyle had decreased their participation in communal activities, saying, "You can't be everywhere at once." I commented that there was a Yiddish saying with that meaning, and he immediately recited, "Me ken nit tantsn af ale khasenes" (You can't dance at all the weddings). It was Shmuel-Arn who made me realize that South Philadelphia Jews knew Yiddish proverbs well, could use them with little effort, and frequently drew upon them in Yiddish and English speech.

Sometimes when residents could find no words to express their strong emotions, they used Yiddish proverbs, even during a conversation in English. For example, I was talking to Izzy over the phone the evening after his wife had undergone surgery for cancer. The operation had taken them by surprise, forcing them to cancel plans they had made. In our English conversation Izzy offered the Yiddish, "Der mentsh trakht un got lakht" (literally, People think and God laughs, or, Man proposes and God disposes).

In another situation, Itke was overtaken by grief when she described to me her inability to adjust to life after her husband's death. As usual in our conversations, she had started in Yiddish but then changed to English. She attempted to tell me how she harbors an ever-present inner sadness. Pointing to her chest, she said to me in Yiddish, "Like you say, di gedikhte, di shiter un di gedikhte blaybt du ot o du" (The thick, the thin and the thick stays here right here). There are circumstances, it seems, when an English word will not suffice. The Yiddish proverb is a valuable tool for expressing grief, disappointment, faith, and humility.

People do not easily share the thoughts and events that worry them the most in life, except with intimate friends. I had known Libe and Izhak for a few years and had heard about their son but had never discussed his marital status. One afternoon I spent a few hours with them in the store. When

Izhak went out, Libe initiated a discussion about their son. At that very moment, the son telephoned. When she got off the phone, she exclaimed to me that she wished he would get married, but she said, "Eyb me brit zikh op af heysns, blozt men af kaltns" (If you burn yourself on hot things, you blow on things that are cold). She implied that his negative experience during his first marriage, which ended in divorce, kept him from trying again. Over time, Libe had begun to feel more comfortable with me, and both she and Izhak shared some of their more private thoughts when I was alone with each of them. I took this as a sign of our growing friendship.

Izhak used more and more Yiddish in our conversations as time went on. One afternoon, I went by Izhak and Libe's store to thank Libe for some delicious poppyseed cookies she had given me. Libe was not in, but Izhak was standing outside the store with a neighbor whom we both knew. When the neighbor left, Izhak invited me in for wine or beer. I told him that I had to leave, but he proceeded to tell me that the neighbor complained about her marriage continually. According to Izhak, her husband had pursued her after his first wife died, the first wife having been very religious and old-fashioned. After she died, the husband just wanted a good-looking woman. Izhak remembered that his father used to say, "Oyb der pots shteyt, der kop geyt"[2] (If your prick can stand up, your head is working, or alternatively, If your prick stands erect, your mind goes astray). Izhak used this proverb to tell me that the husband had made a mistake and had not considered the negative characteristics of his future wife. He had let his *pots* rule his head. At the same time, Izhak was letting me know that aging men like himself and the husband know they are alive as long as their *pots* works. The Yiddish proverb provided a key for us to open the door of shared men's talk.

Izhak used Yiddish proverbs at appropriate times, especially when he was emotionally involved in a narrative. He said that he had learned them from his father. When describing his neighbors who reported him to the health department when one of his drainage pipes broke, he expressed his anger with a proverb: "Ven me leygt zikh mit hint, shteyt men oyf mit flayen" (When you lie down with dogs, you get up with fleas). Izhak told me the story of entering America illegally from Mexico, certain that he would be caught, whereupon he added: "Der tate hot gezukt, afn ganef brent dos hitl" (My father said, the thief's hat burns on him, meaning that when you knowingly do something wrong you remain visibly uncomfortable and guilty). By associating the proverbs with the wisdom of another generation, Izhak attached veracity and venerability to the message and established the linear transmission of knowledge from parent to child.

More than anyone else, Dveyre was likely to interpret her life experiences in religious and moralistic terms and incorporated proverbs unhesitatingly into her speech. She recounted that, unlike her Jewish coworkers in the Health Department, she refused to work on Passover. She asserted herself and was paid anyway. Her conclusion was that she was rewarded for having faith in God: "Ikh trakht bay zikh, eyb er helft, a—eyber got helft af fish vet er helfn af khreyn" (I think to myself, if He helps, if God helps by providing fish, God will also help provide horseradish [ground horseradish is traditionally eaten with *gefilte* (filled) fish]). Similarly Dveyre described her refusal to work on the Sabbath at her job for a newspaper: "Bot ikh hob getrakht bay zikh, eyber got iz gut far di finef teg vet er zayn gut farn zekstn tog, in azey iz geven" (But I thought to myself, if God is good for the first five days God will be good for the sixth day, and that's how it was). When her first husband left her and her three young daughters, Dveyre blamed it on the interference of his sister. She related the story with flair: "Makh nit ken toves, ir zolt veln visn eyn zakh, az vu tsvey mentshn shlofn af a kishn tor zikh ken driter nit mishn" (Don't be mistaken, you should know one thing, that where two people sleep on one pillow a third person should not mix in). The style of Dveyre's verbal delivery and the coalescence of maxims with her accounts of life experiences made the proverbs ring true, as though they conveyed an ethic by which Dveyre lived.

In other instances the repetition of a proverb trivialized its use or left it devoid of ethical or emotional content. Ezra, for example, relished the sound of one proverb, which he repeated constantly regardless of context: "Oles in eynem nitu ba keynem" (No one person can have it all). When I interviewed Yankl B., he resented my questions and repeatedly told me to wait for him to finish: "Khop nit di fish far di nets" (Don't grab the fish before the net, or, Hold your horses, don't be impatient). Such proverbs functioned as personal markers, identified more with a particular individual than with a community moral code.

Shorter formulaic phrases, similar to those Matisoff (1979) called psycho-ostensive expressions, also abounded in the speech of South Philadelphia Jews. Often they were pronounced quickly and delivered parenthetically as an embellishment to the main message, unlike the longer proverb, which was used to communicate the main point or emotion. However, similar to the use of Yiddish proverbs, the shorter phrases were available to a wide spectrum of Yiddish speakers. For example, Blumke, who hardly uttered a Yiddish word, did use the occasional Yiddish phrase in her English speech: "She has a little heart condition so she makes it for a big one, af mir gezuk gevorn" (I should be so lucky—literally, such should be said about me; she then laughed). Shmuel-Arn also used such a phrase in an English speech. He recounted that he had addressed the elderly members of his former synagogue and offered to assume a leadership role with the words, "Some of you are, tsu lengere yurn (you should have long years), passing away, we'll keep the shul going."

Most significant was how such forms were historically integrated into Yiddish speech. The following are a few examples from the speech of fluent Yiddish speakers. Often they indicate the folk belief that the dead can intercede for us on earth, or they are invoked to ensure that no evil will befall a living close family member. For instance, Beyle told me that her grandmother died at the same time her youngest son was born, and that she gave him his great-grandmother's name:

Ikh hob ibergedreyt dem numen, zan numen, zol er zan gezint, nar vos er iz, bot gezint zol er zan, Khunin-Aren, in ir numen iz geven Khaye-Aeny, dus i(z) gevin ir numen, aen e—aen dat waz it.

I reversed the name, his name, let him be well, idiot that he is, but he should be well, Khunin-Aren, and her name was Khaye-Annie, that was her name, an' e—an' that was it.

Beyle, a masterful narrator, easily integrated fixed phrases into her flowing style. While sharing with me her sadness about the absence of love during her marriage to her first husband, the father of her children, she exclaimed: "Fin di dray kinder, zoln zey got mane beyner iberlibn, nit eyns is gevin fin libe gemakht, er flig trinken ekhet" (Of the three children, may they outlive me [my bones] oh God, not one was conceived out of love, he used to drink too).

Marye retraced a story she had told me several times about the rabbi in Belgium who gave her money to come to America, according to her thinking, because her grandfather had been a member of the court of the famed Hasidic rabbi of Chernobyl. This fateful turning point in her life still seemed incredible to her. By using a fixed phrase entreaty, Marye swore to the veracity of the narrative, prefacing her account with the following, "Mayne kinder zoln nit visn fin keyn shlafkeyt, nor azey vi ikh zog aykh rikhtik" (My children should know no sickness, as I tell you truly).

Other common fixed-phrase forms are parenthetical wishful petitions such as *leshulim* (let _____ rest in peace); "loz er ekhet zan a gite beyt far indz ale" (let him intercede positively on our behalf); and "zol er take hubm a lekhtikn ganeydn" (he should certainly experience a bright Garden of Eden, or heaven). But the variety of phrases also encompassed such metaphors as "vern[3] tif tayer in drerd" (to become dearly deep in the ground, or, to fail miserably) and "ikh bin an ofener eyn un draysik" (I am an open thirty-one, meaning, I say outright when I disagree; thirty-one is the numerical value of the Hebrew word for "no").

That this population continued to use these fixed-phrase forms suggests that they continued to function as expressions of strong emotion and as positive personal ways of identifying with Yiddish. Thus, even for residents whose speech repertoire was limited, these forms linked the speakers to their cultural traditions.

Reading, Writing, and High Culture

Yiddish language and culture, as transmitted across the generations of Jewish immigrants and their descendants in South Philadelphia, was primarily imparted orally within the family environment. Yiddish was originally the language of discourse in most social interactions within the community. However, the informal speech of every day was not isolated from other uses of language, especially written forms and the language of literature and the arts.

During their lifetimes, the local Jews heard a more cultivated Yiddish in the language of the theater. The stars of the Yiddish stage performed in Philadelphia, and the American-born residents recalled attending plays at the Arch Street Theater with their families. By the time of my study, the Yiddish-language performances were limited to an occasional singer or actress at the Center or at a meeting of a fraternal order. Some listened to the daily Jewish radio program, which played Yiddish songs. In general, however, they were not familiar with the works of Yiddish literature and did not report attending Yiddish lectures.

Leye was the only one in the neighborhood who knew Yiddish literature as a child in South Philadelphia. In fact, she distinguished the "kikhn yidish" (kitchen Yiddish) of home with the cultural language of her uncle's literary group. As a child she traveled to Fairmount Park on Sundays with the group, where she learned to recite and act out works of Yiddish literature. With little coaxing she was able to assume her childhood roles and recite without hesitation. Yet the Jewish groups to which she belonged during her life featured mostly English-language programs. Thanks to the Yiddish course at the Center, Leye was learning to read and write Yiddish. She and a half-dozen other members met weekly with Gedalye, their teacher, who was active both in the Center and in Adath Shalom. He was familiar with religious practice and knowledgeable about Hebrew and Yiddish.

Although the Center had explored the possibility of teaching Hebrew, the members always demanded Yiddish. Hebrew is a common cultural component of programs at most Jewish community centers, but South Philadelphia Center members related more closely to their own first language, Yiddish, and expressed little interest in Hebrew. The local public Southern High School offered Hebrew to adult learners on Saturday mornings.

Three of the South Philadelphians expressed their loyalty to the Yiddish press. All three were European-born: Avrum, Marye, and Yisrul. Avrum read the weekly *Forward* sitting by the doorstep of his store. At home, Yisrul kept the paper on the kitchen table and read while eating or while drinking a glass of tea. Marye could not do without her *gazet* (paper), since in her isolation, the Yiddish news was her only window on the world. Her one weekly trip out of the neighborhood was to the newspaper stand in town. Although the Center subscribed to two weekly Yiddish papers, no one read them. Dveyre was the only non-European-born resident who expressed an interest in the Yiddish newspaper. She had read it when her husband was alive and decided to renew her subscription, having found it superior to the English-language *Jewish Exponent*.

When Beyle started working at the Center as a senior aide, she noticed the Yiddish papers that arrived in the mail, but found them difficult to read. She asked me if I would tutor her so that she could improve her reading ability. I agreed, although I harbored misgivings about functioning as a language teacher. She progressed quickly through a children's primer and a university Yiddish text to easy literary selections. Since Beyle knew the spoken language so well and used it so often, she had no trouble pronouncing the words according to her Ukrainian Yiddish dialect. Other than Beyle, only Yisrul read Yiddish literature. Of the Center members, he was the lone borrower of Yiddish books from its library.

There appeared to be few occasions on which residents wrote Yiddish. Two neighbors who moved to Israel sent letters to Yisrul, Avrum, and Malke in Yiddish, but otherwise there was little correspondence in Yiddish. My own move out of the area gave some of the community members a chance to write a Yiddish letter. For example, Yankl A. wrote that his letter to me was his first Yiddish letter in more than 60 years. Of the few American-born residents who could write Yiddish most were women, taught by rabbis or family members. I was surprised to receive long Yiddish letters from Dvoyre and Tsipe-Khashe. Rivke A., who came to America at age twelve, recounted that her husband had asked his future father-in-law to hire a teacher to teach Rivke to read and write Yiddish before their marriage: "A yidishe meydl darf kenen, in ikhl tsuln" (A Jewish girl should know, and I'll pay).

The only creative Yiddish writer was Tsipe-Khashe. When she was ill in the hospital at age twenty, her father taught her to write letters home to her parents, grandparents, and aunt and uncle. Later on, with her mother, she wrote plays, stories, and novels in Yiddish, one of which she translated into English. With this voluminous manuscript Tsipe-Khashe searched for a publisher, without success. She continued, however, to write poems in Yiddish and sometimes read them at the Center. A polished writer in English, this imaginative individual was also a talented painter. In 1985 she won the Pennsylvania contest for the best poster in the state drawn by a senior center member.

Although all the elderly Jews in South Philadelphia understood Yiddish and almost all could speak the language, far fewer could read or write. The several community members who could, however, were proud of their skills. Reading a newspaper or a novel, responding to a letter, or composing a poem or song in Yiddish were acts that counted significantly in their Jewish identity. At first glance, matters of Yiddish culture other than speaking or singing seemed unimportant to the population. However, the members responded positively to the occasional literary recitations and worked hard in the Center's Yiddish class. And for a minority of the residents, other forms of Yiddish cultural expression constituted an essential part of their Yiddish linguistic biography.

CHAPTER EIGHT

Yiddish Fluency

In common parlance, fluency of speech refers to a way of talking that we associate with native speakers. This contrasts with the speech of second-language learners and of most immigrants. Many of the Jews of South Philadelphia were native speakers of Yiddish, but because of the history of immigrant communities, few immigrants and their children retained their immigrant language as their major mode of discourse throughout their lives. Therefore, even I was surprised to find fluent Yiddish speakers in South Philadelphia. The concept of fluency was a useful one for me in comparing different speakers, first in South Philadelphia and later in New England. In searching for a precise definition of fluency, the most compelling construction I found was in the writing of the linguist Fillmore. His criteria meshed with the array of features that I found useful for comparing American Yiddish speakers:

1. the ability to talk at length with few pauses . . . ,
2. the ability to talk in coherent, reasoned, and "semantically dense" sentences . . . ,
3. the ability to have appropriate things to say in a wide range of contexts . . . ,
4. and the ability . . . to be creative and imaginative in . . . language use. (Fillmore 1979: 93)

Fillmore's list covers aspects of performance that reflect knowledge of appropriate ways of speaking in different situations, the ability to innovate rather than just accommodate to an interlocutor, the capacity to convey information and emotions, and the ability to speak rapidly, the quality most often associated with fluent speech. Native speakers typically exhibit all of these characteristics.

The references to fluency of speech in this study are based on general assessments of the speakers over time. The motivation for using this subjective evaluation is to dispel the popular impression that immigrants, and especially their children, have lost or never had the ability to speak Yiddish. In addition, variations in Yiddish speech style, for both the individual and the general population, are presented to explain their social functions and to correlate the variation with changes in individual life experience, Jewish identification, and communal organization.

Among the South Philadelphia residents, fluency in speaking did correlate with immigrant status, in that all of the European-born residents were fluent in Yiddish. However, when the population was divided into age cohorts, it did not follow that the older American-born Jews spoke more fluently than the younger ones. One of the most fluent speakers, for example, was the American-born Beyle, who at the age of 60 was the youngest of the core respondents I interviewed. She spoke more fluently than Surele, for instance, who was 86 and also part of the American-born sample (although Surele was actually born in England and arrived at the age of two). But Beyle also spoke more fluently than European-born Izhak, 77, who arrived at twenty and claimed he did not speak much Yiddish during his 50 years of marriage to European-born Libe, part of the core group of 30 (see Appendix B). Rivke A. came to America at the age of twelve, spoke Yiddish some of the time with her husband, and remained a fluent speaker. Rivke B. arrived at the age of seventeen; she did not speak Yiddish with her husband but spoke it with other family members and friends, including her mother, and remained fluent. In general, fluency in Yiddish within the elderly population was not strongly influenced by age, or by specific age at immigration, but mostly by the pervasiveness of Yiddish speech throughout the respondents' lives and whether they were born in Europe.

In order to better understand the way of talking that I have labeled as fluent, let us examine the speech of Beyle and her sister Elke. Their speech illustrates the abilities described by Fillmore as constituents of a fluent style; I will also show instances of variation in fluency.

Beyle and Elke lived together and spoke both Yiddish and English. Beyle's animated delivery when recounting the reunion of the *zekste* (Sixth Street) is a good example of fluent speech (see Appendix D for the Yiddish text and English translation). Referring to Fillmore's four criteria, we are first struck by Beyle's ability to talk practically without pause or hesitation. Second, her narrative clearly conveys the setting and the sequence of the reported conversation; meaning and sarcasm are conveyed by manipulation of voice quality. Although the third measure of fluency, appropriateness in a variety of contexts, cannot be measured by one speech event, she describes someone's appearance and dress appropriately and vividly, presents reported speech effectively, and expresses her own opinions and values. The echoing style of her Yiddish oral storytelling is appropriate and convincing—for instance, "hob ikh ir gezukt, zug ikh"; "ikh bin zakh gevin on di Riviere, iz zi gevin" (so I told her, I say; I was after all on the Riviere, she was). Fourth, Beyle is creative and imaginative in her use of qualifiers, contrast, dialectal prestige markers, and metaphor to convey sarcasm and irony.

Beyle conveys her strong emotional experiences expressively, readily locating an appropriate fixed phrase. The next sequence illustrates her sense of humor as she describes how her second husband could exaggerate her good qualities and how she appreciated this.

> B.: In ba im bin ikh gevin sheyn, in dar, in klig, klig, kliger fin mir iz nit gevin, s'hot nit gekent zan. Iz gevin git azey. Far
>
> R. P.: Git far di igo.
>
> B.: Far azeyne shvartse yurn vus ikh hob gehot iz dus gevin far mir azey vi gevintshn.
>
> B.: And according to him I was beautiful, and thin, and smart, smart, smarter than I did not exist, it couldn't be. So it was good that way. For
>
> R. P.: Good for your ego.
>
> B.: For such dark years that I had this was as if prescribed.

Beyle, the youngest of the American-born informants, was a fluent Yiddish speaker. Beyle's sister Elke was also a fluent Yiddish speaker, more so than most South Philadelphia Jews, but less fluent than Beyle. Elke was quieter, speaking more softly and less often, and was not as demonstratively emotional. Although her overall "ability to talk in coherent, reasoned, and 'semantically dense' sentences" was comparable to Beyle's, on the three other counts she was less proficient than her younger sister. The contrast between the sisters did not, however, appear as great in English. Since both were raised in the same household and Elke was older, one might have expected her to be more fluent in Yiddish. That the reverse was true might be explained by their Yiddish language use in more recent years. Beyle had moved back to her parents' house thirteen years earlier and lived there with her second husband, an immigrant nineteen years her senior. Even as, one by one, her mother, husband, and father died, she was surrounded by Yiddish speakers during those years. Elke, however, returned only for periodic visits, until the recent deaths of her father and husband. For ten years before Beyle's return to South Philadelphia, both sisters had lived in St. Thomas and continued to talk to each other in Yiddish. But in more recent years Beyle had had more occasions to speak Yiddish.

During an hour-long conversation with me in her living room, Elke's style of speaking Yiddish varied. The changes reflected topic shifts, differing degrees of emotional involvement, recognizable translations of English speech patterns, and specific verbal performance genres. Elke spoke quickly and with the fewest pauses when telling a story. She seemed most at ease and innovative in Yiddish when recounting her youngest years.

But, the house to which we moved, where we now live, had belonged to my mother's sister. And one time my mother was in the hospital, and I went—came here for a day with my aunt, my mother's sister. And my grandfather told her, her name was also Elke. And he told her. You should watch the child. My aunt was a very fancy-dancy, and she had rugs in the house. This is the story Beyle wanted me to tell you.
[I say, "yeah."]
And I entered the house. I was a good child, but somehow I lifted the rug. My aunt started to scream at me. And I thought that she was going to hit me, so I told her, "You shouldn't bother me, I'll tell grandpa." She says, "Woe is me, don't tell grandpa. Don't tell my father anything. You know what, if you'll be a good child and say nothing I will buy you a diamond ring." I say, "For sure you will buy me a ring?" She says, "Yeh I will buy you a—," and that is what she did. As soon as she bought me the diamond, I went and told my grandfather.
[I laugh.]
What took place, because he wanted to know how come she's giving me—that she bought me a diamond ring? Don't ask what he gave her with the diamond ring and without the diamond ring. Afterwards when my mother left the hospital my father bought the house, from my aunt, and she moved away. We had good years here, we were poor. (See Yiddish original of narrative in Appendix D.)

Like Beyle, Elke spoke with few pauses and hesitations, but they lasted longer. Elke also used fewer contractions. In addition, she was less theatrical and did not manipulate the pitch of her voice as much. Her descriptions evaluated people in unmistakable terms, and she ended the narrative with a summary of the topic, in this case referring to the house the family had inhabited for the past 63 years.

Another narrative, in which Elke described the dilemmas facing a Yiddish-speaking child in the public schools, also was vivid and flowed easily (see Appendix D for the Yiddish original and the English translation). Most likely she had told these narratives in Yiddish many times during her lifetime.

Like most Yiddish speakers in America, Elke borrowed and translated from English in her Yiddish speech. This was especially evident in a description of a later period in her youth, which emerged as a word-for-word translation. In this story, about music conservatory and high school, she summarized facts in a fashion that is not typical of the speech of a fluent Yiddish speaker. In other words, when Elke was not telling a story or recounting facts about family relations in early childhood, her Yiddish speech became more halting, with pauses, and contained more English. This was effectively illustrated in her report on the population living in the Virgin Islands. Yet, a bit later on, while still talking about her time in the islands, she became more animated when recounting the story of helping her boss arrange to adopt a child. The pace of her speech increased, the pitch and loudness of her voice varied, and there were no hesitations. When telling a story in which she was emotionally involved, Elke once again demonstrated characteristics of Yiddish fluency. Thus, Elke's speech demonstrates that Yiddish fluency can vary within one speaker, and even within a given topic. The factors affecting such variation may include speech genre and the attitude or mood of the speaker. Using Yiddish to discuss topics that are not typically discussed in Yiddish can be problematic. English speech patterns will be called upon in such instances.

Beyle and Elke were the most fluent American-born pair of speakers who spoke Yiddish with each other. But Reyzl, who claimed she was no longer accustomed to speaking Yiddish, demonstrated many differences in style within a short span of conversation. Her Yiddish speech was full of hesitations, but she retold a nostalgic memory from her childhood at a quicker pace and in a more coherent, logical order than the compliment she paid me when summing up how much I did for the Center members. The latter, more abstract, evaluation seemed a greater challenge to her speaking abilities than the description of an event she experienced as a Yiddish-speaking child:

In indz hobm gemuft in a kleyne strit in Triy Striyt. In ikh gedenk. I—i—indz hobm nisht gehot ken badrum, in hoyz, in gedaft geyn in yad. In ikh gedenk az indz fleygn e—krign a bud in a—. In a groyse shisl. In di mame fleyg e—, oyfzotn vaser afn ge—nit afn gez reyndzh, ikh gedenk nish ken gez reyndzh, af a oyvn, a shvartse dus, fratik fleyg zi, polishn mit e—. Shvartse peynt. In ikh gedenk, inem mitn af de tir, de kleyne tirz vus i geveyn af de oyvn, in silver, end e—.

And we moved to a small street on Tree Street. And I remember. I—i—we didn't have a bathroom, in the house, and had to go in the yard. And I remember that we used to get a bath in a—. In a big bowl. And my mother used to e—, boil up water on the ga—not on the gas range, I don't remember a gas range, on an oven, a black this, Friday she used to, polish with e—. Black paint. And I remember, in the middle on the door, the little doors that was on the oven, in silver, and e—.

In contrast with this rambling recollection, Reyzl deliberated and seemed to weigh every word that she spoke as she described my role at the Center.

Ikhl akh zugn de reyne emes e—Rakhmiel, a, ir (h)ot gebrenkt, aza vunder af idishkayt tse de mentshn vus gekimen tsim Senter vus (h)ot, fa—fargesn dus idish-kayt iz nokh du.

I'll tell you the pure truth e—Rakhmiel, that, you brought, such a wonder of yid-dishkeit to the people that came to the Center who, fo—forgot that yiddishkeit is still here.

It is possible that Reyzl would talk at such a slow pace, utter incomplete sentences, and use unusual syntax (for example, the auxiliary missing before *gekimen*; the lack of agreement regarding number in the second example of the auxiliary *ot*, which is used instead of *obm*; or the omission of *az* [that] before *dus idishkayt*) when faced with similar circumstances in her English speech. Nevertheless, the stylistic variation in fluency is partly explained by differences in the topic and type of speech event.

Beyle spoke more fluently than Elke, who spoke more fluently than Reyzl. The age of these American-born South Philadelphians played no role here since Beyle was 60 and Reyzl 72; however, the amount of Yiddish each used after childhood may well be an explanatory factor. In addition, fluency within a given speaker's repertoire is enhanced in contexts in which the speaker has had previous experience talking Yiddish.

In rating the fluency of Yiddish speakers, I also considered the South Philadelphia Jews whom I did not directly observe speaking Yiddish. Often, I was surprised to hear Yiddish from individuals I had prematurely judged to be nonspeakers. I considered the whole community as Yiddish speakers: there are no "semi-speakers" in this report (see Dorian 1981: 107).

Some of the residents understood Yiddish but were not comfortable speaking it or refused to speak it. Shmuel-Arn, for example, spoke Yiddish on only two occasions that I noted. The first was a brief comment from the microphone at the shul Hanukkah party. The second was in the Center lunchroom, where I introduced Marye to Shmuel-Arn and his wife, Ester-Beyle, a Yiddish speaker, who were sitting at the next table. They both spoke Yiddish to Marye. Shmuel-Arn gave her the common advice that it was important to speak English in America. He also shared with her that he had understood Yiddish but did not learn to speak it until he went into the paperhanging business with his father. I later learned that his mother, although born in Europe, was educated in America and spoke and read English, but his father "did not accept American ways."

During a tape-recorded conversation among Shmuel-Arn, Ester-Beyle, and myself in their living room, Shmuel-Arn repeatedly spoke in English during our primarily Yiddish conversation. At two points when he did speak Yiddish, he did not articulate clearly and used words and syntax that were not common to Yiddish speech. About the decision to have his father live with them, he said: "He was living alone. An(d) then I said to Ester-Beyle, Ester-Beyle, I can't take it, az der tate voyn eyk(?) eyner aleyn (that my father live [?] all alone), what, what do we do if he ge(t)s sick?" Describing his father's arrival in Philadelphia, Shmuel-Arn recounted: "He came in New York, and the uncle said, 'Shik im du aend firn(?) makhn aen fin im a dzhab (send him here and we'll[?] make a job from him).' So my father came to Philadelphia." His Yiddish anecdotes frequently referred to his father. Shmuel-Arn used no Yiddish to describe his life with Ester-Beyle and the children, although she discussed a variety of subjects in Yiddish.

Moyshe B., the Sephardic Jew in the neighborhood, was not a fluent Yiddish speaker, but he must be counted in the larger group of those capable of speaking Yiddish. In a conversation with him and his wife, Rive-Rukhl, he understood everything and finished her Yiddish sentences. He injected Yiddish words and phrases easily, for example, when describing a Sephardic friend: "He got landsmen, you know countrymen." He uses the word "a pur" to refer to a couple of Jews and the phrase "ert gemakht a shidik(h)" (he made a match). When Rive-Rukhl tried to read a letter to me, he jokingly recited a typical salutation for a Yiddish letter: "Mayn libe fraynd ikh vintsh dir di beste zakhn" (My dear friend I wish you the best things).

Another neighborhood resident with whom I usually spoke English was Basye A. Since her husband died she had rarely spoken Yiddish. At the beginning of our conversation, which I recorded in her kitchen, I suggested that we speak Yiddish. She did not wish to speak but claimed to understand everything, so I proceeded in Yiddish and she in English.

R. P.: So oyb ikh red yidish, ir farshteyt alts vos ikh zog? (So if I speak Yiddish, you understand everything that I say?)

B. A.: I can't always answer you, but yes I understand it all.

R. P.: Great, uhm.

B. A.: You want me to try to mess up the Yiddish language?

R. P.: Oyb ir vil—oder ir darft nisht, ir kent redn af english, vus iz beser. (If you want—or you don't have to, you can speak in English, whichever is better.)

At certain junctures Basye A. did, however, respond in Yiddish. For example:

R. P.: Ir hot gehat brider un shvester? (You had brothers and sisters?)

B. A.: Nor a shvester, a yinge shvester. (Only a sister, a young sister.)

And, in another such instance:

> R. P.: Dos iz geven vayt fun aykh in de—siz geven vayt fun ayer heym?
> (This was far from you in th—it was far from your home?)
> B. A.: N—n—nit azey vayt. (N—n—not so far.)

When quoting her mother-in-law, Basye A. also used Yiddish. She remembered that when her children misbehaved and did not treat their mother respectfully, *bub* (grandma) would say to them, "Men tur nisht, di mame" (You are not allowed, she is your mother). In addition, when her mother-in-law's grown son, Basye's husband, demanded his due, *bub* would exclaim, "Ikh hob dir oysgekakt, nisht dir mir" (I shit you out, not you me).[1] In short, when I met her Basye A. was capable of speaking Yiddish but did not choose to do so. The reasons for her reticence included lack of confidence and the sense that Yiddish did not fit into her life.

Two additional South Philadelphia Jews who did not speak Yiddish, even in my presence, were participants in the Gleyzele tey sessions. Two regular attendees, Feyge and Blumke, never spoke during the meetings. Feyge was generally quiet and had few friends at the Center. Some members did not know she was Jewish until she started showing up at the sessions. On one occasion she described herself to me as *sheymevdik* (bashful); another time she managed "Siz a sheyner tuk haynt, varemer" (It's a nice day today, warmer), and before the official start of one session, her voice was recorded as saying to another participant, "Dus iz emes" (This is true). Thus, although the generally quiet Feyge rarely spoke Yiddish, she did understand and could speak.

Blumke, on the other hand, was a talker and joker in English but virtually silent in Yiddish. When I recorded our conversation in her kitchen, she understood my Yiddish but responded in English. Only once did I hear Blumke resort to Yiddish at the Center. She asked Yisrul, 95, about his injections for a blood clot, comparing it to the injections she administered to herself daily. Her brief Yiddish comment was delivered at a quick pace and with the pronunciation and intonation of a native speaker.

These descriptions of the Yiddish speech of South Philadelphia Jews report primarily on the variations in fluency of children of immigrants. Besides fluency, I have also examined the factors that determine the frequency of Yiddish-language exchanges. These influences relate to how talkative people are in general, their confidence in their ability to speak Yiddish, how much they spoke in the past, and whether Yiddish seemed appropriate to the circumstances.

My efforts to determine how spoken Yiddish had changed over the years in South Philadelphia and the meaning of ethnic language to Jewish identity were furthered by my observation of all the individuals who were able to speak Yiddish at some level—those who were very fluent as well as those who were almost silent but able to speak. Fillmore's parameters of fluency put Beyle, who was fluent and had spoken much in recent years, at one end of the continuum, and Shmuel-Arn, whose speech was halting and simple, and who rarely spoke, at the other.

The properties that Fillmore attributes to fluency include the ability to use language creatively and appropriately in a variety of contexts. These abilities often distinguish native speakers from language learners. Most of the Yiddish speakers of South Philadelphia were versatile in their ability to be descriptive, to express their emotional state, and to be innovative yet sound authentic and appropriate. Rivke A., for instance, described the perpetual snow in Ukraine of her youth: "In Yurop az se folt oys a shney ligt er abi gezint" (In Europe when a snow falls, it lies forever). The idiomatic usage here is not meaningful in English (the literal translation is, It lies as long as you're healthy). Upon hearing of the death of the person she held responsible for her misfortune, Dveyre controlled her resentment toward her by posing a rhetorical question: "Vos iz do nikome in teyt? Si nito ken nikome" (How can there be any revenge in death? There is no revenge). Leye jokingly remarked that her husband Yankl A.'s customers did not shun him during the McCarthy era because he was a Communist, as long as he could repair their leaks: "A se rint ba dir in se gist zikh vaser vest nisht, vest nisht zayn zeyer forzikhtik tsi siz a komunist tsi siz, hot er rumatizm tsi komunizm" (If you have a leak and the water is gushing you won't, you won't be very careful if it's a Communist or if it's, if he has rheumatism or Communism).

I found variation in style and structure, but relatively little variation in attitude. Whether in the senior center, an organization sponsored by the Philadelphia Jewish community, or on the shopping street, the Jews I met had a positive feeling for Yiddish. If I was unsure at the outset of my stay in South Philadelphia just how much Yiddish I would find, by the end I was analyzing the universal love for the language.

Variation in the style and structure of speech, once studied only in terms of geographic parameters, is now a mainstay of sociolinguistics. Research on Yiddish, however, has been late in turning attention to this issue (see, for example, Prince 1987; Peltz 1990a; 1990b). While students of language variation look to social and contextual factors, issues of gender, class, age, and ethnicity, the field of contemporary Yiddish studies has been delayed in trying to understand sources of variation. Researchers have largely focused on the normative language of Eastern Europe as the standard. Thus, when I embarked on my South Philadelphia adventure, my training had prepared me to view American Yiddish as substandard. Yet, without knowing exactly why, I felt ready by then to appreciate the nonfluent speaker and the silent speaker, as well as all varieties of Yiddish speech, as rich resources for understanding American Jewish culture. The histories I compiled of the neighborhood, of families, and of individuals authenticated the expression of identity by all the Yiddish speakers I met in South Philadelphia.

Who's Accommodating Whom?

For the duration of my research I was conscious of my influence on the language behavior of the neighborhood people. Documentation and analysis of my role are especially critical for interpreting the observed behavior because, to a certain extent, I reintroduced Yiddish into the neighborhood. As Fabian has stated with much insight, cultural knowledge is not something that even most native speakers express in speech: "This sort of knowledge can be represented—made present—only through action, enactment, or performance. . . . The ethnographer's role, then, is no longer that of questioner; he or she is but a provider of occasions, a catalyst in the weakest sense, and a producer (in analogy to a theatrical producer) in the strongest" (1990: 6–7).

If it is true that I was a catalyst in bringing together forces and traditions that both I and the neighborhood people had been rehearsing throughout our lives, I feel comfortable that the opportunities I helped to create were natural and enmeshed in the context of the community. In that case, the residents did not simply repeat my cues or follow my choice of language or linguistic form. We were actors reacting to each other, acting out rather than controlling subtle power relationships.

My own language choice was not uniform; it was largely determined by the responses I received to my initiating exchanges in Yiddish. Thus, although at first I used Yiddish primarily when I believed my conversational partner understood Yiddish, I eventually shifted to the language chosen by my partner. The configuration of participants in some discussions and specific settings, such as the Gleyzele tey meetings, swayed conversation toward Yiddish. But even then, on occasion I responded in English to someone who understood Yiddish but spoke only English in the group. A comment made in English was sometimes a signal for the next speaker to use English. And, when a Yiddish speaker began to speak in English before the start of a session, I likewise responded in English.

Although I usually spoke Yiddish to Yiddish speakers, sometimes the emotion I wished to convey was more easily expressed in English. For instance, in a phone conversation in Yiddish with Beyle, one of the most fluent speakers in the neighborhood, I asked her if she was "still on a high from Saturday night," when her family gave her a surprise birthday party. Subsequently, our conversation proceeded in English before returning to Yiddish. Another example is a telephone conversation I had with Ester A., who was in the hospital with heart trouble. The first half of our conversation was in Yiddish, but her speech became more halting, and I sensed that speaking Yiddish at that time was tedious and stressful for her. When I switched languages, her speech became quicker, and we concluded our conversation in English.

Generally, I either matched the language of response or selected the language that I sensed would provide my companion with the most comfort. On my first visit to a delicatessen on the zibete, I conversed with the proprietors in Yiddish. At one point, the wife asked me in Yiddish if I also spoke English. I felt that speaking Yiddish was somewhat difficult for her, that she preferred English, and so I answered her in English. After she left, I continued to speak Yiddish with her husband.

More typical is the pattern illustrated by two consecutive phone conversations, both with Yiddish-speaking members of the Gleyzele tey group. In both instances I started in Yiddish; the first woman continued in Yiddish and I did likewise, whereas the second woman responded in English and I changed to English. I always began with Yiddish when speaking with someone who understood, even in response to English, but the language in which I continued depended on them.

Upon reviewing the tape recordings of my conversations with individuals and couples, it became apparent that I used two particular conversational techniques unintentionally. In interviews with people who spoke English almost exclusively, I developed a consultative style, asking many questions. In interviews with people who spoke mostly Yiddish, I let them speak at length, only rarely asking a question. In retrospect, I believe that I let them speak because I valued Yiddish speech more, perhaps found it more interesting, did not wish to interrupt its flow, and wanted to record as much as possible for posterity.

The second technique made apparent by the recordings was my frequent posing of questions in Yiddish to people who were speaking English. At the time, I did not realize how much I wanted the residents to speak Yiddish. The Yiddish question was a signal from me for a Yiddish response, a switch from their previous English comments. Sometimes after the Yiddish question speakers switched to Yiddish, but more often, despite my Yiddish questioning, speakers continued in English. Thus, my influence on directing the interview toward Yiddish speech varied.

In the interview settings, I also spoke English. Once, in a conversation that was almost all in Yiddish, Rivke A., a conversational star of the Gleyzele tey group and an adroit Yiddish storyteller, cried when telling how her deceased husband had helped her sister's children. She then summed up his character with a trite phrase in English. I tried to sympathize and show solidarity by asking a question about her sister in English. It was primarily in discussions with couples when both members were speaking English that I did not maintain my Yiddish speech but joined the conversation in English.

Although I did not usually encourage people to use English when they were having difficulty expressing themselves in Yiddish, on one occasion I did just that. In an interview, rather than switch to English, Ester A. said, "I'm at a loss of words," and then was silent for a few seconds. I then said softly, "Af English" (In English). She then quickly switched to English and eventually returned to Yiddish.

Some people spoke Yiddish spontaneously during informal conversation at the Center, but I never saw this happen in the presence of non-Jews. However, once in the lunchroom, two Jewish women and one non-Jewish member who did not understand Yiddish were seated together talking. I joined them and we continued to talk. Although I spoke English, both women recounted life experiences in Yiddish, even though their non-Jewish partner did not understand a word. My presence was a cue to speak Yiddish.

The phenomena that influence language choice in the examples just discussed can be understood in terms of the social-psychological theory of speech accommodation (reviewed by Thakerar, Giles, and Cheshire 1982; and Giles and Coupland 1991: 60–93). Speech accommodation refers to the adjustment of speech by a speaker in order to be more acceptable to the other interlocutor or in order to convey a specific personal identity. Thus, speech accommodation has to do with presentation as well as with individual and group identity. Speech converges when participants seek approval and when the rewards outweigh the perceived costs (Thakerar, Giles, and Cheshire 1982: 218). A person who maintains divergence or a different speech pattern in a conversation may wish to stress a particular group identification or to dissociate him- or herself from a specific way of speaking. The extent of accommodation to a conversational partner is a function of a speaker's abilities or repertoire and a variety of personality and contextual factors. In addition, investigators have found that speakers are not necessarily aware of the manner or direction of accommodation, as producers and receivers of speech. Low levels of awareness of accommodation even characterize switches between recognizable dialects and languages (Giles and Coupland 1991: 77–78).

Experiments with speech accommodation have examined the interaction between individuals, but the results have been interpreted in terms of group identity and stereotypes. Another line of investigation, which measures language trends in large populations, has established a related theoretical framework for individuals and societies, entailing the phenomena of focusing and diffusion: "The speaker is projecting his inner universe, implicitly with the invitation to others to share it, at least insofar as they recognize his language as an accurate symbolization of the world, and to share his attitude towards it. By verbalizing as he does, he is seeking to reinforce his models of the world, and hopes for acts of solidarity from those with whom he wishes to identify" (Le Page and Tabouret-Keller 1985: 181). The speaker's language behavior will become more regular or focused as it is reinforced in a particular context. If the speaker accommodates to others, the behavior may become more variable or diffuse. On a group level, however, Le Page and Tabouret-Keller hold that language behavior becomes more focused over time. This view, based on Creole studies, a field that has long viewed languages as continua and not discrete entities (De Camp 1971), is quite relevant to the analysis of Yiddish usage in South Philadelphia.

Trudgill points out that in settings that are often labeled "multilingual" a relatively diffuse situation may prevail. "Speakers may have no very clear idea about what language they are speaking; and what does and does not constitute the language will be perceived as an issue of no great importance" (1986: 86). In Belize, which has a relatively unfocused speech community, some circumstances require only one language, but others are facilitated by the use of English, Creole, and Spanish (Le Page and Tabouret-Keller 1985). Similar circumstances were not uncommon in South Philadelphia, as later examples will show. Yiddish-speaking communities throughout history may be considered multilingual, with a strong tendency to accommodate the language choice of others (see Kulick 1992: 261–62).

Le Page and Tabouret-Keller interpret linguistic focusing as "acts of identity" (1985: 182), which include the capacity to modify or accommodate behavior, the ability to recognize groups and behavioral patterns with which one wishes to identify, and the positive and negative motivation to identify oneself with a group. But "how is a balance struck between identification and differentiation?" (Hewitt 1989: 166). In South Philadelphia, many residents who wished to identify with a Yiddish-speaking community and/or develop a friendship with me responded to my Yiddish in kind. Some spoke Yiddish at any opportunity and extended their network of Yiddish speakers to include me. Others would not accommodate to my use of Yiddish for a variety of reasons, which only rarely involved the inability to speak. For some of them, using Yiddish was only appropriate for the world of their parents and a Yiddish-speaking community was a relic of the past.

Even I, the ethnographer, could be diverted from my mission. "Diffuse" or irregular language behavior also reflected my own associations with speaking Yiddish and English, and on occasion I deviated from my policy of speaking Yiddish with Yiddish speakers. I saw the issue of choice of language as focal in encouraging rapport and developing relations with the neighborhood residents.

My influence on the dialectical features of the residents' speech was also an issue, since I do not follow the parameters of any one European Yiddish dialect. My dialect mixture is composed of the Yiddish school standard, which largely reflects the phonology of the northeastern dialect and the grammar of the southeastern and central dialects, and the southeastern dialect of the region of eastern Poland from which my grandparents had emigrated. Although at times I matched the dialects of the residents, I eventually decided to keep my dialect and presentation of self as intact and consistent as possible. It is possible, of course, that the dialectal differentiation of my own Yiddish affected my partners' language during our conversations. Concerning the immediate responses of others to my own speech, there was very little positive accommodation (Thakerar, Giles, and Cheshire 1982) or convergence that related to dialectally specific phonological or lexical items. In other words, very rarely did the Yiddish speakers accommodate themselves to my pronunciation, vocabulary, or syntax. On the contrary, there were more examples of divergence, especially in response to my questions.[2]

Social-psychological studies have documented divergence in conversations between two people that reflect different social identities (Giles and Coupland 1991: 80). My conversations with South Philadelphians may illustrate their limited exposure to dialects other than those present at home during childhood (see Chapter 7). Perhaps it would be more appropriate to view their language behavior as maintenance of ways of talking Yiddish characteristic of a previous era, rather than the negotiated dynamics of divergence. I do not believe that the variation I observed in the Yiddish speech of South Philadelphia can be accounted for by convergence with my speech. Although my language choice sometimes induced residents to talk Yiddish, the Yiddish they spoke was largely from their own repertoires and unrelated to any attempt to copy my Yiddish. Of course, such behavior is also a statement of identity.

CHAPTER NINE

Facets of Speech

English in Yiddish Speech

The interplay of language and identity in the South Philadelphia Jewish community was without doubt shaped by the residents' use of their English-language resources while engaged in Yiddish speech. In Chapters 7 and 8 I discussed stylistic variations by a given speaker and within the population. In less fluent speakers, I observed borrowing and calques (loan translations, lexical borrowings that are translated into the target language) from English and hesitancy in talking about unfamiliar subjects in Yiddish. Almost all of the fluent Yiddish speakers were also fluent English speakers, but the variation in their Yiddish speech was not easily correlated with characteristics of English speech.

I have not treated separate languages as definite abstractions with discrete boundaries, but have accepted that different groups have evolved distinguishable linguistic behaviors over time. The patterns of linguistic behavior that inhere to communities that maintain multilingual repertoires are in a state of flux, as is language in general. Although this study focuses on Yiddish speech, it also documents the symbiosis of Yiddish and English in South Philadelphia, and, indeed, the hegemony of English in most domains.

Studies on bilingualism have utilized the concept of interference, the intrusion of a linguistic element or rule from one system or language into the second system or language (U. Weinreich 1953: 1). Interference implies that the speaker cannot maintain two discrete linguistic systems and subverts the rule-governed borrowing language. The more recent literature on code-switching, defined as "the alternative use of two or more languages within a single stretch of discourse, a sentence, or constituent" (Berk-Seligson 1986: 337), or more simply, "the use of more than one language in the course of a single communicative episode" (Heller 1988: 1), deals exclusively with synchronic language behavior rather than analyzing integrated historical borrowings. There has been a controversy in the literature over whether code-switching occurs only where the grammar of two languages overlaps—in other words, whether there is a shared grammar at the site of code-switching that is amenable to the rules of both grammars (Poplack 1980). Also, it is thought that "code-switching errors" occur—that is, people may use the grammatical rules of one language to express themselves in ways that normally do not occur according to the grammar of either language (Berk-Seligson 1986). Although this is a level of linguistic abstraction not addressed in this book, the debate recognizes that code-switching, or synchronic borrowing, empowers the speaker with communicative capabilities that exceed those of the monolingual speaker. In agreement with Myers-Scotton (1992; 1993a: 6; 1993b: 163–228) and others (Gysels 1992), I am referring to the mechanism of borrowing and code-switching as the same; differences between the two relate to time in history and frequency of occurrence.

One may view the language behavior of the bilingual individual as integrated and interpret the borrowing function as a means of achieving a supplementary pool of linguistic resources that facilitates better communication. Such a positive function seemed to direct the language behavior of the South Philadelphia Yiddish speakers as they manipulated their Yiddish and English language. I agree with Eastman's admonition: "It is clear that once we free ourselves of the need to categorise any instance of seemingly non-native material in language as a borrowing or a switch, we will be much further along in our effort to understand the way cognitive, social, and cultural processes work together in urban linguistic contexts" (1992a: 1). Evidence from a variety of communities has shown code-switching to be not only widespread but actually the norm for in-group talk in certain instances and for intergroup communication in others. Code-switching is embedded in conventionalized behavior, just as it is an indicator of change (Heller 1988: 7, 12). Residents of neighborhoods where more than one culture and language are common are at home in the area of overlap. They learn how to keep the languages and cultures separate, as they also learn how to mix them.

Languages that descend from the stock languages of Yiddish are coterritorial vernaculars that have influenced the standardization processes in Yiddish, both in toward-German (or Hebrew or Slavic) developments and away-from-German (or Hebrew or Slavic) developments (reviewed by J. Fishman 1981). As has been the case for many languages and cultures, the evolution and establishment of norms and standards has occurred both spontaneously within the speech community and as an organized planning process within communal institutions, such as school systems, the press, theater, and language academies. Just as in certain social circumstances borrowings from modern standard German (*daytshmerizmen*) were either encouraged or frowned upon, the same was true for borrowings from English, *anglitsizmen* (M. Weinreich 1938; 1941; 1971; Mark 1938; Niger 1941). Researchers have studied the influence on Yiddish of other languages and cultures.[1] The utilization of English-language resources in South Philadelphia Yiddish speech represents the continuity of a tradition in Yiddish language behavior.

One example illustrates the enlistment of an English-language element into the Yiddish speech of a resident, when a comparable Yiddish element is not available. I have referred to Avrum as an example of a dominant Yiddish speaker: he normally spoke Yiddish with his wife, Malke. One morning he and I were talking in Yiddish about the mother-in-law of Elie Wiesel, whom Avrum had known in Vienna. Avrum was searching for a word to describe young people, and I offered "yungelayt," but he was not satisfied with that and mentioned the word "youngsters"; I then suggested "teenagers," which turned out to be exactly the word he was seeking in this Yiddish conversation. No readily used Yiddish equivalent was available. In this case, the speaker judged a word from English to be appropriate. Thus, focusing on what constitutes a word in the Yiddish language is not as pertinent as observing that when speaking Yiddish, speakers selectively use elements generally associated with English in order to best communicate their ideas.[2]

Since English was the dominant language of most residents, it was not surprising that Yiddish speech was framed by English at the beginning and end of a sequence. The endings were frequently more striking and related directly to the topic just discussed in Yiddish. Even if one narrative in Yiddish was followed by another, the weaving in and out of English made Yiddish seem to be a normal part of everyday life, in which English was the usual language of discourse. Thus, when Beyle concluded her story in Yiddish about the reunion (see Appendix D), which she told to me and her sister Elke, she turned to Elke and said, "Didn't she?" The English was a way of addressing Elke, since the Yiddish narrative had mostly been directed to me. Beyle normally spoke to me in Yiddish and to Elke in English, although they sometimes spoke Yiddish to each other. Yiddish could be used for a narrative, but confirmations, commentary, and closure were more suitable in English.

In some cases, a speaker terminated a narrative in English even when the final statement was not the punchline or a summary or recapitulation; stylistically, English seemed to be suitable for closure. In the following short Yiddish narrative about her cousin, Libe used English internally in a kind of dialogue with herself, and then again when she ended the story in a terse summary statement:

[Laughs] He—se azey vi undzer a kozin iz gegangen mit a meydl [laughs], mishtame (ho?)t(e)rem geshtert. Nu. E—gornisht, hot gezokt er geyt in—in e—e—e—in—e—e—I don't remember where he went, maybe he went to Mexico, ikh veys nit avu, iz e—zol me—hot er gehat di sutkeyses, un— [laughs]. Zey(hob)n o(p)geredt az zi geyt ekh mit em, but zey(hob)n nit gezokt di femeli. Zeyn gekumen tsu der bos, iz er aruf afn bos un avekgeforn mit em(?), un fertik. [Laughs] He was a nice handsome fellow.

[Laughs] He—it's like our cousin went with a girl [laughs], probably they made trouble for him. So. E—nothing, he said he was going to—to e—e—e—to—e—e—I don't remember where he went, maybe he went to Mexico, I don't know where, so e—they should—he had the suitcases, and— [laughs]. They made up that she was going along with him, but they did not tell the family. They came to the bus, he went up onto the bus and went away with him (her?), and finished. [Laughs] He was a nice handsome fellow.

The most accomplished Yiddish narrator, Rivke A., used English in limited fixed phrases, for the dialogue of non-Yiddish speakers, for addressing the interviewer within the narrative, and as the final statement in a narrative. In the following example, Rivke A. used English to summarize one narrative and then directly to begin another, as a framing device. She was describing her husband's kindness to her parents by telling Rivke A.'s mother that she could always leave the old age home and come to live with them and by purchasing a house for his in-laws.

[Husband speaking to his mother-in-law] Ir zolt visn ir geyt avek fin donet farlirt ir nit ayer heym, eyb ir glakht dos nit iz di tir ile mul ofn far akh, siz ayer heym in ir kent kimen du libm mit indz, biz got e—e—git akh yurn. Azoy hot er zi u(p)gehit. He was very good to my parents, well, when I was married only one year that's all, iz er avek in gekoyft a hoyz. Zukt er vi lang, man shvester iz shoyn gevorn elter, bekoz ven ikh hob khosene gehot i(z) man shvester gevin fir yur olt. [Continues]

[Husband speaking to his mother-in-law] You should know that as you leave here you are not losing your home, if you do not like this the door is always open for you, it's your home and you can come here to live with us, until God e—e—gives you years. That's how he cared for her. He was very good to my parents, well, when I was married only one year that's all, he went off and bought a house. He said as long, my sister was older then, because when I got married my sister was four years old. [Continues]

In Rivke A.'s narratives, the last lines summarized, in English, the main point. For example, "He was a out of the ordinary good person," or

"That's the type of person he was," or "If there was angels on earth he was an angel," or "He's just like his father, a heart of gold."

This type of succinct evaluation of a person's character in English usually appeared at the end of the narrative, but wherever placed, it functioned together with other short English stretches of speech to convey a strong opinion or emotion. For example, when Ester A. described her father, a freethinker, she exclaimed, "Got hot nisht gemakht mentsh, mentsh hot gemakht got (God didn't make people, people made God),[3] he didn't buy it, that's the way he felt." Libe recalled that her mother died soon after they arrived in America. She finished in English:

R. P.: Zi iz geven krank nokh in Eyrope?
Libe: No zi iz nit geven krank. (Mir) zaynen geven grine, un nit gekent reydn. Un mi(ho)t nit gekent visn gornisht. We went to the hospital to see her, that's all. That was the end of it.

R. P.: Had she already been sick in Europe?
Libe: No she wasn't sick. We were greenhorns, and didn't know how to speak. And we couldn't know anything. We went to the hospital to see her, that's all. That was the end of it.

In another instance, while lamenting the death of her husband at a young age, Itke cried and said, "Rakhmiel, I had it so good." Rivke A.'s English compliments about her deceased husband, which I quoted, were also delivered with great emotion and sometimes accompanied by crying. Libe, when recalling how observant she had been when she came to America, added the English fixed phrase, "I mean it," to show how surprising that may seem today. "Ikh ho gekent zayn a rebetsin ven men(iz) gekumen aher. I mean it" (I could have been a rabbi's wife when I came here. I mean it).[4]

U. Weinreich discussed borrowing from languages of high cultural prestige when speakers and writers regard their language as inadequate because it is not ornate or elegant (1972: 51). The turning toward English for platitudes and expressions of strong emotion by South Philadelphia Jews may have been rooted in similar motivation, or may have reflected their greater ease with such expression in English, since English was their major mode of discourse.

Short fixed-phrase forms in English, including idioms and formulaic expressions, were also enlisted: "What the hell you want" (Izhak), "borderline genius" (Feygl-Asye), "blackballing of a kind" (Leye), "a wonderful man" (Dveyre). In addition, there were examples of reflexively oriented speech uttered when a speaker paused, seemingly to collect his or her thoughts: "Let me see" (Leye); "I think that's all I remember" (Tsipe-Khashe). Even a very fluent Yiddish speaker, Beyle, ended a telephone conversation with me that we had conducted entirely in Yiddish, with the English leave-taking forms: "Bye Rakhmiel, have a safe trip, thank you so much." Interestingly, there was no similar tendency to use English proverbs in Yiddish conversation.

Another property of the Yiddish spoken in South Philadelphia was the glossing of English and Yiddish words. These pairs of Yiddish and English equivalents included commonly used words replaced by equivalents of English origin, Russian words, and words from the Hebraic and Aramaic components of Yiddish, as well as names. Here, I have listed the words in the order in which they were spoken. English appeared first in: to begin—*untsufangen* (Ester A.); kindness sort of pays off—*se batsolt zikh* (Dveyre); a little basket—*a beskitl*[5] (Feygl-Asye); happy—*tsufridn* (Rivke A.); in and out—*aran in oroys* (Elke); candles—*lakhter* (Roze); boys—*yungelayt* (Tsipe-Khashe). Yiddish preceded English in: *farzikh*—selfish (Dveyre); *mikane*—jealous (Dveyre); *a maseskaye*[6]—a shop (Yankl A.); *link-geshtimt*—left wingers (Yankl A.); *shver*—father-in-law (Reyzl). Other formulations used were: look Franny—*ir nomen iz Frume* (her name is Frume) (Dveyre); *poln heyst* (means)—floors (Rivke A.); *a mime*—that's an aunt (Ester-Sosye); a well—*a brunin* no *a brunin*—a well (Tsipe-Khashe); desert—*midbor vi zokt men?* (how does one say?) (Tsipe-Khashe).

There are several explanations for why such translation pairs were used. Historically, in the spoken and written language there is evidence that speakers used near-equivalent word pairs from different components of Yiddish or from Yiddish and a coterritorial language.[7] In the modern spoken language, it was common to hear elements of the Germanic component paired with Slavic borrowings.[8] The phenomenon in South Philadelphia Yiddish may also be related to an older aspect of Yiddish, perhaps analogous to the word-for-word method of translating or studying the Bible in the Yiddish vernacular (Leibowitz 1931; Noble 1943), to a general sensitivity to the components of Yiddish (M. Weinreich 1980: 656–57), or to an ongoing negotiation process carried out by the multilingual speakers regarding the boundaries between Yiddish and coterritorial speech.

One may assume that some of the South Philadelphia speakers were unsure of their Yiddish usage because they had not recently spoken Yiddish. A possible model for the structure of their spoken language is a word-for-word translation from English. However, since the fluent Yiddish speakers also used the translation pairs, there must be other explanations for their function. In some instances speakers found themselves indulging in English speech and corrected themselves by switching to the corresponding Yiddish word. In other cases, residents used both equivalents separately as interchangeable synonyms in their Yiddish—for example, Dveyre used both *veykeshin* and *vakatsye* (vacation) and *butsher* and *katsev* (butcher).

The repair of Yiddish speech was also related to the phenomenon of translation pairs. The phrase *hoykhe fentster* (high society; *hekhe fentster* in Ukraine) was pronounced by Elke as *haye fentster*, and then she immediately repeated it as *hekhe fentster* (in this instance she first inflected the English adjective "high" before the Yiddish noun). Tsipe-Khashe, a fluent American-born speaker of Yiddish, also corrected her Yiddish speech, reacting against the borrowings from English. For example, she corrected her borrowed *soldzerz*[9] with *soldatn* (soldiers), and after recalling the name of a play as *Froy agenst froy* said *Froy akegn froy* (Woman against Woman). Ester-Beyle, in contrast, changed her pronunciation of the borrowed verb *gemu:vd* to the commonly used American Yiddish *gemuft tsu Miflin Strit* (moved to Mifflin Street).[10] One speaker showed sensitivity to more than one level of language by using one member of the pair of equivalents derived from English and a word in his own Yiddish, *konfidents*, and the other member of the pair associated with his father's language, *betukhn*: "Eniwey, ikh ho(b) gehat konfidents, in vi azoy de tate heyst a betukhn" (Anyway, I had confidence, in what my father called faith. —Izhak).

Most of these examples were taken from conversations between myself and the residents. The speakers knew that I spoke Yiddish, yet I symbolized to them a generation that, as a rule, did not understand or speak the language. Even when speaking to me, they felt impelled to provide translations of Yiddish words. At the same time, some residents articulated their awareness that they were using non-Yiddish words as part of their Yiddish speech, indicating that during conversation with me they believed they should only speak what they considered to be Yiddish. Feygl-Asye, for example, said the word "butcher," then acknowledged that in Europe this word was not used, and soon thereafter used the word *katsev* (butcher). Marye, a Russian speaker, shared her thoughts as she spoke to herself during a search for the Yiddish equivalent of a Russian word: "A dank got ikh hob nit vos tsu—af R—ikh hob zikh nit vos tsu, krasteyen, iz af Rusish, ikh (hob) nit vos tsu ergern zikh" (Thank God I don't have reason to—in R—I don't have reason to, *krasteyen*, is in Russian, I don't have reason to worry).

Studies in Yiddish historical linguistics have discussed differences in the use and structure of whole Hebrew and merged Hebrew. These insights are relevant to the symbiosis of English and Yiddish in South Philadelphia. Merged Hebrew or the integrated Hebrew component generally follows the phonological, morphological, and syntactic patterns of Yiddish, as contrasted with whole Hebrew, which is a citation form in a Yiddish text that agrees with Hebrew patterns (M. Weinreich 1980: 30). In addition, there are mixed text forms, in which elements following Yiddish patterns are interspersed with those of Hebrew in the same sentence (U. Weinreich 1958).

In the study of borrowing in historical linguistics and in the general investigation of languages in contact, one of the most common ways that one linguistic system accommodates elements from another linguistic system is through loan translations, or calques (Haugen 1950: 211; U. Weinreich 1953: 51). In this study, it was not always possible to distinguish influences from English that had been processed by speakers over many generations from those that were specific to the social circumstances in contemporary South Philadelphia. Some words, such as *koyt* (coat), *lontsh* (lounge, parlor furniture, couch), *geyn gebrokhn* (to go broke, go bankrupt), and *opleygn* (to lay off), were so widespread that I assumed they had been integrated into the Yiddish of my informants for many years. Other usage seemed unique and individual.

At certain junctions, speakers verbally dissected their translation process for me: "I wish I could express it in Yiddish. Imprinted in my mind. Iz mir azoy in gedanken." (It is so much in my thoughts. —Ester A.) Izhak shared the following calque and then commented, *vi me zokt* (as one says), suggesting that he was not so certain of this Yiddish usage: *ugehat gemakht dem de—maynd* (made up one's mind). In many of these instances, the resulting Yiddish rendition did not agree with conventional Yiddish grammar. In the previous example, the verbal prefix was added to the auxiliary *hobn* instead of the verb *makhn*, and the borrowing *maynd* (mind) presented gender confusion so the speaker offered two definite articles, *dem* and *de*.

In other instances part of an English phrase was directly borrowed and the rest translated word-for-word, and no attempt was made to translate phrases into idiomatic Yiddish. As a result, uncharacteristic word order in Yiddish revealed an underlying English structure:

Ikh bin geven zayn aepl fun zayn ay. (I was his apple of his eye. —Itke)

Mayn eltste shvester iz elt iynuf tsu zayn mayn mame. Shiyz kinore tsvey un akhtsik yor alt. (My oldest sister is old enough to be my mother. She's, may the evil eye spare her, eighty-two years old. —Itke)

Der ershter komershil stuwdent ever tsu krign a skolership. (The first commercial student ever to get a scholarship. —Ester-Beyle)

Bot zit nisht gevolt nemen no far an anser. (But she didn't want to take no for an answer. —Ester-Beyle)

Ikh nor gedenk. (I only think. —Reyzl)

Di milkhome iz geven iber. (The war was over. —Reyzl)

Indz hobm nisht gezeyt oyg tse oyg. (We didn't see eye to eye. —Reyzl)

Zi olemul shpilt far undz. (She always plays for us. —Reyzl)

The preceding examples of South Philadelphia speech are indicative of the stereotype of spoken Yiddish in America: word-for-word translation and direct borrowing from English, without regard for the conventions of Yiddish word order and phraseology. Such blatant incursions of English forms into Yiddish speech are not necessarily pervasive, but they seemed acceptable enough to the population when spoken, since self-correction or reaction by other speakers was rare.

Even some of the most fluent Yiddish speakers allocated room in their Yiddish speech for English. Dveyre, for example, almost always reverted to English when directly quoting English speech, including her dialogue with non-Jews and with her children. Beyle also did this when quoting her son. For certain speakers who could maintain a conversation in Yiddish on a variety of topics, specific subjects signaled a switch to English. The reverse was also true. Memories of childhood generally evoked Yiddish speech. Thus, Ester-Beyle turned to Yiddish when she recounted memories of the Passover holiday as a young girl:

One of the things I remember. Es iz gevin yontoyvim. Gevin Peysakh. Yedn kind hot gehat ale naye kleyder. Afile az me(ho)t nisht gehat vus tse esn hot men gedarft hubm a naye kleyd. En me(ho)t gen—geshpilt mit nis. Ae—mir(hob)n gehat aza gut taym af de peyvment. De kinder.

One of the things I remember. It was holidays. It was Peysakh. Each child had all new clothes. Even if you didn't have what to eat you had to have a new dress. And you—played with nuts. And we had such a good time on the pavement. The children.

Residents drew upon their English-language resources when speaking Yiddish, using words at the end of narratives to express strong emotions and stylistically to serve as a summary, as an additional store of formulaic and idiomatic expressions, as part of a glossing style of dual-language word pairs, and in calques and lengthier word-for-word translations. Because of the focus on Yiddish speech, this study does not document the Yiddish forms found in the English speech of South Philadelphia Jews, even though there were many.[11] My major interest was the social situations that favored Yiddish talk, as well as the significance that conversing in Yiddish had for the personal and group identity of the multilingual members of the South Philadelphia Jewish community.

Earlier I discussed language choice in relation to accommodation to the investigator and in regard to naturally occurring events and social settings in the neighborhood. Having provided descriptions of the residents and their connection to Yiddish language during their lifetimes, as well as some samples of stylistic variation in their Yiddish speech, it is now possible to further examine factors that influence the residents' choice of language: Yiddish or English, or, Yiddish and English.

As discussed earlier, although my initial tendency in social interaction with Yiddish speakers was to speak Yiddish, I did not always persevere and sometimes accommodated to their choice of English. In small groups, I noted that the normal choice of language in my absence most usually determined the language choice in my presence. Thus, my conversations with Beyle and Roze individually were usually in Yiddish. But because Beyle and Roze usually used English when speaking to each other, when the three of us talked together at the Center, we spoke English. A second example: when I visited Libe and Izhak we mostly spoke English, although little by little Izhak spoke more and more Yiddish with me. When Rivke B. stopped in at the linoleum store when I was visiting Izhak, the three of us conversed in Yiddish. In this example, Rivke B. was likely to converse with us separately in Yiddish. A third example: Malke spoke Yiddish very often to her husband and other neighborhood residents. One day, I had been speaking English with Libe and Izhak when Malke sat down in the store. It was she who urged the four of us to shift to Yiddish.

In conversations that I recorded with couples, the two interviewees would sometimes become engrossed in interaction with each other. As sociolinguists have noted, group interviews are generally more informal than one-on-one interviews and provide revealing data on language choice (Labov 1984: 48–49; Wolfson 1976: 199–201). In a conversation involving Rive-Rukhl, Moyshe, and myself, the Yiddish-speaker, Rive-Rukhl, persevered despite the fact that her husband and I were speaking English. After speaking mostly Yiddish with the two of them in their living room, I realized that the conversation had neglected Moyshe's early life. I addressed him in English, and Rive-Rukhl immediately understood this as a signal that she should not participate, and she said as much in English. But she continued to interrupt my dialogue with Moyshe in English with her comments in Yiddish:

> R. P.: So, so Maury you you ca—you grew up here too.
> R.-R.: All right I'll shut up.
> M.: Yeah. [In low voice)
> R. P.: You can talk in i—the middle, it's O.K., whatever you want.
> R.-R.: That's all right. [In low voice]
> M.: Grew up here.
> R. P.: So you grew up on where?
> M.: On Seventh Street. We had a store there, in the twenty-three-hundred block.
> R.-R.: Er iz geboyrn in Nuw York. (He was born in New York.)
> M.: I was born in New York, yeah.

In this exchange, a speaker clamors for the chance to continue to use Yiddish, and demonstrates this in circumstances in which one of the interlocutors cannot maintain the conversation in Yiddish.

In the second illustration of the situational constraints on language choice, all three participants eventually conversed in English. The topic of discussion was the decision to remain in South Philadelphia and the opportunities to move away. Ester-Beyle talked in English, I asked questions in Yiddish, Ester-Beyle switched to Yiddish. But, as if remembering that her husband was present and uneasy about speaking Yiddish, she returned to English:

E.-B.: Many youngsters Friday night at services, would get together after services.

R. P.: So in der tsayt hot ir nisht getrakht vegn baytn di gegnt. Ir hot keynmol nisht getrakht az ir zolt voynen in e- the Northiyst? (So at that time you didn't think about changing your neighborhood. You never thought that you should live in the Northeast?)

E.-B.: No, I didn't, I didn't.

S.-A.: No, we were satisfied to stay in South Philly.

R. P.: This was fine?

E.-B.: Yeah.

S.-A.: We were satisfied to stay in South Philly.

R. P.: So siz gevern gevorn erger nor in di letste yorn. (So it become became worse only in recent years.)

S.-A.: Letste (last) five, in the last five years.

E.-B.: Yeah.

R. P.: Ven di kinder zenen shoyn avek. (When the children had already left.)

E.-B.: Di—di kinder hobm nokh gevin in der heym ven zayn brider hot gevoyn(t) in em—, Lombard Strit. Aend ert indz gezukt fin nokh a dokter vos der futer hot gevolt farkoyfn de hoyz en ert es nisht gekent farkoyfn. Aend siz gevin in Aedison Striyt. (The—the children were still at home when his brother lived on em—, Lombard Street. And he told us about another doctor whose father wanted to sell his house and he couldn't sell it. And it was on Addison Street.)

S.-A.: At that time that was the beginning of the renovation, of South Street area, Lombard Street, en that e—

R. P.: It's still going on. It takes a long time [unclear].

S.-A.: It's still going on. I know, sure.

E.-B.: Right. And at that time, when I heard about it we figured gee it might be nice.

S.-A.: To get out.

E.-B.: It was like e—e—father son and a holy ghost type home, e— three storeys.

R. P.: Uh—hum .. Probably smaller than this.

E.-B.: Smaller in some ways and larger in some ways.

S.-A.: You were never inside. You never saw the inside.

E.-B.: Yes we were inside.

S.-A.: We were inside?

E.-B.: I—I—oh I'm not I don't remember.

If an interlocutor persisted in speaking English, the conversations generally switched from Yiddish to English. An alternative scenario was a mixture of English and Yiddish, as in the following exchange between Beyle and Elke in their kitchen, where Elke has been preparing dinner.

B.: Beser gib a drey dortn. Ikh hob es no(kh) nit gedreyt. Ver(ho)t gerifn frier? (You'd better stir it over there. I haven't stirred it yet. Who called earlier?)

E.: Your man from the T.V. called, Rita called, and the lawyer called me.

B.: And?

E.: He hasn't heard anything from them yet.

B.: Khob meyre az si(ve)t blabn gurnit (I'm afraid it'll remain as nothing), Ellen.

E.: S(ivet) blabn gurnit, si(ve)t blabn gurnit. (It'll remain as nothing, it'll remain as nothing), I lost more than that in my life.

B.: Darfst nit shrayin. (You don't have to yell.)

E.: I'm not shrayin (yelling). He said he hasn't heard from them yet and fartik (finished).

Another tendency was to use English when it was easier to do so and when it added a dimension not present in the Yiddish repertoire. In such cases, one member of a couple was the Yiddish authority and main speaker. Ester-Sosye, for example, addressed Shmiel-Leyb in English, and he spoke more Yiddish than she did:

R. P.: Bi-biz biz ven hot ir dortn gearbet in Witmans? (Ti—till till when did you work at Whitman's?)

E.-S.: Ikh ho(b) gearbet nukh mon khosene. (I worked after my wedding.) Didn't I work after I got married?

S.-L.: Ye, far a shtikl tsat hot zi gearbet. (Yeah, she worked for a short while.)

In the next exchange about her sisters and their suitors, Ester-Sosye reverted to the English "send off" for the Yiddish word *opzogn* (dialect: *upzugn*) and asked Shmiel-Leyb for the word. He continued with a mixture of Yiddish and English, a phenomenon that occurred in South Philadelphia Yiddish speech when the absence of mutual facility in Yiddish led to the absence of reciprocity in the language.

E.-S.: Zey (hobn) nit khosene gehot. (They did not get married.)

R. P.: Khveys. Ober zey zenin gev— (I know. But they were—)

E.-S.: Ze(yhob)m uge—yeydern. (They e— off everyone.)

R. P.: Uhu.

E.-S.: They se—sent em off, how e—e—

S.-L.: Ze—z(ih)ot ir up— (Sh—she, sen her)

R. P.: Upgezukt. (Dismissed.)

E.-S.: Upgezukt. (Dismissed.)

S.-L.: Upgezukt. (Dismissed.) They had a very high opinion of themselves.

R. P.: Aha.

S.-L.: They thought they deserved the best of the best. Nu (so) the best of the best ho(bn) gefinen ondere (found others).

R. P.: Aha.

S.-L.: Zanen zey ibergeblibm. (So they were left over.)

R. P.: Aha.

The fact that English played an important part in the Yiddish speech of South Philadelphia is not surprising. In the history of Yiddish culture multilingual Jews interacted with speakers of different languages. In this neighborhood, however, the majority of Jews were more fluent in English, the non-Jewish language. Boundaries existed between their English and Yiddish repertoires, but the boundaries were fluid enough to allow certain individuals to use a mixture of Yiddish and English at specific times. Stretches of Yiddish speech that were word-for-word translations from English were not characteristic of fluent Yiddish speakers. Speakers who exhibited such a style were neither creative nor imaginative, according to the definition of fluency I am using (Fillmore 1979: 93). But their speech may have been "appropriate . . . in a wide range of contexts" in the South Philadelphia speech community.

The examples of self-correction that showed sensitivity to the permeability of the boundary between Yiddish and English usually derived from fluent Yiddish speakers. The maintenance of a style that constructed barriers and prevented conversations from switching to English could be supported only if there were sufficient pairs of interlocutors who could speak Yiddish and wanted to do so. Such dyads are limited in number today. Heller has pointed out that although code-switching contradicts language separation, it is the concept of separate domains and relaxation of boundaries that is the key for understanding its use in organizing communication and social life (1988: 7). Code-switchers of the second generation could transmit the Jewish ways of thought and life of the immigrants to a new generation through the use of Yiddish in their English speech. One observant child of immigrants in Greensboro, North Carolina, ascribed her mother's mixing of English into her Yiddish as a conscious understanding that this was the only way to render the child receptive to Yiddish, to make Yiddish a part of the child's own world (Min Klein, "This I Remember," American Jewish Archives, Oral Histories File, Klein Family, p. 19).

My investigation of Yiddish use across the lifespan demonstrated that when my elderly Jewish subjects were young there were clear domains for English and for Yiddish. The domains in which Yiddish culture and the personalities who transmitted it thrived diminished markedly with time. As languages and cultures changed, so too did their interface.

The Dialects of Eastern Europe in the New World

Linguists and Yiddish speakers often classify Yiddish by regional dialect. There are some compelling reasons to compare the current linguistic features of Yiddish in South Philadelphia with the European regional dialects spoken before World War II. Rather than highlighting the loss or corruption of European features, this study underscores the retention of pan-Yiddish features or dialect-specific properties. This view is broader than that of U. Weinreich, who wrote: "In centres of immigration like the United States no uniform dialects have developed, but certain noticeable regionalisms of the European varieties have been leveled out. Substandard American Yiddish, like the languages of the other immigrant groups, have been heavily influenced by English" (1973: 893).

Just as our understanding of sociolinguistics and dialectology has grown to accommodate variation, more recent studies of dialects have demonstrated a complex picture that leaves room for more than "dialect leveling" (the reduction or attrition of dialect-specific features; see Trudgill 1986: 98). Many traits of European Yiddish, particularly ones identified with dialect stereotypes, have been maintained. At the same time, deviations from archetypal markers that appeared in European Yiddish were also observed. The Yiddish speech I observed in South Philadelphia attests to a high degree of maintenance of pan-Yiddish characteristics. And the English language added a potential pool for stylistic variety in Yiddish.

Trudgill (1986) has discussed dialect contact—what happens when speakers of different dialects interact and communicate with each other— from the point of view of linguistic development. The mechanisms he considers include accommodation when interlocutors have face-to-face contact, and focusing on a community level (see Le Page and Tabouret-Keller

1985 and discussion in Chapter 8). He describes the process of simplification—when new intermediary forms appear as a result of the interaction of many dialects. He has shown that even after minority dialect forms are lost and simpler forms emerge, some variant forms live on and even acquire new meanings. Thus, Trudgill shows that the development of homogeneity occurs simultaneously with the development of variation.

More than one hundred years after the arrival in South Philadelphia of Jewish immigrants from East Central and Eastern Europe, very little is known about the circumstances of their initial contacts with one another. They came from various regions, including Congress Poland, Lithuania, Belorussia, and Transylvania, but the majority arrived from Ukraine (including Volhynia and Bessarabia; see Appendix B).[12] The residents reported that in their youth they spoke Yiddish primarily at home with their parents and grandparents, not with their siblings and peers. There were a few exceptions, including the older immigrants Khatshe and Yisrul, who used Yiddish with friends and coworkers. In most cases, linguistic transmission did not take place in communal institutions but relied on parents, relatives, neighbors, and landsleit. In some cases, the survival of Yiddish was complicated by marriages between families from different regions.

Several residents did not know from precisely where in Europe their parents had emigrated and were only able to identify it as Russia, for example. Others could locate the place of origin of one parent but not the other. The reasons for their lack of knowledge may have been their immigrant parents' failure to pass on information, the children's lack of interest in the old country, or a general distancing of American-Jewish culture from its European roots. The implications of such possibilities for my own investigation are significant. Because the ethnic identity of the South Philadelphia Jews was grounded in American society, the evolution of Yiddish structures and ways of talking likely diverged from those characteristic of European Yiddish. But dialect mixing[13] and dialect retention can still be examined for all residents, regardless of whether their parents came from the same location, whether they married, or whether they continued to speak Yiddish as adults.

Itke was the only resident who repeatedly and vociferously proclaimed her regional identity as a *litvak* (a Lithuanian Jew), "a gebrutene af beyde zaytn" (roasted on both sides), and flaunted her clearly defined dialect. It is comic that in the words of her proclamation she pronounced the stressed vowel in *gebrutene* as [u]. In Yiddish dialectology the cardinal marker for the northeastern or *litvish* dialect is vowel 12, realized as [o], not [u].[14]

At 62, Itke was one of my youngest Yiddish-speaking informants. She was born in South Philadelphia, the youngest of seven children, and was the only one remaining in the neighborhood. Her parents were born in a small town in Lithuania near Kovne, and two of her siblings were born in Europe. Itke and her husband lived with Itke's mother until her death in 1968. At home they spoke Yiddish with her mother, and Itke claimed to still speak Yiddish to her older sisters. She did not hesitate to declare proudly how much she loved to talk Yiddish. Upon entering school at age five, she did not know English well (see narrative in Chapter 7). Although she used many Yiddish idioms and sang Yiddish songs, she was not a fluent Yiddish speaker.

During my stay in South Philadelphia, I tried to avoid making comments about the residents' spoken Yiddish. I did not want them to become self-conscious, nor did I wish to become the arbiter of correct usage. Nevertheless, after almost a year of hearing Itke pontificate that her dialect, *litvish*, was the best, and commend me when I pronounced words according to the dialect of northeastern Yiddish, I raised the possibility with her that "a bisl fun der rusisher shprakh" (a little of the Russian language) of her husband's family had rubbed off on her. First she responded, "My husband spoke a good Jewish like I did." Then she admitted, "You know we talk we say, *kum* (come), I got away from it a little bit, *kum*, *puter* (butter)." But when I suggested that it was due to her husband's influence, Itke responded, "No, all of us married Russian backgrounds, none of us married a Litvak. All through the years it rubbed off."

Itke maintained a strong *litvish* identity yet spoke a Yiddish influenced by the phonology of the southeastern dialect, which she attributed to the influence of the "Russian" Jews who had married into the family.[15] One can imagine that there were other opportunities in the neighborhood to be influenced by the language spoken by the majority, the Ukrainian Jews. That there was a *litvish* presence, however, is clear; B'nai Samuel, the predecessor congregation in the synagogue building of Congregation Adath Shalom, was called the *litvishe shul*. Itke continued to insist that it was her husband who was swayed to speak according to her family's dialect, since he lived with them. Her mother used to exclaim, "Oy, ikh hob im upgeshmadt"[16] (Oh, I converted him). Itke recalled that her husband had business dealings with older Jewish men, with whom he spoke Yiddish. After their marriage, the men told him that he spoke differently. She claimed that after their marriage "he never said *piter*" (butter, pronounced according to the southeastern dialect).

Let us examine Itke's pronunciation, as she told how her brothers and sisters helped support the family:

Siz geven finef peyz aen zeym ale arayngetshipt, aen di mame (hot) gekokht aen gebakt, aen di hoyz hot sheyn gekost nit a sakh rent, si geven kimat vi opgetsolt en zeym upgetsult. So siz geven gringer.

There were five salaries and they all chipped in, and my mother cooked and baked, and the house already didn't cost much rent, it was almost paid off and they paid it off. So it was easier.

The noticeable deviation from the pronunciation of northeastern Yiddish is the substitution of *upgetsult* for *opgetsolt*. It is striking that she realized [u] in both positions in the word only two words after she pronounced the same word with [o]. Both forms actively co-existed in Itke's language, a transitional phenomenon discussed by Trudgill (1986) resulting from dialect contact situations. Whether this reflects a universal sound change in progress or a word-by-word borrowing cannot be determined from these data. Note that in the above passage Itke did not realize certain vowel pronunciations common to the majority of South Philadelphia speakers (e.g., i_{25}: *gevin* [been]; o_{11}: *mome* [mother]).

Other examples of Itke's speech also deviated from the phonological pattern of northeastern Yiddish. The deviations were realized in only some words, some of the time. Although her speech contained several examples of southeastern vocalic features, they had entered Itke's pronunciation on a single-word basis.[17] However, the dialectal variation in her speech in no way stopped her from being an avowed dialect chauvinist, loyal to a minority variant in this neighborhood, the language of her parents' household.

As a contrasting example shows, certain speakers retain major features of their dialect, even if theirs is a minority way of talking in the Yiddish speech community. Tsipe-Khashe, at 69, was close in age to Itke and was also born in America. She had lived in her house for 63 years. Her father was born in the *gubernye* of Kovne and her mother near Minsk, both districts in the area of the northeastern dialect. Tsipe-Khashe was a high-school teacher in Philadelphia, had never married, and had lived with her parents until their deaths. She was a fluent Yiddish speaker whose speech often reflected English phraseology. However, phonologically, unlike Itke, Tsipe-Khashe's Yiddish deviated little from northeastern Yiddish (see Tsipe-Khashe's narrative in Appendix D). I noted only three deviations in my many conversations with her.

Northeastern Yiddish has a pattern of hissing and hushing sibilants that does not exist in other dialects; this phenomenon is known as *sabesdiker losn*—a stereotypic wordplay meaning "Sabbath language," generally pronounced in Yiddish as *shabesdiker loshn*.[18] Although the phonological and lexical constraints have not been clearly identified by linguists, the phenomenon was widespread in the speech of informants who lived in the region in the early twentieth century. Itke exhibited the deviation in only one word, *zi* (she), which she pronounced some of the time as [zhi]. Its absence in other words could mean that the phenomenon had largely disappeared from her parents' language or that in the evolution of Itke's Yiddish it had become stigmatized. Itke actually attested to both facts. Her grandmother, whom she knew, was born in a different shtetl (small town) from her parents and exhibited *sabesdiker losn*. Itke asserted that there were two kinds of litvaks, those who spoke that way and those who did not. She reported that her entire family would laugh when their grandmother spoke, and she claimed that neither her parents nor her siblings spoke that way. In a Gleyzele tey session, both she and Leye were able to recite tongue twisters that presumably mimicked *sabesdiker losn* speakers. These two American-born residents kept alive the stigma and derision associated with this way of speaking.

In Tsipe-Khashe's narratives, unlike Itke's, there were many examples of the pronunciation of sibilants that differed from Yiddish from most regions, such as *gestanen* versus *geshtanen* (stood), or *shekhl* versus *sekhl* (wisdom) (see Peltz 1990a: 63–64). A phenomenon that was viewed negatively and was disappearing had been retained by a child of immigrants. Tsipe-Khashe spent the summer through her teens living with her grandmother in Baltimore, in surroundings in which she may have spoken Yiddish more than in Philadelphia and in which she was exposed to the language of a person older than her parents. Not having married into a family from a different dialect area, as Itke had done, and not having conversed with her siblings in Yiddish as Itke reported, Tsipe-Khashe was able to maintain a language that retained more of the dialectal features of the older generations.

Yiddish dialectologists have focused their studies on the phonology of vowels, which are the features that speakers identify most with dialects. Itke was a speaker of a mixed dialect, while Tsipe-Khashe was a speaker who retained the phonological system of a single European dialect, including even a feature that was archaic and stigmatized. Similar dichotomies and variations were apparent within the population as a whole, even among the speakers who hailed from Ukraine. From the dialectological data, because of differentiation exhibited geographically within northern Ukraine, for example, we do not find a single uniform dialect for all the original immigrants from the entire region (Herzog 1969; Peltz 1990a: 64). But I did find individuals who rather faithfully replicated features of their geographic dialect.

This was the case for the sisters Beyle and Elke, children and grandchildren of immigrants, who continued to speak Yiddish to each other as elderly women. In analyzing a narrative of Beyle's, I identified only one variation from the vocalic pattern expected for her dialect of northern Ukraine. She realized one instance of u_{51}, instead of [i]. I interpreted this as Beyle's desire to mock her interlocutor's supercilious air by using a pronunciation characteristic of the prestigious northeastern dialect (see Appendix D). However, in most examples of varied pronunciation by single speakers, I was not able to ascribe semantic or stylistic differentiation to such usage. It is the variation of pronunciation of the same word, sometimes within one breath, that indicated a certain linguistic insecurity, which might reflect a sound change in progress and/or specific competing forms in the speech of individual speakers. For speakers who derived from Ukraine, the most variation focused on words exhibiting vowel 11 (*khate/khote* [hut], *ander/onder* [different]).

Izhak left Transylvania at age twenty, married Libe, a native northeastern Yiddish speaker, and did not often speak Yiddish anymore. In his speech I noticed dual realizations of vowel 22, [ay] and [ey], in close proximity to each other:

Geveyn a shayne fro, ye, a fayne sheyne fro. (Was a beautiful woman, yeah, a fine beautiful woman.)

Mayn tsvay, di tsvey onkls, in di tsvey tsvay vi heyst es, tantes, in di tsvey tantes hobm khasene gehat du in Amerike. (My two, my two uncles, and my two two how do you call it, aunts, and my two aunts got married here in America.)

Lists of words cannot convey how variations occur in context, in actual use. Most speakers in South Philadelphia exhibited variability along with uniformity of speech. However, sociolinguistics, by studying variation, has made us aware of this universal property of language and society. Although we do not possess much information on variation in the speech of previous generations of Yiddish speakers, we should not assume that South Philadelphia Yiddish speakers were different from their predecessors. The data from the largest study of spoken Yiddish, the Language and Culture Atlas of Ashkenazic Jewry at Columbia University, have not been analyzed for variation within the speech of individuals. One older study in Belorussia that examined in detail the hissing and hushing sibilants in a few towns did indicate great variability for single words and single speakers (Veynger 1928: 619–30).

Reyzl, a child of immigrants, who spoke Yiddish with characteristics of English speech, demonstrated the existence of alternative forms. I do not know whether one or both of her parents came from the large southern Ukrainian region in which vowel 11 is realized as [o]. This subdialect of southeastern Yiddish is popularly termed *tote-mome-loshn* (*tote-mome-* language) to indicate the pronunciation of the common words for "father" and "mother." For most Yiddish speakers, this vowel realization is a stigmatized form, not used in the language of high culture. Therefore, one might expect to see realizations changing away from o_{11} toward a_{11}, since prestige forms would serve as models. Interestingly, Reyzl's pronunciation of the words *tate* and *mame* contained a_{11} exclusively. Most of the immigrants came from the o_{11} dialect area, and thus it is surprising that this vowel exhibits the most variation. However, the language reflects processes that started in Europe and continued in America in which prestige forms were not necessarily the forms of the majority.

With a few exceptions, alternative forms did not usually appear close to each other in speech. However, one narrative included repeated alternation of the same forms containing vowel 11. This example demonstrates this variation within a speech context and also indicates that there is a constancy and order to the spoken language. It is interesting to note also the relative lack of variation in pronunciation of vowels other than vowel 11 (see Reyzl's narrative in Appendix D).

An examination of Reyzl's narrative for the pattern of realization of vowel 11 uncovers four instances of *vaser* (water) in proximity to each other, two with [o] and two with [a]. In the two instances of *kalte* (cold), one contains the realization of [o] and the other [a]. In the latter two occurrences of the same noun phrase, *kalte vaser*, the adjective and noun exhibit the same vowel realization in one case and a different realization in the second example. In addition, one example each of *gehat* (had), *gegan* (went), and *hant* (hand) were realized with [o], and one instance of *shmate* (rag) as [a]. She also pronounced two hypercorrect forms with [a]. Hypercorrections are defined as forms that represent efforts to take on prestige constructions, but involve overgeneralization and realization of forms that are not present in the target speech (Trudgill 1986: 66; for a more detailed analysis of Reyzl's narrative, see Peltz 1990a: 67).

Although hypercorrections are sometimes seen as temporary and part of the speech of only some individuals, they can lead to integral "interdialect forms" that remain in a particular dialect, as Trudgill has pointed out (1986: 76). We do not have sufficient evidence to determine the age of these hypercorrections, but we do know that immigrants and children of immigrants maintain such interdialect forms in their speech.

The kind of variation I have described was greater in the second-generation cohort in our sample than in the immigrants. But the picture is not simple (see Peltz 1990a: 68). The generalization that immigrants speak relatively uniformly, as contrasted with the variable way the children of immigrants speak, does not hold for the speech of some second-generation residents. For example, the phonology of Beyle, Elke, and Tsipe-Khashe indicated less variation than that of immigrants Libe, Izhak, and Rivke B.

Variation in Yiddish speech does not have its basis only in the dialects; earlier I noted the differential role of English and the variability of fluency. Additional examples of variation take morphological and syntactic forms

(Peltz 1990a: 69–71). Intimate family contacts influence language the most. Therefore, children of immigrants who had extensive contact with their parents and grandparents and did not marry into families from different dialect areas retained the characteristic speech of their ancestors. However, the internal variation in their dialects and the value judgments related to specific dialectal features continued to affect Yiddish speech patterns in South Philadelphia.

The social process that started more than a hundred years ago—that of immigrants from different European areas living as neighbors and inter-marrying—created a much more complex contact situation in the new country than existed in Europe. Even in South Philadelphia, a Jewish community in which most of the residents came from one region, there were examples of leveling and retention of dialect features, mixed dialect speech, and relatively intact dialect speech. The circumstances in which children of immigrants continued to speak Yiddish almost exclusively with their parents and English in more general social intercourse prevented the process of simplification from occurring, as is generally seen in the survey of dialect contact studies (Trudgill 1986). The changes that have occurred in Yiddish in South Philadelphia, including those attributable to the role of English or to dialect contact, have, however, allowed communication in Yiddish to persist. In social situations, especially in the meetings of the Gleyzele tey group, I never heard the complaint that the Yiddish language as used by one participant was unintelligible to another neighborhood resident.

The widespread co-occurrence of alternate forms does not reveal the direction and extent of language change within the individual speaker. The small group of individuals in South Philadelphia who used variant forms most often were the less fluent Yiddish speakers; they frequently used forms characteristic of English speech. Since some of the language changes had already started within the greater Yiddish speech community, as reported by other researchers, it is possible for us to speculate that this group of speakers was actually a vanguard for change.

General conventions for Yiddish speech that were developed over the centuries have coexisted with changing patterns of features. The variation in South Philadelphia illustrates patterns that are present in modern Yiddish as a whole, as well as specific changes in language that reflected the mix of immigrants in the neighborhood. Moreover, these studies demonstrate for the first time that the investigation of the speech of children of immigrants is necessary and revealing. This generation constituted the majority in Jewish South Philadelphia in the mid-1980's. The language behavior of the second generation developed in harmony with the social experience of the family and the neighborhood. Opportunities to marry into families from other European areas enabled new dialectal complexions to arise, just as English-language culture aided the evolution of new ways of talking Yiddish. The children of immigrants who formed new Jewish institutions, such as the Jewish center, the Young People's Congregations, and the war veterans' groups could not be expected to remain fixed in a European-based Yiddish culture. Historians have shown us that this was not even the case for the immigrants, who started new world groups and fashioned new identities for themselves. Perhaps what is surprising is that the children were still motivated to share in the language and culture of their parents.

PART IV

Philadelphia and Beyond:
The Evolution of Ethnic Culture

CHAPTER TEN

Language and Identity

One hundred years after the mass immigration of East European Jews to the United States, the connections of contemporary descendants to their immigrant culture have hardly begun to be uncovered. As a student of Yiddish, I became aware that this major culture of Jewish immigrants had only been scrutinized on the institutional level—in the press, the theater, the cinema—and in the texts of poetry and belles lettres. But what about the language and culture of the primary institution—the family, the household? What can be unearthed in the archaeology of the contemporary woman or man in the street? By turning the ethnographic microscope onto the Jewish residents of South Philadelphia—people of varying relation to the first generation of immigrants, including newer immigrants—I focused on their involvement with Yiddish language and culture. Although I was committed to learning as much as possible about history, my emphasis was on the residents as I saw them, as they presented themselves to me.

My major research technique, speaking Yiddish with all those who could understand the language, revealed a treasure trove of behaviors, attitudes, and identifications. Language was a valuable guide for revealing feelings about family and neighborhood, the depth of self-identity, and the extent of group identification. The succeeding generations are able to utilize elements of immigrant culture creatively to carve out identities and communal supports that serve them well in the decisions they make throughout their lives. Although this collaborative effort between the South Philadelphia residents and myself reveals much about Yiddish speech and attitudes toward language, even more emerges about personal and group identifications of contemporary Jews in America.

The fieldwork I have conducted in other communities and the work of others with a variety of ethnic groups have further demonstrated to me that our understanding of ethnic identity in America can be expanded to accommodate the historical and psychological attachment to the culture of the immigrant household and neighborhood. The picture of Yiddish in South Philadelphia points to fundamental trends in ethnicity and life-cycle changes in personal identity in the United States.

This book is about people—how they communicate with their contemporaries, their ancestors, and their offspring. The ethnographic venture on which I embarked shows that language is intimately intertwined with a feeling for place, a connection to tradition and religion, and above all a sense of self. The American Yiddish voices themselves have guided me in my understanding of what it means to be a Jewish American. The treatment of Yiddish throughout its history is a story of marginalization. Yet, from my work in South Philadelphia and other communities, I have found a cultural undercurrent that may actually drive the mainstream of American Jewish life. A Yiddish proverb says: "Di gantse velt shteyt afn shpits tsung" (The whole world hinges on the tip of the tongue). The symbolic strength of speech became clear from the behavior of the South Philadelphia residents. The centrality of language to the ethnic culture they embraced was proclaimed in their voices.

Language, Identity, and Place

This book has focused on members of an aging population. During their youth, Yiddish language was much more evident in their neighborhood than it was during the period of my research there. My presence in the neighborhood, my relatively young age, conversation with the residents in Yiddish, and facilitation of the weekly discussion group catalyzed the expression of positive attitudes toward the ethnic mother tongue. As Myerhoff demonstrated for a community of aged immigrant Jews in Venice, California, the marginality of their existence within the larger society made the specific ethnic culture they possessed invisible and precariously subject to terminal neglect (1987: 145). Although different from the Venice group in many ways, including the fact that a majority of its members were second-generation Americans, the South Philadelphia Jewish community shared an invisibility that not only conferred inferior status on the neighborhood but also did not allow for the development of a community with cultural continuity.

My presence in the neighborhood elicited in the residents a nostalgia for their youth and provided some of them with the hope that their language and culture would not terminate with their death. From their biographies and neighborhood history, notwithstanding a history of ambivalence, on the whole they had developed in their old age a positive relationship with Yiddish culture. The genesis of this attitude predated my arrival on the scene. Although at the beginning of my sojourn in South Philadelphia I was confused by my role of injector of Yiddish into the neighborhood, I now understand better. The ethnographer is dramaturge, not creator (see Fabian 1990: 7). Much of the work of ethnography is interpreting the interactions of all the actors, including the ethnographer. My experience with South Philadelphia Jews was a continuation of their life's repertoire. What was meaningful to them, how they did things, most often cannot be encapsulated in words; rather, it was acted out in life, together with me. The documented enthusiasm of the residents demonstrated how the use of an ethnic language that normally does not appear in the public and private domain can be a valuable research tool for the anthropological study of matters of personal and group identity.

The focus on language in a multiethnic neighborhood was one of the topics addressed in Suttles's (1968) study of the social structure of the Addams area in Chicago. He had the insight to appreciate the interconnectedness of language, gesture, personal appearance, and clothing. My more limited investigation follows a tradition in the study of language in which an urban neighborhood is the locus of observation (Labov 1982 [1966]: 89–179; Hoffman and Fishman 1971). It is necessary to explore the linguistic history of the community and the individuals in order to understand language use synchronically.

The changes in the South Philadelphia neighborhood had affected the frequency with which people spoke Yiddish. Because the Jewish population was largely elderly, the Jews who came into contact with other Jews shared a fairly common background: they were Yiddish speakers—immigrants or children and grandchildren of immigrants—who had heard Yiddish spoken at home and on the street during their youth. Most South Philadelphia Jews had a positive attitude about their venerable Jewish community and their low-prestige neighborhood; this was part of the general local pride in their ethnic roots.

My survey of institutional succession and development found a decreased incidence of Yiddish as a language of organizational activity. Its use was limited to occasional conversation in the Orthodox synagogue and to some cultural programs at the Center. According to the residents, the major public locus for Yiddish speech used to be the zibete, but in recent years Jewish merchants had moved away, and their children did not want to assume responsibility for the businesses. A new shopping center nearby attracted the local trade, and as a result, Yiddish had become increasingly restricted to the private domain.

Important services and opportunities for forming "intimate secondary relationships" (Wireman 1984) did exist within the Jewish institutions of South Philadelphia. However, because the neighborhood Jewish population had shrunk so much since their childhood, South Philadelphia Jews had to look inward to personal and family history for the ethnic foundations of their upbringing, rather than to the street, synagogue, club, or Jewish Center.

I portrayed Izzy as a central figure who linked social networks, led several Jewish institutions, and provided a daily open door on the zibete for neighborhood residents. Izzy had tremendous influence both within the local Jewish community and in its relations with non-Jews. For many, he was their link to life as they checked in daily on the zibete, and to the Jewish community, as he kept Y.P.C. Shari Eli, the Jewish masonic lodges, and the Pruzhaner landsmanshaft alive. Izzy closed his luncheonette in 1985 right before his wife Sure died, and he died in 1988. In 1997 all three synagogues still functioned, and the Center had attracted some new Jewish members. But without Izzy, the neighborhood and Jewish community were in some ways less vibrant, depending more on professional help, on the services of a rabbi, social worker, and Center personnel. And the Jewish zibete is no more. The hundreds of hours I spent in Izzy's luncheonette, in Libe and Izhak's linoleum store, in Basye A.'s kitchen over her upholstery store, and on the doorstep of Malke and Avrum's notions store cannot be again.

This study provides an integrated picture of the use of Yiddish in institutional life and in various functional allocations, the stylistic variation for a single speaker in changing contexts, and the differing attitudes toward Yiddish. This picture bridges the gap separating micro- and macro-sociolinguistics (J. Fishman 1980; Hakuta 1986: 165–92). Talking was a touchstone of sociability in the South Philadelphia Jewish community and an activity that remained possible for the residents after other limitations had been placed on their lives. The study of Yiddish conversation in Jewish society and culture has recently been recognized for both its linguistic and its literary value (J. Fishman 1981: 61; Harshav and Harshav, eds., 1986: 14–15; Harshav 1990). Most sociolinguistic studies have concentrated on either microstyle, such as variation in a phonological feature, or macrostyle, such as strategies for refusing requests (Irvine 1985: 561). The present investigation has looked at both; no previous study has analyzed the overall dynamics of Jewish language in a contemporary American community.

Language is a vital component of personal and ethnic group identity, but researchers who have attempted to portray the forces operating in the development of Jewish neighborhoods and communities have apparently thought otherwise. Thus, the sociological and social historical studies of Jewish life in Brownsville, Brooklyn (Landesman 1969; Sorin 1990; see, however, p. 16); Boro Park, Brooklyn (Mayer 1979); and Portland, Oregon (Toll 1982) ignored changes in daily language use and personal identification with language. Although Lowenstein (1989) writes much about the language use and attitudes of German Jewish immigrants to Washington Heights, Manhattan, because of his focus on one group, he largely overlooks the neighborhood's other Jewish and non-Jewish groups and their languages. In a classic study of three generations in the Jewish community of Providence, Rhode Island (Goldstein and Goldscheider 1968: 225–27), the authors analyzed the changing meaning of Yiddish for American Jews by examining the answers to the one item of a questionnaire that asked whether some Yiddish is spoken at home. Their conclusion was that "linguistic assimilation among Jews was rapid and complete in three generations."

If the authors of the Providence study had done a qualitative analysis of the ways Yiddish is spoken to a Yiddish-speaking fieldworker, different data may have been generated about Jewish residents of Providence. The results of the present study demonstrate that an examination of Yiddish speech and attitudes toward Yiddish can reveal much information about the development of Jewish communal life, personal identity, and linguistic structure. The study of Yiddish in South Philadelphia challenges the judgments of Yiddish linguists, such as M. Weinreich (1941; 1971) and Mark (1941), that an investigation of spoken Yiddish in America would be unfruitful. On the contrary, at least with regard to second-generation American Jews, using spoken Yiddish as a research tool can unravel the complex dynamics of changing personal and group identity. By concentrating on the neighborhood, this study shows that Yiddish was alive in a place no one had thought to look before.

Overriding many identifications and closely bound to the attachment to Yiddish was the residents' strong feeling for place. It appeared as a stabilizing factor in a larger society in which cultural change was perceived on a daily basis. The attachment to place has been heralded as a valuable but missing ingredient in the contemporary United States, where few people benefit from the advantages of "staying put" (Sanders 1993). Yiddish was part of these residents' constancy of place. I am speaking more of a state of being, a state of mind, than a physical or social reality. Indeed, I have chronicled large changes in neighborhood, family, and personal history. Although the place had changed, since most had never lived anywhere else, the feeling of being grounded in the most familiar of places, the parental environment, remained. It is this constant reassurance that strengthens the building and maintenance of self-recognition (Hummon 1990).

Gaining sustenance from being rooted in a place does not necessarily come naturally, but as a result of rejection of or isolation from the dominant cultural and economic forces. The universalizing, abstract, postmodern landscape facilitates the erosion of locality, "the annihilation of the archetypal place-based community by market forces" (Zukin 1992: 240). South Philadelphians who upheld the vernacular, the local, the Yiddish, were part of the powerless in society. Zukin asks if they will be able to make a cultural imprint, if their "identities are oppositional or Orwellian relics" (1992: 242).

Ever since the establishment of this Jewish community by immigrant families, mainly from Ukraine, more than one hundred years ago, the mental and emotional image of place has been in flux, be it the hometown in Russia, or South Philadelphia, or Northeast Philadelphia: "The ability of people to confound the established spatial orders, either through physical movement or through their own conceptual and political acts of re-imagination, means that space and place can never be 'given,' and that the process of their sociopolitical construction must always be considered" (Gupta and Ferguson 1992: 17).

The feeling for place is fundamental to the negotiation of the community member with others during the processes of developing personal and group identity. It also colors the perception of the physical and social surroundings. No South Philadelphian reported an aesthetic attraction to the neighborhood, an area of drab brown-brick attached houses, blocks without trees, and only a one-square-block park. The critic Howe, a child of Jewish immigrants, remembers his childhood Bronx, New York, neighborhood similarly: "It was rare for a building of red or tan brick to break the monotony of muddy browns and grays; what I remember of the streets is notable for flatness of color, sameness of shade" (1982: 2). Yet a strong feeling for place, for the identity of the Jewish South Philadelphian, pervaded the neighborhood. Culture is place, kitchen and street, smells and sounds. South Philadelphians did not give up easily on any of these components of the identity of place.

Language and Ethnic Culture

The changing patterns of Yiddish language behavior during the lifetime of multilingual Jewish Americans and during the concomitant evolution of their local community can be evaluated in light of research on ethnic language and ethnic group identity, particularly those studies that stress the relevant attitudes of speakers to their ethnic language and culture. Notwithstanding the different approaches to defining an ethnic group and an ethnic language, there exists a rich literature on the markers in speech that indicate ethnic group membership (reviewed in Giles 1979).[1]

Milroy and Milroy discuss a number of cases throughout the world in which "social norms" for speech that have wide acceptability conflict with "community norms" that pertain to a smaller group (1985: 108–14). Ethnolinguistic group members will adopt higher-status social speech norms on the one hand, but also maintain over centuries language forms in accordance with community norms. Speakers may accept the unfavorable judgments made by the larger society regarding their dialect or language, yet view these linguistic varieties as valuable symbols of group cohesion. Although the literature on language shift analyzes language choice of the majority language in terms of the desire of the speaker to be associated with the positive status of the majority rather than a stigmatized ethnic identity, less effort has been expended to understand how the locally based conceptions of self and difference that groups develop guide their members in their interpretation of social worth (Kulick 1992: 9, 262–63). There can be social pressures toward vernacular use that differ from the norms favoring use of the standard. Use of vernacular forms "increases with the degree of membership in core community peer groups, with the density and multiplexity of social networks, and with the importance of dependency and reciprocity" (Woolard 1985: 744). For example, on many levels, speaking Yiddish in South Philadelphia at the time of my study provided the Jewish English-speakers with acclaim from peers and associates that it may not have earlier in their lives and in history. As Yiddish speakers, they were the only ones able to rescue the culture of their parents from oblivion. From another perspective, in an aging community, the possession of a resource that engenders feelings of beauty and intimacy eases the difficulties of old age and is viewed this way by the individual and the group.

Le Page and Tabouret-Keller have established principles of research based on many years of studying creole language in the Caribbean. Their views were particularly valuable in constructing the theoretical background for evaluating the data in this study. Le Page and Tabouret-Keller (1985: 2) adopt Giles's definition for ethnic group: "those individuals who perceive themselves to belong to the same ethnic category" (1979: 253). Le Page and Tabouret-Keller are less interested in defining ethnic group or language than in exploring the ways individuals project their concepts of language and ethnicity on others and thus help to determine the nature of groups (1985: 247–48). Moreover, these authors believe language to be the focus of "acts of identity," an overt way individuals symbolize themselves and their world. It is this type of self-definition that I have used in grappling with what it means to be a South Philadelphia Jew, from the residents' perspectives.

As I interpreted the social life of people and language in the neighborhood, it became clear to me that I was uncovering not only language behavior and attitudes, and not only related issues of personal and group identification, but also the culture of this Jewish community. My understanding of culture in this book is close to that of many contemporary anthropologists, who see culture as the social knowledge that people constantly negotiate, create, and reform (e.g., Geertz 1973; Ochs 1988; Fabian 1990). By bringing to a focus on language the various behaviors and identities within the community, I support the view that communication and language behavior constitute and generate culture (Cronen, Chen, and Pearce 1988).

My inferences reflect the priorities that South Philadelphia Jews expressed. Communication in Yiddish was a focus for a cluster of factors that contributed to the Jewish identity of community members. The task was to investigate the constituent influences on language behavior within a framework that took into consideration the significant emotional consequences of such behavior for the residents as they themselves interpreted them.

This research concentrated primarily on people. The importance of the use of one abstract form of language or another can only be argued based on an understanding of who these Jews of South Philadelphia were. There are relatively few secondary sources or autobiographical materials that stress the specific individual experience of Jews in this neighborhood. Most of the data emphasize the life of institutions and public figures. Therefore, I relied increasingly on the informants' reports for their recollections of the history of the neighborhood. What emerged was a picture of a compact area of residence that contained myriad Jewish religious, educational, business, and social service enterprises. Although subject to population shifts within the area and within the greater Philadelphia region, South Philadelphia continued as the most traditional Jewish community in the city. From its inception, the residents had contact with neighboring ethnic groups. The opportunity for such contact increased as the relative size of the Jewish community diminished, but the social interaction and affiliation of the aging residents remained preponderantly Jewish. This tenacious affinity for other Jews facilitated the development of newer Jewish institutions, such as American veterans' groups and innovative Conservative synagogues. Moreover, community members actively maintained old friendships with other Jewish residents and formed new ones at the Center and other Jewish institutions.

The residents recalled the time of their youth when the neighborhood showed a much stronger Jewish presence and, in contrast, felt deprived by their current marginality. The general historical trend of leaving them behind was reinforced by members of the larger Philadelphia Jewish community, often relatives and friends who had left the neighborhood, who then disparaged the South Philadelphia Jews and abetted the formation of a lower-class image. Although other white ethnic groups of South Philadelphia shared such an image, the Jews were more vulnerable to such deprecatory judgments because of their dwindling numbers. But Jewish residents simultaneously accepted their inferior status and asserted a strong neighborhood identity. These conflicting positions are often difficult for outsiders to understand.

There were economically disadvantaged Jews in South Philadelphia, but, according to local social service workers, they probably constituted a smaller proportion than the poor within other ethnic groups. The individuals included in this study were mostly lower middle class. They had run small businesses, worked in the hand trades, or been employed as factory and office workers; a smaller number were in the professions. Those experiencing financial difficulties reflected the general predicament of the aged living on fixed incomes. The residents who had remained in the area had not generally done so because of financial limitations, but to be near parents, to remain in a house in which they had felt comfortable for many years, and to stay in a neighborhood that was familiar and supportive, a place where people knew their names and showed concern for their wellbeing. A large proportion of community members were the siblings who cared for their parents in their last years.

Yiddish, the dominant language for the immigrants, remained such a force in the neighborhood because of the local age structure, during a period when the language was being used less in other Jewish communities. But occasions for speaking Yiddish had gradually dwindled, and most of the Jewish elderly expressed remorse that this avenue of social communication was not open to them.

A critique of current research on human aging has called for the study of ways to expand functions for the aged (Rowe and Kahn 1987). "Successful aging" has been shown to be especially enhanced by two psychosocial factors: autonomy and social support that promotes autonomy. My project on ethnic language in an elderly population has shown the positive value of promoting ethnic language use for first- and second-generation Americans. Pride in a heritage that this population viewed as its own and the strengthening of a current ethnic identity by using the language of childhood tended to counter the negative effects of their relative isolation. The success of the Gleyzele tey group and the members' interaction with me, as reported by the residents, points to the value of developing intergenerational programs focused on ethnic language (Peltz 1990c).

Yiddish and Yiddishkeit

I had become the main interlocutor in Yiddish for some of the residents. For example, after Yankl D.'s mother died, he explained that now that his mother was gone he needed to talk to me in Yiddish. Was this desire solely an exercise in nostalgia? Certainly the residents could share both the language and the experience of looking backward with numerous South Philadelphia Jews who understood and spoke Yiddish. When I asked Reyzl whether the return to yiddishkeit at the Center was only nostalgia, she replied that it was, but she continued by saying: "Di host zey dermant vus zeym gehat, in zey hobm dus nisht yetst. Dus iz zeyer harts." (You reminded them of that which they had, and they don't have now. That is their heart.) The Yiddish discussion group stimulated essential emotions within the participants.

There is much evidence that South Philadelphia Jews associated speaking Yiddish with the quintessence of being Jewish, yiddishkeit. The local Jews used the term yiddishkeit to connote not only the fundamental state of being Jewish, but also the conglomeration of traditional Jewish ways that they once knew. To the residents, my use of Yiddish marked me as a "real Jew," as Yisrul referred to me. Many people assumed that because I spoke Yiddish I must be religiously observant. Twice, individuals I met in the neighborhood called me "rabbi."

This identification of speaking Yiddish with traditional Jewish observance was not, however, restricted to the way people viewed me. On many occasions, Yiddish was associated with the customs the residents remembered from their parents' home. Repeatedly, when we discussed speaking Yiddish, the conversation shifted to talking about yiddishkeit. For example, in one breath Reyzl mentioned both: "Bot dos idishkayt o—redn idish, nor geredt ven a mentsh (h)ot geredt idish tsu mir" (But yiddishkeit o—speaking Yiddish, only spoke when someone spoke Yiddish to me). When I asked Basye A. if Yiddish speaking had decreased in South Philadelphia over the years, she responded, "The yiddishkeit went with the older people." When I asked Roze with whom she spoke Yiddish after her grandmother's death, she replied, "Vi ikh hob gekent ikh hob never gevalt dus fargesn, di yidishkayt" (Any way I could I never wanted to forget it, yiddishkeit). For them, Yiddish and yiddishkeit were intimately entwined.

Similarly, Dveyre described being the only one of her American-born siblings who preserved Yiddish and "vos firt dem yidishn din in hoyz and in di shul" (who observes Jewish law at home and in the synagogue). Surele said she learned Yiddish from her parents and told me that her brother built a synagogue in the town he moved to in Pennsylvania. Tsipe-Khashe too linked Yiddish with traditional observance. Although she did not marry, she imagined that had she married she would have had a kosher home and that her children would have learned to speak Yiddish. Rivke B. valued speaking Yiddish because it guaranteed that the speakers would retain their Jewishness, their yiddishkeit:

Ikh ho(b) tsvey plimenitses red ikh nor idish mit zey. Farvus? Ikh vil a(z) (zey)zoln unholtn dus yidishkayt az zoln epes visn, a nit e—der tote zeyerer iz shoyn long nitu.

I have two nieces and I speak only Yiddish with them. Why? I want them to maintain their Jewishness that they should know something, if not uh—their father has been gone a long time already.

Ester-Sosye mentioned Jewish education, Yiddish literacy, and the dietary laws in one thought. Directly after talking about her lack of a Jewish education, and thus never learning to read and write Yiddish, she declared with pride that she still kept kosher. Speaking Yiddish, along with keeping kosher, was part of a constellation of memories and practices that constituted living like a Jew for most South Philadelphia Jews. Even though they did not always observe them, these practices symbolized true yiddishkeit for them. Although children of Jewish immigrants have been known to denigrate Yiddish and to laugh when a Yiddish word is spoken, I do not recall hearing one disparaging remark about Yiddish during my work in South Philadelphia. In this community of aged Jewish immigrants and children of immigrants, Yiddish language was an integral part of individual and ethnic group identity.

For some of the immigrants, Yiddish remained the only meaningful way in which to express themselves. American-born residents and those who immigrated as children wanted to hear and speak Yiddish because it made them feel comfortable and at home. The Yiddish conversation group at the Center became the most popular program there in recent years. Even people who spoke English most of the time looked forward to talking about current politics in Yiddish. And people who could barely speak Yiddish but understood perfectly struggled gleefully to express an idea in Yiddish. Speaking Yiddish signified belonging and in-group status for these elderly Jews, who frequently felt isolated.

The second-generation Jewish Americans' warm association with their ethnic language demonstrated a common situation, in which expressions of ethnicity characteristic of childhood experiences provide resources to draw upon in old age (Myerhoff 1980). Accordingly, the positive attitude toward Yiddish in South Philadelphia did not necessarily reflect the same emotional attachment to first language that the residents felt as children, but rather a renewed interest in an aspect of their youth. Their attitudes over the intervening years are another matter.

In his treatment of language and identity, Edwards has noted that ethnic language may remain longer in limited and private domains than in public communicative use (1985: 97). This generalization applied as well to the use of Yiddish in South Philadelphia. The institutions themselves did not cling to Yiddish as the major language of discourse, and individuals did not insist on speaking Yiddish to all Jews they met. Residents who continued to speak Yiddish spoke to their family and close friends. Yet despite these changes in this one element of identity, language, residents continued to associate Yiddish strongly with their identity as Jews.

That language persists as a symbol of personal and ethnic identity beyond the period in life when an individual's first language is spoken every day is testament to the theory of Le Page and Tabouret-Keller that language itself is "the focal centre of our acts of identity" (1985: 248). In addition to demonstrating the first- and second-generation speakers' retention of Yiddish communication skills, this study of Yiddish in South Philadelphia also describes the durable association of Yiddish and yiddishkeit that accompanied personal and communal changes in language use.

CHAPTER ELEVEN

Aging and the Life Course
The Memory of Language

Children of Immigrants and Yiddish

Despite the danger of depicting the second generation as a uniform generation or cohort, several common themes relating to language use and attitude are indicated for many children of Jewish immigrants alive today. The variation in patterns of Yiddish language behavior seems to relate to factors such as the age of immigrant parents at the time of immigration, the presence of immigrant grandparents, and the position in the birth order of siblings, as well as the degree of interaction with parents during the life cycle. To be sure, these are precisely the issues that need further clarification in the future. Nevertheless, we can make some general observations at this point.

Children born of immigrant parents reported that the most intensive time of exposure to Yiddish was during the years before they started school. Their Yiddish was restricted to the domain of house and family, used with other immigrants, relatives, friends of parents, and neighbors. If they spoke Yiddish with their siblings, it was at home, not on the street. This crucial period of initial language contact was followed by comparatively little use in later years. When active Yiddish speech did continue, it was typically with a parent: sometimes both spoke in Yiddish; sometimes the parent spoke in Yiddish and the child responded in English. And in these later years sometimes both switched to English. When the child initiated involvement in a

Yiddish-related activity, it was often during a period when parents were no longer alive to serve as interlocutors.

A variety of sources confirm these patterns, including autobiographies of Jewish communal leaders that both illustrate these trends and elaborate on the embeddedness of language in ethnic culture and religion. For example, we read of the cocoon-like Yiddish environment that enveloped a young child in Brooklyn: "I knew no English, mine was a Yiddish speaking house. When I got into public school, for the first time, I began to understand that the language of this country was not Yiddish but was English. And I had a few difficult years in accommodating myself to what was happening in public school. But obviously I made it" (Sol B. Kolack, in Cohen and Wexler, eds., vol. 6, B 2–3). Similarly, growing up in Coatesville, Pennsylvania, Benjamin Epstein was comfortable at home in Yiddish: "Yiddish was the second tongue and frequently the tongue that many of us used in our homes. My father and mother could not converse in Yiddish to keep a secret from me because I understood Yiddish which they had taught me. On the contrary, when they wanted to talk privately, they would talk Russian, and I was always trying to get into the act by trying to learn some Russian from them" (ibid., vol. 1, A 9–10).

Even if immigrant parents normally conversed in English, the Yiddish culture of the home could greatly influence the life of a youngster, as we can see from the memoirs of Conservative Rabbi Simcha Kling, who grew up in Newport, Kentucky:

Although my parents spoke English to each other as well as to my brother and myself, Yiddish was often used at family gatherings and I was able to follow conversation. As a young teen-ager, I learned to read Yiddish and occasionally went over *Der Morning Journal* which my father received daily. And much later, after I had become proficient in Hebrew I improved my Yiddish and was able to turn to Yiddish articles for research. (American Jewish Archives, Cincinnati, Ohio, Biographies File, p. 1)

One description of the Sabbath as a special day in the life of a rabbinical household points to the integration of Yiddish in traditional Jewish family life. The father tested his son's ability to translate portions of the Bible into Yiddish. The mother read the children stories from the week's Yiddish newspapers, as well as Yiddish classics, although "later she read them to us in English." At the end of the day the farewell to the Sabbath was recited in Yiddish and Hebrew (American Jewish Archives, Manuscript Collection, Box 548, Rabbi Herman Elliot Snyder, "Memories").

Although the autobiographical fragments above cite persons in leadership roles within the Jewish community, similar reminiscences are often shared by children of immigrants with far less visibility in their neighborhoods and in public Jewish life. South Philadelphia residents, too, recalled an intense Yiddish-speaking environment at home as children, and in the few instances in which immigrant parents did not use Yiddish at home, the surrounding Jewish life of the neighborhood facilitated language learning for the American-born children.

During the years after I left South Philadelphia, I did fieldwork in smaller cities in Massachusetts. The picture I obtained of the relationship between Yiddish and Jewish identity was different in some ways, but surprisingly similar in others. In contrast to the larger cities, which had compact immigrant neighborhoods, in smaller cities the support of neighbors, relatives, and fellow townspeople from the old country as agents of language acquisition was far less evident. Residents recalled with humor an immigrant mother's futile use of a Yiddish word to a local Northampton, Massachusetts, policeman. Those who grew up in larger urban environments in New England, such as Worcester or Springfield, spoke more fluently than those raised in smaller towns, such as Northampton. But all of the children of immigrants understood Yiddish to varying extents.

Within the family, there was usually one person most readily identified as a Yiddish speaker, and the child's connection to the language was colored by this familial relationship. In Worcester, Massachusetts, for example, both Rokhl-Leye and Minke recalled speaking Yiddish exclusively with their mothers and English with their fathers. Freyde-Nekhe was very close to her grandfather and spoke only Yiddish with him. The first time she realized that he could speak English was when he was in the hospital close to death and spoke English to a nurse. She described this discovery and the ensuing exchange with her grandfather:

> *F.-N.*: Zeyde, di kenst take redn english? (Grandpa, you can actually talk English?)
>
> *Grandfather*: Ikh hob gevist a(z) di vest lernen english ober (i)khob gevolt az di zolst visn yidish. (I knew that you would learn English but I wanted you to know Yiddish.)
>
> *F.-N.*: [summing up] In derfar de gantsn leybm ikh hob nor geredt yidish tsu eym un er tsu undz. Aen ikh dank em ale tug derfar ikh hob es zeyer lib. Un ikh denk, a sakh mentshn in mayne yurn ken nit redn yidish un ken nisht farshteyen, un ikh dank em ale tug az er hot mir gelernt un ikh ken farshteyen. (And therefore my whole life I only spoke Yiddish to him and he to us. And I thank him every day because I love it. And I think, many people my age cannot speak Yiddish and cannot understand, and I thank him every day because he taught me and I can understand.)

However, American-born children of immigrants also felt a certain amount of ambivalence and shame about speaking Yiddish. The immigrant language, after all, was a badge of peculiarity, and a child might choose to reject this distinctiveness, as this memoir of childhood in Altoona, Pennsylvania, relates: "At the end of every afternoon Mama rested briefly, cleaned up, put on a fresh apron and sat on the front porch on the swing, reading the *Yiddish Daily Forward* in full view of the neighborhood. What an agonizing experience that was for us kids, to have our mother flaunt her differentness! I used to cringe at the sight of the Jewish paper that proclaimed to the world that we were not exactly like our neighbors, that we were not quite Americans" (Karp 1983: 30).

In an autobiographical essay, the literary critic Irving Howe, a child of immigrants raised in the East Bronx, New York City, recalled his first day in kindergarten. The teacher held up a fork and Irving identified it by its Yiddish name, "gupl." Shamed by the laughter of the whole class, five-year-old Irving informed his parents that afternoon that he would never again speak Yiddish to them (1946: 364). This silence of the second generation belied a knowledge of the language and culture at the same time that it halted transmission to the next generation. Howe also recalled the humiliation caused by his father's Yiddish accent: "He would shout my name from afar, giving it a Yiddish twist: 'Oivee!' I would always feel a sense of shame at hearing my name so mutilated in the presence of amused onlookers" (1946: 364).

Being reminded that as Jewish children they were indeed different was often painful, as we see in another autobiographical account. Although he possessed an English name, Lionel, this child was called Leybele by his parents, the loving diminutive of his Yiddish name: "But all others—Jews and non-Jews alike—called me, until I went to public school, simply 'Laby.' Imagine being called 'Laby' in a town like Waco, Texas. I recall being unmercifully teased with taunts like 'Laby, the cry baby,' and much worse" (Lionel Koppman, "What I Remember," American Jewish Archives, Biographies File, p. 1).

The ambivalence is clear. The culture of the home was nurturing and reassuring at the same time that it broadcast to the child and the outer world that a barrier must be overcome in order to fully participate in that world.

Henry Roth's novel *Call It Sleep* (1991 [1934]) has been acclaimed as a classic portrayal of urban immigrant life in the United States during the early twentieth century. In the novel, an immigrant child, David, tells the story of his life in the United States from age two through age eight. In this linguistic marvel Roth builds a complex but consistent code whereby the major language of the immigrant home is Yiddish, written by Roth in standard English. The children on the street and among themselves speak in a New York dialect of English, sometimes with a few borrowed Yiddish words, transcribed in the text to reflect pronunciation. Adult immigrants,

Jews and non-Jews, speak to people outside their group in an accented English that is influenced by their mother tongue. Added to these are Hebrew and Aramaic of the religious school, and Polish, which David's mother uses to keep secrets from him.

At no point does this orderly language system break down in David's mind; he controls all parts and knows their place. Language is present in the foreground as intense, mind-boggling events and emotions confuse and overwhelm David, as we follow his education in matters of sex, love, family relations, physical abuse and violence. Yet in this passionately psychological novel, language is not a threat or puzzle for David, even though the different components seem to push against each other. As the processes of becoming American ensue, language is hearth and home for the immigrant child.

This does not mean that the rest of David's world is also able to use his delicately balanced language system. Right off, when the immigrant couple (David's parents) is reunited upon the mother and child's arrival in America, marital conflict and cultural disintegration are clearly presaged in the symbol of a broken Yiddish, one of the few times that Roth does not use standard English (1991: 16).[1] Not only is there disorder in David's family and its culture system, but the outside non-Jewish world does not accept his language system. In a frightening scene in which David gets lost, this English-Yiddish bilingual cannot make the name of his street understood (1991: 97–100). He seems destined to be a prisoner of the Jewish street, able to communicate only with those who speak Yiddish and Jewish English. For little immigrant David, his inability to communicate is terrifying. Henry Roth, who himself arrived in America at the age of two, likely vividly remembered being similarly fettered by the language of his youth.

No one has better articulated how the supportive and caressing nature of the language of the hearth can, at the same time, impede growth and development in the larger society than the writer Richard Rodriguez (1983). In his book *Hunger of Memory*, Rodriguez poignantly and powerfully analyzes his own life in terms of the bittersweet decision to divorce the language and culture of the home from his public voice. Writing at age 39, Rodriguez conjures up the boy in himself to relive the shamefulness of his first language and the hope that his second language sets forth for him. He argues for a distinction between private and public culture. The memory of his ethnic and religious roots remains strongly embedded in his personal identity, but separated from his maturation as a thinker and writer in contemporary American English-language culture. Rodriguez's story of his childhood as a Mexican American is similar to the stories I heard from elderly Jewish Americans: "It is not possible for a child—any child—ever to use his family's language in school. Not to understand this is to misunderstand the public uses of schooling and to trivialize the nature of intimate life—a family's language. Memory teaches me what I know of these matters; the boy reminds the adult I was a bilingual child" (Rodriguez 1983: 12).

The turning point for young Richard and his family in their quest to maintain an intimate world at home and to conquer the larger culture outside came when his parents decided to speak only English at home. Rodriguez reports that English unsettled the family and upset any hope of communication between children and parents. As a child, the Spanish sounds had said to Rodriguez, "You belong with us. In the family." Spanish had "become the language of joyful return" (Rodriguez 1983: 16).

The Middle Years

The children of immigrants I interviewed in South Philadelphia during the last stage of their lives shared with me memories and evaluations of their middle years; our conversations concentrated mainly on their careers, on marriage and children, on relations with their parents. They said little about their involvement with Yiddish language and culture during this time. In South Philadelphia, residents remained physically close to the immigrant generation, but as members of that generation died, less and less Yiddish was spoken.

Their memories of their involvement with yiddishkeit during their middle years revealed a variety of choices. Some became less observant, while others became more active in religious activities. Basye A. reintroduced Jewish custom into her household when she began living with her mother-in-law. Her children and others, members of the third generation, had less opportunity to learn Yiddish than the previous generation. The third generation, to be sure, had much less exposure to Yiddish at home and in the streets of South Philadelphia. Yiddish, after all, was mainly the language of the neighborhood's immigrants, few of whom were still alive during my fieldwork. In the smaller cities in Massachusetts, most of the second generation never spoke Yiddish, and in adulthood only understand (rather than speak) the language they heard as children. In their middle years, there was little contact with the language, other than the limited Yiddish their parents still used while they were alive. It was never the language of the shopping street, as in South Philadelphia. Thus, the third generation learns very little Yiddish in the smaller Jewish communities. The children of immigrants in these communities, however, throughout their life, including the middle years, maintain close friendship ties with their Jewish contemporaries, with whom they share a common past.

In South Philadelphia, Izzy, more than the other second-generation residents, maintained a high level of Jewish religious and organizational commitment and leadership throughout his middle years. Although there was limited use of Yiddish at home when he was growing up, Izzy managed to learn the language, since it was all around the neighborhood. He welcomed opportunities to speak Yiddish:

I had—in fact I had a strange experience. A man calls us on the phone speaking Yiddish. My wife answers the phone. She said, "vel shteln mayn man tsu redn" (I'll put my husband on the phone to talk). I got on the phone and uh- we- un- his father told him, after about a half hour conversation, if your name was Emanuel, and his name was Emanuel, he came from uh—he hardly could speak, uh, Y—Yiddish, he y—only could speak Yiddish and uh Hebrew. If your name was Em—second name was Emanuel, you had to be related. So he was going down the whole phone book, we got pages of—years ago there was only two of us in the phone book by the name Emanuel. And I spoke to him for about a half hour, I really enjoyed speaking Yiddish. I enjoy speaking it anyhow every opportunity. And at the end of the conversation was, "Kum tsi un mir'n hobm a glezl tey un a shtikl keyk un mir veln redn" (Come over and we'll have a glass of tea and a piece of cake, and we'll talk).

The glass of tea symbolized a way of talking and getting to know one another better that belonged to the past. In my work, I offered elderly children of immigrants an opportunity to share that glass of tea, to encourage communication about and among themselves, in Yiddish.

The Later Years

In my research in various cities I located very few instances of spontaneous Yiddish conversation in public and residential settings. At the senior center, however, the elderly Gleyzele tey group members responded enthusiastically to the opportunity to speak Yiddish in a relatively unstructured setting.

Although the main thrust of the Gleyzele tey activity was Yiddish conversation, its nature and evolution were shaped by the special history of the neighborhood, the senior center, and the residents. Similar experiments have taken hold in the United States since the 1970's. Elderly Jews, preponderantly children of immigrants, have formed hundreds of Yiddish cultural clubs in a variety of institutional settings. Some are connected to synagogues, Jewish community centers, and residential centers for the elderly. Others take the form of adult education courses or informal meetings of friends. Since most Jewish communal institutions are not accustomed to offering any Yiddish-language activities, this new interest in Yiddish on the part of children of immigrants is perhaps the major shift in Jewish cultural programming in the United States in recent years. Yet the resources of most Jewish communal institutions have not been expended to meet the cultural needs of these new Jewish elderly (Peltz 1990c). This largely spontaneous grass-roots endeavor usually survives with volunteer facilitators rather than professional staff. The Yiddish club activities include telling stories and jokes, singing songs, guest lectures, films, and reading and speaking Yiddish.

At a seminar devoted to utilizing Yiddish conversation as a resource for club meetings, leaders of such organizations agreed on a set of characteristics that various groups hold in common. For example, the leaders often partake in the world of high Yiddish culture, support the theater and the press, and have difficulty identifying with the Yiddish cultural interests of the elderly children of immigrants in their groups. The leaders usually defend high standards in language, norms for a language of culture that ordinary group members find quite foreign. Since the members have difficulty understanding the literary language, the leaders complain that they cannot read aloud from Yiddish belles lettres to the group. In addition, they avoid conversational activities because they do not have patience to wait for less fluent members to come up with the proper words.[2]

The 1986 inception and subsequent evolution of the Yiddish cultural group I attend in Northampton, Massachusetts, epitomizes the recent shift of elderly children of Jewish immigrants to their ethnic mother tongue, Yiddish.[3]

From the beginning, the focus on Yiddish attracted a loyal following, although only a few members were fluent Yiddish speakers. While the South Philadelphia Gleyzele tey was devoted exclusively to Yiddish conversation, the Northampton does other things as well. My role in the Philadelphia group was largely facilitator, but I did not very often speak out on issues. In Northampton, although I do not attend every meeting, usually I am much more active at the meeting, supplying Yiddish words, reading stories, or teaching songs I have selected. The Northampton group has developed into a Yiddish cultural club that supports many ventures.

The most ambitious undertaking of the group was the organization of a Yiddish-English musical comedy. The play, which took almost a year to write and produce, was called *Vos iz geven un vos iz yetst* (What was and what is now) and was a history of the local Jewish community. Although the group planned the entire production, members of all ages were invited to act in the play. This project established the group as a vehicle of intergenerational ethnic education. But Yiddish speaking and Yiddish language remain the sine qua non of the group.

Very few Jewish communal endeavors relating to Yiddish existed in

Northampton before 1986. Although most of the local Jewish elderly can understand spoken Yiddish, they hardly ever used the language themselves, even as young children. Yet, in this small town with so few connections to the Jewish past, Yiddish serves as a vital link to the Jewish culture of their youth. With tenacity and originality, these aging offspring of immigrants refashion their recently reacquired language and culture.

The strong attachment to Yiddish language as a component of yiddishkeit is a sign of identification with an oral culture of the immigrant household. The fundamental transmitters of Jewish tradition are not the synagogue, the local federation of Jewish agencies, or Zionism and the state of Israel, but family members, who pass on the immigrant cultures of the kitchen, of holidays, and of Yiddish.

Changes in Language and Ethnic Identity

My fieldwork findings in Philadelphia and later in smaller New England cities are in agreement with the view that ethnic identity is malleable, changeable over time and according to situation. The factors that affect variation in the individual and the group are numerous and interrelated. Children of immigrants develop multiple identities that interact and overlap in different contexts. In the earlier literature, when theories of ethnicity were emerging but case studies were still limited, Barth asserted that ethnic identity is "imperative, in that it cannot be disregarded and temporarily set aside by other definitions of the situation. The constraints on a person's behaviour which spring from his ethnic identity thus tend to be absolute" (1969: 17). However, analysis of empirical data, such as that of Sinhalese-Buddhist identity in Ceylon (Sri Lanka), soon uncovered a far more complex and flexible conception: "When an individual's commitments to his other identities have weakened, his commitment to his ethnic identity will be enhanced. . . . With the dissolution of these other identities the ethnic identity, often revitalized and refashioned to suit the changed social conditions, helps to give a sense of meaning and coherence to the individual's existence" (Obeyesekere 1975: 256).

The idea of ethnic identity as a pliable social construction was embraced by Kellogg (1990: 28) in a treatise that emphasizes the centrality of ethnic identity in contemporary American family life. Kellogg, furthermore, in trying to account for the persistence of ethnicity, localizes it in the private and family realms, as I have in my discussion of the contemporary yiddishkeit of elderly children of Jewish immigrants: "Ethnic identity symbolizes a history that families mediate for individuals, particularly children. It allows children to form a sense of belonging and attachment to both the family and the larger ethnic group" (Kellogg 1990: 37). Our evidence supports the theory that ethnic identity is flexible, changing with time and situation. Children of immigrants exhibit multiple identities that influence one another. There is choice and creativity in the ongoing process of ethnic identification (see Waters 1990; Sollors 1989). As Holzberg reminds us: "Ethnicity is a resource—an identity that older people can turn on or off as needed. When ethnicity is called into play, it sustains a familiar cultural setting that provides opportunities for continuity with the past and instrumental contributions to the present" (1982: 254).

One aspect of the development and meaning of ethnic identity that has received relatively little notice is that of change over the life cycle. Many of the insights gained from gerontology come from the underlying supposition that flux and growth are constant in life. The anthropologist Myerhoff and her colleagues have stressed the cyclical nature of ethnic involvement over the life cycle: high levels of engagement in the early years followed by an eclipse in the middle years and a subsequent intensification during the later years (Simic 1985: 68; Weibel-Orlando 1988: 329). In general, however, longitudinal studies of aging have not carefully examined organizational affiliation, behavioral acts, or psychological orientation relating to identification with the ethnic group. In addition, perhaps because ethnic culture is usually transmitted early during primary socialization, although theorists accept that all social identities change over the life cycle and history, ethnic identities are viewed as relatively stable (Liebkind 1989a: 40). Such assumptions should also be tested.

Even though language has been identified as the "focal centre of our acts of identity" (Le Page and Tabouret-Keller 1985: 370), linguists pay little attention to the changing attitude toward and use of ethnic language during the life cycle. To a great extent, this reflects the paucity of interest in broadly treating language and aging (Eckert 1984: 230–31). When language behavior of the nondiseased elderly is scrutinized, it is seen purely as a series of deficits, either speech impairments, poor intelligibility, or memory loss (Emery 1985; Light and Albertson 1988; Zelinski 1988). This attitude parallels the once standard approach to aging and the aged that viewed older people as cultureless and incapable of interacting within the social system and dominant cultural tradition (Simic 1978). The field desperately lacks a serious inquiry into the transformations in ethnic language during the life changes of members of ethnic groups. Does the significance of ethnic language and culture indeed intensify as other identities subside, and vice versa?

Seliger (1989) has worked on the attrition of first language over the life cycle, and Clyne (1984) was one of the few to show interest in whether first language reversion in elderly bilinguals is related to monolingualism or

bilingualism during childhood. At the present time, we have only fragmentary evidence of correlations between increased ethnic cultural awareness and greater interest in and use of ethnic language on the part of the
elderly. This has been depicted for Jewish Americans in a study that posited
a variety of cultural and religious involvements as related to greater satisfaction and self-esteem (Saul 1983). In addition, we learn of the utility and
popularity of programs in Yiddish instruction for staff at a Jewish long-
term care facility (Berman, Weiner, and Fishman 1986). However, at least
in these specific cases, second-generation immigrants are not differenti-
ated. This is not the case for Doi's (1991) analysis of the ritual of the sixti-
eth birthday celebration among children of Japanese immigrants. And
Rempusheski's (1988) work on second-generation Polish-Americans is an
exception, showing that this group does seek out an environment in which
to express its ethnic identity, and that its members tend to appreciate and
use Polish more as they get older. Although researchers have largely ignored the confluence of language, culture, and aging with an expressed
interest in the descendants of immigrants, the field of family therapy, which
values the interlocking relations of different generations as keys to understanding family dynamics, has highlighted the ethnic language behavior of
such diverse groups as Cuban, Greek, Irish, and Vietnamese Americans
(McGoldrick, Pearce, and Giordano, eds., 1982).

Among ethnic minorities in this country, we find a wealth of data on
the increased identification of elderly Native Americans with their ethnic
culture and language in present-day America (Saunders and Davis 1974;
Svensson 1974; Amoss 1981). The most striking examples relate to the migration of urban Native Americans back to the reservation after their re-
tirement, but also pertain for those who remain in Los Angeles (Weibel-
Orlando 1988; 1990; 1991). A role they play that Jewish Americans rarely
assume nowadays is that of cultural conservator and instructor of the
grandchildren. The youngest speakers of Arizona Tewa spend much time
with their grandparents, who serve as informal Tewa teachers (Kroskrity
1993: 103).

Not all studies, of course, indicate that older ethnic Americans univer-
sally embrace the language and culture of their youth. For example, di
Leonardo (1984) found that second-generation Italian Americans in northern California demonstrated fluency in the native Italian dialect only when
talking with aged relatives. Overall, attenuation and not enhancement of
cultural involvement was predominant.

My own research gives little attention to those who do not already identify with cultural organizations and ethnic language. Consequently, I may
have neglected elderly American Jews who have no interest in Yiddish. Another warning that the process of cultural return may not be universal

comes from Luborsky and Rubinstein (1990: 238), who caution that revitalization may also activate anxieties associated with loss of family members and cultural heritage. We may also question whether the phenomenon of return is limited to this time in American history and may not be a characteristic of aging children of immigrants in the future.

The patterns that relate to Yiddish in the United States are not restricted to second-generation Jewish Americans, but apply to other groups as well. Krause's (1979) comparison of Italian American, Jewish American, and Slavic American grandmothers, mothers, and daughters showed some use of the European language by 81 percent, 58 percent, and 12 percent, respectively, of the three generations. But when asked if learning the ethnic language should be a priority, 75 percent of the mothers, the group with the bilingual childhood experience, answered positively; only 52 percent of the grandmothers and 53 percent of the daughters did so. Although isolated examples of long-term retention of ethnic language use persist (Thomas 1979), a survey by J. Fishman (1985) reports that in the United States only those communities that ensure stable residential and cultural segregation maintain their ethnic mother tongues beyond the second generation. In fact, S. Fishman (1982) has exhorted the secular Yiddish speech community to secure Yiddish in its primary institutions and to effect physical and ideological separation, in order to guarantee continuity of language and culture.

Studies of the language of school-aged children of Italian immigrants to Australia have revealed that the pattern of language use that the Jewish Americans describe for their youth also pertains to this ethnic group, on another continent, a half-century later. Generally, Italian dialect is restricted to interactions with the ethnic elders, not with siblings, and increasingly a mixture of English and Italian is used as the language of the home. In addition, going to school marks the beginning of English use for as many as 35 percent of the pupils (Smolicz 1983). Punjabi youths in California today, like generations of other immigrant children before them, speak Punjabi with adults and English with peers, but they tend to maintain a separate Punjabi identity. They come in contact with the English-speaking majority but affirm their primary social identity within the ethnic group (Gibson 1988: 138–39; 170). The children may respond to their parents in English, as happens in other language groups; however, the lack of production of language does not imply the inability to perceive and comprehend (Troike 1970). Indeed, this asymmetry of production and perception obtains in households in which parents speak one language and children another.

The emphasis in linguistic research on production and the inventory of losses associated with language shift has often resulted in neglect of what

Dorian (1982b) has termed the "working margins" of the speech community. Nonfluent speakers, like some of the second-generation American Yiddish speakers I have studied, can be significant members of the Yiddish speech community, since they have mastered both receptive skills and sociolinguistic norms of appropriateness (Dorian 1982b: 30–31). Gal (1989) has emphasized that continued use of the ethnic mother tongue can be a strong statement of group solidarity and that the new social and linguistic forms that emerge parallel with language shift are worthy of further scrutiny. In the present study I have attempted to make this point regarding the group cohesiveness that is engendered by speaking Yiddish. I have presented the forms of Yiddish speech of the second generation as a topic that can help us better understand the history of Yiddish. Gal (1989) pleads with linguists to abandon the pastoral position that focuses on the old conservative "authentic" forms and to turn to the newer changing forms associated with cultural contact and shift.

Future work on the variably contracting and expanding use of Yiddish can also benefit from empirical and theoretical approaches to second-language acquisition. As Anderson discusses, just as second-language learners rarely come in contact with speakers who use the language, so too do second- and third-generation speakers rarely have the input necessary to remain competent speakers (1989: 385).

In short, the most striking findings in the present research are the fervor, enthusiasm, and deep passion that characterize the new engagement of elderly second-generation Jewish Americans with Yiddish, which was either their first language or the first language of their parents.

In a review of ethnicity and aging, Gelfand discusses the conflicting views of older individuals: they are described either as reverting to the class and ethnic characteristics of their youth or as maintaining values of their ethnic culture throughout life (1982: 43). Gelfand states that even individuals who do not belong to ethnic organizations and do not live in a homogeneous ethnic neighborhood may have internalized attitudes of the ethnic culture of their youth that accompany them into old age. My own research has shown that attitudes toward yiddishkeit remain strong even for Jews who reside in a predominantly non-Jewish neighborhood and without the influence of living immigrant parents.

These elderly Jewish Americans actively pursue their ethnicity in the present. Kaufman sees such pursuits as their way of adapting to their environment "by symbolically connecting past experience with current circumstances" (1981: 84). Indeed, for many the symbolic strength of their ethnic language has outweighed the effect of their involvement in speech, through production and/or reception. Theorists of ethnic identity have acknowledged that all cultural features, and especially language, can be used emblematically (De Vos and Romanucci-Ross 1975a: 369; De Vos 1975: 15). According to Eastman and Reese, in order to identify strongly with ethnic language one does not have to understand or speak it, but only feel associated with it, since "language is an aspect of our self-ascription" (1981: 110).

However, we should not deemphasize the intensity of feeling toward Yiddish that we have observed and the concentrated linguistic and cultural experience of their youth that these children of immigrants recalled so vividly. The prediction of Gans (1979) that the third and fourth generations would not have intense ethnic identity needs and would be content with empty diluted symbols does not apply to the second generation. They can benefit both from the symbolic strength of Yiddish and from the enjoyment of active involvement with Yiddish speech, albeit in some cases only as listeners. Cultural expression undergoes historical change, and we should not expect the Yiddish cultural elements of children of immigrants to replicate those of the immigrants. Simply to treat the process as dilution does not contribute to an understanding of the complexities of identity development and attitudinal change. As a social critic approaching vernacular culture, I have come to grasp that Yiddish, "like other traditions, may be invented on the basis of an imagined past, or restored as a basis of an entirely different landscape" (Zukin 1992: 242).

Language and Memory

People living in the present are inevitably affected by the past, even in the most future-oriented groups and societies. Whether consciously or not, human beings continually adjust to and reinterpret the lessons and treasures of the past. It is these processes of remembering and reintegrating of children of immigrants that I have strived to explain.

Memory and remembering are the result of an individual or group's invocation of the processes of recall and interpretation of the past—in other words, memory is a socially constructed phenomenon (see, for example, Halbwachs 1992 [1925]; Connerton 1989; Schuman and Scott 1989; Middleton and Edwards, eds., 1990). Erikson, who pioneered a model that views life as a cycle of discrete developmental stages that turns on itself and is linked to previous and future generations, should also be credited for the concept that past stages of the life cycle are always connected with and serve as the bases for the present stage (see Erikson 1968; 1975: 17–22; Erikson, Erikson, and Kivnik 1986: 13–53).

The term lifespan is currently preferred to life cycle, which is thought to stress inaccurately the existence of identifiably separate stages (Coupland,

Nussbaum, and Grossman 1993: xiv–xx; cf. Woodward 1991: 21). Giddens, in charting a theoretical construct for contemporary identification of self, has underscored the notion that discrete stages for identity development do not exist and that identities are always being renegotiated (Giddens 1990: 120–24; 1991: 14, 52–55, 74–80, 145–49, 215).

My research shows that in focusing on discourse at different life stages, on both the symbolic and the conversational level, matters of identity play a central role (see Coupland, Nussbaum, and Grossman 1993: xx, xxvi).

The gerontologist Butler (1963; 1970), who saw the life review as a normal and healthy part of aging, also criticized a static view of identity. According to Butler, because people change at all ages, they can never know who they are. The lifelong search for self-understanding, as opposed to the process of defining and consolidating one's past identifications, is thus a sign of health. The reconstruction of concepts of one's self represents a human need to alter the present in light of the past, or vice versa, and an "intellectual capacity" to change (Bruner 1990: 109, referring to Gergen). Shotter has called "the possession of a developmentally susceptible identity . . . living a life susceptible to a biographical account" an essence of being human (1989: 146). From this viewpoint, the process of life review would not redefine one's youth or resolve old conflicts; rather, it would integrate past experiences and emotions with current, ever-changing lives.

From her anthropological research on elderly Jewish immigrants, Myerhoff (1980) insisted that the processes of remembering during old age were vital for the integration and reintegration of self. In other words, the elderly person was "re-membering," constructing a life, composing a whole. I would argue that this is a vital imperative of the present, and a much more complicated phenomenon than merely looking back. From her work with the elderly, Myerhoff learned to appreciate their need to have others hear their stories and through them witness their lives (1988: 283). My use of Yiddish with elderly Jews helped them to do just that. As a member of the younger generation, both akin to and different from them, I helped them bridge the generations and regain connections to the language and culture of their youth.

The German writer Christa Wolf, remembering the Nazi Germany of her youth, reminds her readers that "what is past is not dead; it is not even past. We cut ourselves off from it; we pretend to be strangers" (1984: 1). Other authors, too, have insightfully underscored the power of childhood experience as a focus for a dialogue with the past, and as a resource for interpretation and integration. For the subjects of my current research, who often view the first years of life through the prism of the last years, language is at the center of strong identification, a living vehicle that engenders memory within its own structure and use. The writer Richard

Rodriguez characterizes the feelings of warmth and family that remain with the bilingual child during aging, during a time that the child often only possesses the memory of language: "Laughing intimate voices. Bounding up the front steps of the porch. A sudden embrace inside the door" (Rodriguez 1983: 71). For the middle-aged child of Mexican immigrants, as well as for the elderly children of Jewish immigrants, the immigrant language signals memory of emotion, of a young child's warm feelings of hearth and home, of parents and family who embrace, envelop, and nurture.

In May 1988, the Northampton Jewish seniors presented their original musical *Vos iz geven un vos iz yetst* (What was and what is now) in honor of the 25th anniversary of the new synagogue building. This newly formed group, which had not yet crystallized its own identity, decided to organize a performance about the history of Jews in Northampton, with the participation of all generations. They planned to retell and create anew their history through Yiddish, which they themselves had just donned, like a newly found old coat.

As a participant-observer, I was able to follow the development of the performance of this new-old ritual from behind the scenes. They worked a full year in preparing the mini-spectacle. At first, it was not clear that the performance necessarily had to concentrate on their own story—but they adamantly wanted to do something in Yiddish. Some of the members had seen the staged Yiddish productions of *My Fair Lady* and Gilbert and Sullivan; others were acquainted with the bilingual musical pageant on American Jewish life, *The Golden Land*. Possessing home-bred talent, they reveled in the idea of doing something original, lively, and joyous with music and dance.

A 62-year old member, on the verge of retiring as a teacher of English in the local high school, wrote the play together with two assistants. The author's grandmother in Philadelphia had spoken Yiddish to her, but her American-born parents had spoken no Yiddish. Her husband was a child of one of the first immigrant Jewish families in Northampton.

The group determined that in order for the younger people in the audience to understand the play, both English and Yiddish had to be side by side in the production. The planners also understood that the retelling must appeal to everyone in such a way that they viewed the story as belonging to them; accordingly, the actors included local youngsters who were twelve and fourteen, and adults in their thirties, forties, and fifties, as well as the senior group members.

A professional choreographer volunteered her services, as did a local band. Lights, decorations, and costumes were arranged. Serving as the backbone of the play were familiar scenes and personalities from Northampton Jewish life, accompanied by popular hits from Yiddish stage and film, such as "Mayn yidishe meydele" (My little Jewish girl), "Abi gezunt ken men gliklekh zayn" (As long as you're healthy you can be happy), and "Vos geven iz geven un nito" (What was, was and is no more). The show opened with a scene of immigrants disembarking from a ship and ended with a contemporary cocktail party at the synagogue. The actors played their roles with great verve and the audience was ecstatic.

From that time on, the Jewish community associated the group with the Yiddish language. Subsequently, they were invited to perform other Yiddish material for holidays, and to speak about Yiddish and memories of times gone by with children in the synagogue school. In other words, the group of elderly children of immigrants became a force for intergenerational ethnic education. If such a phenomenon can develop in Northampton, the seeds have surely been sown in other Jewish population centers.

Indeed, in Holyoke, Massachusetts, during the summer of 1993, a group of elderly members of Orthodox congregation Rodphey Sholem formed a group devoted to Yiddish culture. The group deliberated long on choosing a name and in the end selected, by an overwhelming majority, the name "Di gantse mishpokhe" (The whole family). For this group and others like it, Yiddish is a family matter. The attempt to establish links with like-minded contemporaries widens the family connection and confirms the existence and validity of their culture. They are attempting to recreate a feeling for family that harks back to the first years in their parents' houses. For the elderly children of immigrants, whether in Philadelphia or Holyoke, Yiddish evokes passionate emotions about family that are allied with powerful feelings relating to both personal and group identification.

I have brought evidence from a variety of sources to identify the language of the family as a formative influence in the socialization and acculturation of children of immigrants. Members of immigrant groups see themselves as different from the dominant culture and are viewed as such by other groups, dominant and minority. Language is a symbol of both self-ascription and imposed stereotype. It is a focus of identity just as speaking it is an act of identity (Le Page and Tabouret-Keller 1985: 140, 248).

The significance of the shared cohort experience should not be underestimated. The insight of Halbwachs is important: "Collective frameworks are . . . precisely the instruments used by the collective memory to reconstruct an image of the past which is in accord, in each epoch, with the predominant thoughts of the society" (1992 [1925]: 40). Along the same lines, Bruner (1990: 59) reminds us that memory reconstructions function dialogically, to convince not only ourselves but also our real or imagined reference group.

At the same time, the elderly fear that they may be the last generation of speakers, that "the 'collective memory' for . . . [the] language may be lost to future generations" (Padden 1990: 190). These native Yiddish-speaking enthusiasts used language to spread roots to the past, to strengthen their social connections, and to join a generationally extended cultural chain.

As Padden points out, "living languages are those in which the speakers agree to remember them" (1990: 190). These speakers have agreed, and their remembered language transforms their individual pasts into collective memories. The widespread phenomenon of a return to Yiddish that is expressed in the formation and flowering of hundreds of clubs across the nation locates the process of remembering and recovery in a group setting. As with much of the process of memory, this phenomenon is socially facilitated and constructed, seldom individualized and isolated. The identifiable group is actually a large one—the generation of children of immigrants.

The mediation of memory by way of language use, besides being a shared experience, also signifies a relationship to time that warrants further explication. I am reminded of a scene from the literary imagination, a memoir written by the Japanese novelist Yashusi Inoue. His elderly mother, suffering from Alzheimer's disease, disappears from home in search of her infant son. Two images merged for the author, the 63-year-old son looking for his 85-year-old mother, and the 23-year-old mother searching for the one-year-old infant: "The years 1907 and 1969 came together and the sixty years converged, then diffused in the light of the moon" (Inoue 1982: 106). Woodward rightly stresses the power of the emotion, a "magical . . . moment of both dread and wonder," when Inoue finds meaning in what it is to be a son to a mother and at the same time to reverse the roles (see Woodward 1986: 141–42). It is this simultaneous bewilderment and illumination that seems to possess the elderly children of immigrants, who retain the memory of their culture as they use the language of their past in the present.

In searching to understand the tie to the future that the elderly Jews yearned for in their last years, I once again gained insight from the discussions of literary depictions of aging by Woodward (1991: 136–45). Drawing on the psychoanalytic theory of the transitional object put forward by Winnicott, Woodward analyzed *Malone Dies* by Beckett (1956: 74). Of all the objects collected around him, Malone is left with only his exercise book—a tangible object, but also a receptacle of language. According to Winnicott, the transitional object helps reduce the anxiety of the infant in separating from the mother and entering the objective world. It is the materiality of the object that is stressed, its tactile nature, not only its symbolic value. Woodward postulates that at the end of life there is a another transitional object that practically eases us into the next stage, death, and at the same time reminds us of our childhood. For the elderly children of immigrants, Yiddish may be that object, facilitating and supporting the changes they undergo in their last years of life.

Just as Butler (1963), Kaminsky (1984; 1992), and Coleman (1991) have understood reminiscence and story-telling on the part of the elderly as life-affirming activities, so too is ethnic language use a stimulus for growth and renewal. Western society has avoided dealing with old age and death (Lowenthal 1985: 125–84; Woodward 1991: 4–8). Yet, if these components of the life course are indeed progenitors of creativity, we should recognize them as such.

Very few elderly children of immigrants embraced Yiddish as a means of daily communication. Rather, they used Yiddish in a ritualized manner periodically to express ethnic identity and culture in a group setting. This renewed use of the language of childhood in diverse locations, institutional settings, and Jewish communities throughout the country has become widespread and operates as an identity marker for the generation. Rituals link the past, present, and future. A most common ritual is the performance of everyday stories that we tell ourselves. The most elaborate and complex performance of group storytelling that I have observed was the performance of the original autobiographical play by and about the Jewish community of Northampton. Using Yiddish in a format that could be understood by the community's youngest members, who knew no Yiddish, the elderly children of immigrants created a story that portrayed continuous transmission, from the time of their parents' immigration almost a century earlier to their grandchildren's participation in the drama itself.

Anthropological theorists of the role of ritual have pointed to the absence of dichotomy between ritual that is sacred and symbolic and that which is practical and profane (Skorupski 1976: 173; Geertz 1973: 113). Kertzer stresses the socially standardized, repetitive nature of symbolic behavior, but reminds us that a given activity can have both ritual and nonritual aspects (1988: 9). The shared ritual of speaking Yiddish provides symbolic strength through social drama and public identity for a group of aging Jews whose alterity within American society might otherwise marginalize them further (Geertz 1983: 64). Geertz has noted that such cultural performances are "models of what they believe" as well as "models *for* the believing of it" (1973: 114)

To understand the changing meaning of life to individuals and to a generation, we should examine "how people develop rhetorical redescriptions of their own life" (Van Langenhove and Harre 1993: 96). The remembering of Yiddish helps to convince these elderly American Jews of the veracity of the stories they tell themselves. From their vantage point, it is as if they are saying: We are the children of our parents, even now that our parents are no longer alive; we possess a culture at a time of life and in a place in which the elderly and their culture are overlooked; and, if the language is still alive, that is a sign that we, too, are still alive. Their stories are not merely a way of remembering the past; they are an active confrontation with the present.

American Yiddish, American Jewish
From Immigrant to Ethnic Culture

When I ventured into South Philadelphia, first as a student doing sociolinguistic fieldwork, then as a researcher in search of a dissertation on Yiddish language in America, my eyes and ears were open to language. Having trained in the areas of linguistics, Yiddish language, literature and culture, Jewish history, and some anthropology, it was natural for me to focus on language, even though I did not know exactly what I was looking for or what I would find.

The South Philadelphians opened up for me a world of complex interpersonal relationships, organizational frameworks, and family and neighborhood histories that sent me hurtling into diverse venues of inquiry. Writing years later, I now can benefit from my earlier studies. My work as a molecular biologist made it easy to delve into diverse frameworks and discourses, for it was natural for me to regard the study of life as interdisciplinary. Yet the fierce emotions evoked in me and in the neighborhood residents by our joint enterprise caught me unprepared. I had not realized that a search for the meaning that South Philadelphians derived from their ethnic culture would touch on intimate images of identity both for them and for me. But together, through reciprocal trust and in mutual respect, we wrote this ethnography.

Moffatt (1992: 212), in his review of ethnographies of American settings, finds that despite the recent criticism and experimentation in new styles of writing, especially relating to the voice of the ethnographer and the inter-action of ethnographer and informant, most ethnographies are still conven-tionally written—that is, they reserve any discussion of the ethnographer's relationship with the subjects to the margins. Although I have explained my relationships with my informants to the best of my ability, the issue of authorship—who is the true author of the story of the Jews in South Philadelphia—is not fully resolved in this book. I realized early on that the residents were determining the agenda of the research work, but I still struggled to present an accurate picture of them.

It was easiest to use the Yiddish speakers' own voices, and I believe the appendix of narratives at the end of this book is in fact the first published collection of spoken American Yiddish. Of course, although the transcrip-tions are as accurate as I could make them from tape recordings, they still represent my selection, editing, and interpretation. My aim is to portray the priorities of the residents, at least as I perceived them. Therefore, in de-scribing the method for this study, the very least I must do is to reflect upon who I am now, and who I was when I did my fieldwork. "Participation in-duces change for both researcher and informant" (Cronen et al. 1988: 80).

If I was unaware before I embarked on this journey, I am certainly con-vinced now that this research activity is itself a part of social life. I related to the Jews of South Philadelphia as if they were my grandparents and I was their adult grandson. In some cases the difference in our ages was only twenty years; but much as a child tends to see grandparents as older than they really are, I saw my informants as accepting elders who embraced and enveloped me with love. I seemed to be searching for the grandparents I had lost, for the irretrievable neighborhood of my youth. By viewing the residents as grandparents, I avoided the conflicts I might encounter with parental figures. By setting up carriers of Yiddish culture who gained en-hanced authenticity in my eyes, I ensured in my mind a more secure place and future for Yiddish than would ever be possible.

From my taped conversations with the residents I can tell that I valued the Yiddish speech of the South Philadelphians more than English. I tended to introduce Yiddish in contexts where it was not typically found, but where it could be spoken. The children and younger residents of South Philadelphia became for me a signpost of a potential future for Yid-dish, yet I knew full well that this wish would never be fulfilled. Although I am writing this book at a time when I have two small children, to whom my wife and I speak Yiddish, I wonder who they will converse with as they mature.

For the children of immigrants I studied, that which was American Jewish for them is mainly American Yiddish. The strong dose of home cul-ture to which they were exposed during their youth was embodied in the

Yiddish of the immigrant parents. This culture belongs to them for life as a resource that can be mobilized at different periods.

The concept of ethnicity, at least as it has come to be understood in American society, usually refers to cultural legacies inherited from immigrants.[1] In the case of Jews in American society, historiography has often neglected an essential dimension of ethnicity that pertains to most Jews: the activities and emotions that inhabit the private sphere, the domain of primary institutions—namely, the family. Thus, scholarship about the experience of the mass of Jewish immigrants who arrived at the beginning of the twentieth century and the lives of their descendants often focuses on institutions, such as the daily press, or on individual leaders. The resulting picture, which omits the thoughts and emotions of the people themselves, is necessarily a limited one.

The typical story of Jewish immigrants covers their settlement in the neighborhoods of primary immigration, the eventual movement of their children to the suburbs of American cities, and the blossoming of Reform and Conservative congregations and community centers, which are depleted of traditional yiddishkeit and of Yiddish. But is this picture accurate? We now have evidence of a more complex portrait. The immigrant generation, for example, was itself distanced from Eastern Europe; and immigrant culture consists of more than remnants from the old country.

My research on elderly children of immigrants reveals them to be crucial interpreters of the culture of their parents' homes. And the evolution of their ethnic culture in the United States was strongly influenced by events throughout their lives. Although I began with a sociolinguistic orientation, the disciplines of anthropology, psychology, and gerontology, as well as family and neighborhood history, helped me see that the continual reinterpretation of memories of the first years of life constitutes a vital force in the development of an ethnic group.[2]

My interactions with elderly Jews, in Yiddish, may have deepened the emotional attachments of these Jews to the language of their childhood, but I also became aware of the extent to which they affected me. I helped extend their attachment to Yiddish and yiddishkeit, and they did the same for me. Yankl B., whom many of the South Philadelphians ignored and discounted since they viewed his behavior as socially inappropriate, on several occasions suggested that to them my mission was like a crusade: "Veymen vilste roteven?" (Whom do you want to save?); "Got hot indz geshikt Rakhmiel" (God sent us Rakhmiel). I wanted to be a well-liked participant-observer, a researcher studying Yiddish, where no one had previously trod, the streets of South Philadelphia. I had no way of knowing then that this work would also influence the future of my own growing family. Yankl B., and probably some of the other residents, understood better than I that we were sharing in a magical adventure, one that would provide us pleasure, connect us to our pasts, and change our lives.

The elderly South Philadelphia Jews (re-)adopted their language and cultural practices with great ease, even exhilaration. At the time, I was unaware that I would be living through a life review of my own, reconnecting to my own past and establishing a living Yiddish presence. Not only would I later facilitate Yiddish groups in Northampton and Holyoke in Massachusetts, but years after the Philadelphia experience, my own young children, living far from their grandparents, would attend meetings of the New England groups.

The intergenerational linkages of intimacy and identity revealed by my research have turned my life in new directions. The knowledge I have acquired about myself and the communities of American Jews uncovered for me the everyday lives of everyday Jews (*yidn fun a gants yor*).

Although Yiddish was the predominant language of East European Jewish immigrants to America, very little effort has been made by scholars to describe the changing patterns of spoken Yiddish in America.[3] The vernacular culture, in its verbal, active, and material expression, in its interactive discourse and negotiation, is usually ignored in the arenas of academia and public culture. Two dissertations on Yiddish as spoken in America (Green 1962; Rayfield 1970) did not consider characteristics of Yiddish that may not derive from the influence of English. And early compendia of English borrowings in Yiddish (Joffe 1936; 1943; Mark 1938; Neumann 1938) defined the limits of concern for future work on spoken Yiddish in America—namely, the influence of English.

The fact that few studies have concentrated on Yiddish as spoken in America seems to reflect the attitudes of the leading Yiddish linguists, who were extremely dedicated to studying normative issues in linguistics but rejected American Yiddish as a standard for normative decisions and deemed it, consequently, unworthy of study. This conviction held that Yiddish in America was "in a state of disintegration" (M. Weinreich 1941: 34). In his last article, published posthumously, M. Weinreich still held to the same viewpoint. He compared the Jews in New York of 1920 who used the word *flor* (floor) in their Yiddish speech with those in Vilna who used *podloge* (floor). He wrote that only the latter group interested him because if their children were alive in 1968 they spoke Yiddish, whereas the children of the American Jews spoke only English (M. Weinreich 1971: 12, 15–16). This book examines the Yiddish of the children of those who said *flor*.

Spoken Yiddish in America is a continuation of a thousand-year tradition in Jewish history. I do not adhere to the view that the only topic appropriate for the investigation of Yiddish in America is the influence of English. When American Jews express themselves in Yiddish they share modes of thought and speech with Jews of previous generations and on different continents. Why should American Jewish settings not illuminate issues relating to pan-Yiddish features? The ethnographer's task is to recognize the locally specific traits that inhabit the same space with the more universal, group-specific characteristics.

One of the least studied areas is the conventions of speaking Yiddish in face-to-face interaction, the most common circumstance for speech. Fishman has called for a change:

Least examined of all is the multilingual repertoire in speech, i.e. the bulk of Yiddish linguistic realization during the entire millennium of its existence. . . . The question here is not that of languages in contact or of language purity but of normative pragmatics in face-to-face interaction. . . . For a language which both Jews and the world at large tend to peg as 'talky' (rather than 'bookish' or 'arty' or 'technical'), what we lack most are studies of Yiddish in conversational action. (J. Fishman 1981: 61)

Even less examined is the realm of the meaning of Yiddish to its speakers. The study of Jews and their culture has largely been defined as the study of Jewish thought: the analysis of classical Jewish texts and the works of Jewish philosophers through the ages. One of my grandmothers was illiterate in all her languages, yet I question whether her Jewish thoughts are unworthy of study. As one ethnographer has noted, "The social forms that cage our intellectual activities remain all too invisible to us," but an ethnographer can enjoy "the giddiness of the new" (Rose 1990: 12). In collecting the stories that Jewish residents told each other in South Philadelphia, I found a path toward the thought of my grandmother, the life experiences and words of the nonelites.

In the same vein, we know about the lives and careers of Jewish intellectuals because they deliberately elected in the nineteenth century to write belles lettres in their maligned mother tongue, Yiddish (Miron 1973; Mendele Mokher Sforim 1967; Shtif 1967). But we do not know much about the ordinary woman or man who lived at the same time. More recently, studies have detailed the limiting scholarly traditions that have prevailed when Old Yiddish literary texts of the Middle Ages have been analyzed and published (Frakes 1989). The position of Yiddish in the history of German society and culture has been described, both as a Jewish secret language and as an object for Jewish self-hatred (Gilman 1986). Reclaiming the worlds of Jewish women as historical venues for popular culture in Yiddish, a variety of studies chronicle the role of Yiddish in women's prayer (Weissler 1987; 1991); as a vehicle of expression for women's poetry (Hellerstein 1988); in literature for the female reader in past centuries (cf. Parush 1994 and Niger 1912–1913); and as the language of radicalism for some women at the beginning of the twentieth century (Klepfisz 1994). To these I add the voices of the Jews of South Philadelphia, who chose to carry on their culture and express their emotional connection to their families and ethnic group through Yiddish.

To unravel the concept of changing ethnic identity, I find it useful to consider several theoretical distinctions. At different points in history, individuals and groups may exhibit multiple identities that vary according to circumstances, life-cycle patterns, and historical change. Thus, I have made reference to developments in Yiddish culture over the past thousand years, as well as to the evolution of the Jewish community in South Philadelphia over the past hundred years. During the lifetimes of the informants, their personal and group identities have evolved, such that they exhibit different attitudes about and different usage of their first language.

As an age cohort, second-generation American Jews share some common features. As the descendants of immigrants, their parents' life experiences colored their own decisions and practices. As fellow travelers through history, a host of circumstances affected the fate of their language and culture, including their own and their children's Americanization, the destruction of the heartland of Yiddish in Eastern Europe by the Nazis, and the growth of the Jewish state of Israel, which has fostered Hebrew alongside the diminution of Jewish languages, including Yiddish. All these factors have helped recast their Jewishness, just as other events have influenced the not specifically Jewish aspects of their lives.

Some contemporary critics of American society who have commented on changes in identification see individuals as unanchored in their personal connectedness to either the past or the future. Absent, they say, is any value for or cognizance of the role of ritual as I described it earlier (see Chapter 11), which through drama, repetition, and stability binds the past, present, and future: "People no longer act either under the guidance of their ancestors' ways of living or with any thought to the impact of what they do on succeeding generations" (Hewitt 1989: 46). Lasch termed this attitude the "culture of narcissism," living for the moment, with little concern for that which is greater than the interest of the individual, of the self: "We are fast losing the sense of historical continuity, the sense of belonging to a succession of generations originating in the past and stretching into the future" (Lasch 1978: 5).

If this is indeed the American way, it seems that the South Philadelphia Jews were going against the grain of history. Despite many deviations from the ways of their immigrant parents, their concern for yiddishkeit, with Yiddish culture at its core, is a statement that they are their parents' children. Although the elderly children of immigrants reported providing their children with some form of Jewish ethnic education, in most cases their children moved away when they reached adulthood, removing the proximal source of intergenerational continuity.[4]

Historians of twentieth-century cultural politics in the United States have documented that between 1938 and 1972 people developed a more conscious identification with their national origins and ethnic groups (Polenberg 1980: 244). This was a throwback in part to the ways of previous generations, in which affiliations outside the workplace had been dominated by ethnic institutions, rather than associations according to class lines (Aronowitz 1992: 37). Sollors, an important analyst of ethnic culture in the United States, has characterized the contemporary situation as one of "consent" rather than "descent," favoring the "achieved" rather than the "ascribed," with ethnicity deceptively "appearing to stem from time immemorial" (1986: 37; 1989: xx). A similar situation applies in contemporary Europe (Liebkind 1989b: 31).

The term ethnicity is itself difficult to define. Scholars have tried to address this issue: "Rather than a thing-like entity, ethnicity is a network of interacting social and historical processes" (Moerman 1993: 88); "It is not a thing but a process—and it requires constant detective work from readers, not a settling on a fixed encyclopedia of supposed cultural essentials" (Sollors 1989: xiv–xv); and "But people's ethnic identity is not a 'thing.' It is rather a complex process by means of which people construct and reconstruct their ethnicity . . . only a part . . . of the totality of their identities" (P. Weinreich 1989b: 45). Sollors stresses the new and the syncretic in ethnic culture over the traditional and supposedly authentic: "If we are all third generation (at least as an ideal), we may have parents who, for all practical purposes, are more ethnic than we are; but we can transcend them by invoking real or imaginary grandparents or founding fathers" (Sollors 1986: 230). By invoking imaginary grandparents among the elderly Jews of South Philadelphia, I position myself to inherit a tradition and then mold it anew.

Ethnicity is often used as a resource. Through their changing ethnic identifications, ethnic group members "construct from historical 'facts' biographical continuities between their ancestry and their progeny as a group" (P. Weinreich 1989b: 67–68). The move away from actual kinship ties brings with it the creation and colonization of new associations. The ethnic senior day center is a fairly recent innovation. At the South Philadelphia center, Itke could claim loyalty to her parents' European dialect while speaking a dialectal mixture. In a Northampton synagogue senior citizen group, elderly children of immigrants can present a musical drama that links their own synagogue cocktail party to their parents' arrival on a European steamship almost a century earlier. The shaping of ethnic identity is strengthened by such interpretive license. Furthermore, contemporary individual and collective memory is loosely constructed, and innovation, in such an atmosphere, is warmly embraced. A few emblematic cultural elements, even if historically inaccurate, are sufficient to delineate a group and to stabilize it (Roosens 1989: 12, 17).

We have yet to explore in detail whether Yiddish as a focus of identity for children of immigrants refers to all communities, including the newer sunbelt cities. Moore's portrayal of the Jews of Los Angeles and Miami suggests that different salient features apply (1994: 264–66, 270). Few markers set the sunbelt Jews apart from their Christian neighbors. They came to the cities and affiliated within new Jewish communities in order to attain individual meaning rather than to continue family or group traditions. In contrast, the Jews of South Philadelphia and New England were more like the more traditional Jews of the New York City area (see Glazer and Moynihan 1963).

From my observations, Jews across the United States share Yiddish as a universal link to their Jewish identity. One finds evidence for this link in the existence of the federation of almost one hundred Yiddish culture clubs in southern Florida, which publishes its own periodical newsletter.[5] The power of Yiddish to unite such a diverse array of Jews reflects the choice these second-generation children of immigrants have made to ally themselves with the language of their early years, the ethnic tongue.[6] Whether this aspect of their American Jewish identity is expressed through silence or speech, is manifested in a sectarian group setting or in a moment of private reflection, it serves to link the generations. Recalling Bruner's reminder that memory reconstructions are dialogic, with the interlocutor physically present or an abstraction, this social construction positions these Jews in history (Bruner 1990: 59). Even though the immigrant generation is no longer present to hear the message, and the third generation rarely appreciates the strength of the link, the elderly American Jews are declaring to themselves and to their peers that, indeed, they are and have always been Jewish in America.

These Jews are members of the same generation as the leading Jewish American intellectuals, who formulated the twentieth century's standards of American literary and high culture. They popularized a canon of European writers and thinkers of modernism who were often quite removed from the "artifacts of a national or subaltern culture" in which the children of American Jewish immigrants had been raised (Aronowitz 1993: 42–43). The American Jewish literary avant-garde is well established, but the widespread Yiddish culture of the family and neighborhood remains invisible. The English-language artifacts of their American lives are the popularly recorded symbols of the Jewish life cycle and calendar, from the kitchen to the bar-mitsvah celebration to the Passover seder (Joselit 1994). The ideologies and identifications of the children of immigrants who rally around

Yiddish must be woven into the story of geographic and economic mobility (Moore 1980). I am convinced of this when the young Orthodox rabbi of Congregation Rodphey Sholem in Holyoke, Massachusetts, tells me, "It's you and Rosh Hashone." The only occasions besides the Jewish high holiday services that bring large numbers of Jews to the synagogue there are the meetings of the newly formed Yiddish group.

Some critics have argued for the return to such social organizations on the local level if we wish to transmit vibrant cultures in the United States, rather than the culture that is promulgated through bureaucratic centers of power (Hewitt 1989: 46–47; Elshtain 1995: 5–21; Lasch 1995: 117–28; cf. Rose 1989: 8). Oddly though, even some state, corporate, and professional institutions have created opportunities for the elderly to congregate locally, fostering the evolution of ethnic identities.

In large part, Yiddish has been relegated to the status of marginality by both the larger American society and the Jewish community; the vernacular has historically been subjected to derision and devaluation, and scholars have paid it little attention. Such double marginality is not a common feature of most minority discourse. I know that Yiddish, and American Yiddish vernacular culture in particular, is at the center of human and Jewish experience, in the midst of a mainstream that I am also a part of. Yet scholars relegate the culture of the masses, of my grandmothers and myself, to an academic backwater, to a minor chord. In writing this book, I have tried to remove Yiddish from the periphery to which it is normally relegated and place it in a central position.

As is the case for other movements of cultural retrieval, relegation to the realm of low rather than high culture makes the embracing of Yiddish as the voice of Jewish peoplehood a struggle. But these Jews have successfully utilized Yiddish culture as source of self-esteem and belonging during old age. It has no pejorative connotation in their minds; its expression symbolizes resistance to assimilation and domination (Liebkind 1989a: 2; Wilpert 1989: 20).

Voices of minority cultures must specify both their commonalities and differences. Their shared experiences include antagonism and subjugation as well as the creativity generated through dialogic discourse within their own traditions (JanMohamed and Lloyd 1990a: 1, 6–7, 15; Hartsock 1990: 35; Lloyd 1993: 8–9). Cultural critics who have argued for the centrality of minority cultures have warned that the "mere affirmation of achievement can lead to recuperation into the dominant culture" (JanMohamed and Lloyd 1990a: 7). For example, placing Yiddish literature in a general anthology of world literature assigns it a meaning that is very different from that afforded by positioning it within the context of Yiddish cultural history. The works of Sholem Aleichem and Isaac Bashevis Singer may on occasion enter the canon, but not (yet) the culture of South Philadelphia, which remains unnamed, untranslatable, subaltern.

In providing South Philadelphians an opportunity to *kumen tsum vort* (express themselves), I have stressed their similarities with other immigrant groups and children of immigrants and with other neighborhood residents who were members of the same age-specific cohort, gender, and socioeconomic group. But I have also attempted to set the voices within the historical specificity of the Jewish community and its institutions, of the post-Holocaust period, of the societal position of Yiddish language and culture.

I chose South Philadelphia in part because it has been of little concern to the scholars of Jewish history, as well as to the chroniclers of minority culture. I believe every voice in that community counts as an expression of culture, as do the rhetorical and psychological strengths of the individual and the ethnic group. In answer to the question Spivak asks, "Can the subaltern speak?" (Spivak 1988), I say of course. In agreement with Christian, who rejects the binary framework that is implied in the use of the terms "minority" and "discourse" and points out that "many of us have never conceived of ourselves only as somebody's other" (1990: 40), I am attracted to the Yiddish voices because they lack self-consciousness about their Yiddish culture. It is that innocence in the face of a world that obliterates the appreciation of the small and local that has drawn me so close. Like Christian, who asks, "For whom are we doing what we are doing?," I question whether this book represents my own struggle for a cultural voice, the Jews in South Philadelphia, or the right Jewish history.

I am reminded of the account of the field experience of anthropologist Ethel Albert in Rwanda, discussed by Sanjek (1990: 39). One day Albert found her native field assistant interviewing a local resident and taking notes. He responded, when asked by Albert what he was doing, that he too was doing research and that his work would be better than hers because he knew the language. Unlike many anthropologists who go off to the far corners of the earth, I went off to neighborhoods that were not that far from my mother's kitchen. Although I spoke Yiddish, I had to learn to speak in a fashion that would seem natural and comforting to them and to me.

Despite our similarities in language and culture, I have learned just how much "ethnographers' voices cannot, strictly speaking, be their own. By the same token, the voices in ethnographic prose or films cannot be strictly those of whom we represent" (Stoller 1994: 359). Indeed, my informants and I experienced "crossing over, assimilation, appropriation, juxtaposition, and fusion" (D. Rose 1990: 44). The numerous accommodations all of us made throughout the year included my transition to the dialect of my family of origin from the cultural standard I learned as a student of Yiddish, Beyle's purchase of the university Yiddish text and a Yiddish dictionary, and the increasing frequency and intensity of my relationships with elderly individuals. However, even in these instances of a Yiddish-speaking American Jew studying Yiddish-speaking American Jews, "the space of discourse that we have not named contains the edges of incommensurable cultures" (D. Rose 1990: 53).

Rosaldo painted the picture of an observer as "more a busy intersection through which multiple identities crisscross than a unified coherent self" (1989: 194). Certainly my own identities have changed during the years of fieldwork and writing—from cell biologist to student of Yiddish culture, from student to fieldworker to professor, from Yiddish-speaking student to Yiddish-speaking father. All people lead complex lives. As for those who never left South Philadelphia, I am ever more conscious of my limitations in depicting their rich complexity. While concentrating on the local, I overlooked the global, ignoring the impact of modern technologies and a world economy on the residents' lives. I am especially concerned about my inability to accurately explain the life decisions of women in South Philadelphia. As they are in all older populations in our society, women were in the majority, yet I did not examine their leadership and resourcefulness in such areas as single parenting, wage earning, defining religious and ethnic legacies, and risk taking in general. I also gave insufficient attention to that which was painful or difficult for the residents about their lives in the neighborhood. Most of all, I regret that I did not tell the South Philadelphia story in book form when most of the residents about whom I write were still alive. Although they were never the primary intended audience, I did want them to hear their own voices and know that others were listening.

Anthropologists recognize that ethnographers are an integral part of the situations they analyze (Escobar 1993: 383; B. Tedlock 1991). My personal agenda, to give voice to my own Yiddish culture and its carriers, is evident in the way I do my work. As do other anthropologists, I write for myself, for the community I am writing about, and for more general audiences (see Rouch's comments on his films, Stoller 1994: 363).

Although I wished all along to engage in a dialogue on the meaning of Yiddish, in many cases the residents showed no desire for such a dialogue (cf. Mascia-Lees et al. 1989: 25; Escobar 1993: 383). I believe that their narratives must be integrated into the historical record if Jewish culture is to be understood, just as I am certain that understanding the vernacular styles and concerns of other ethnic groups would rewrite their ethnic cultural histories from the points of view of the group members. At least future generations of ethnic group members who do not have an opportunity to engage in contemporary dialogue would hear an echo of their voices. In this respect this ethnography does "engage with historicism" (see Vincent 1991).

In this book I have interwoven tales of the past and present because I believe that the principles of developmental biology apply equally well to ethnography. Any synchronic state is a process of continual becoming, perpetual development. Any contemporary ethnography, like any personal narrative, cannot disregard the past without risk of distorting the present and the future. To describe individual complexity and community diversity from the perspective of a single ethnographer, I have made use of the residents' narratives and my own, in addition to expository prose and history (cf. Stoller 1994: 362; 1989: 140). My goal is not only to chronicle a culture but to explain the survival of that culture. Unabashedly, I can echo the words of Christian, "I hope to ensure that their tradition has continuity and survives" (1990: 48), and of Lloyd, "I have made some attempt not simply to revalue marginal elements of Irish culture, but to reinsert them in the dynamic of identity formation" (1993: 5).

In reporting on the dynamics of contemporary ethnic identity development and expression, I did not want my analysis to rely on the depiction of individuals alone. Thus, for example, I looked at the social construction of Izzy's identity as it was influenced by his synagogue and Sunday school, his landsmanshaft and lunch counter.[7] I approached the history of Jewish culture in South Philadelphia by alternating the discussion of the cultural aspects of Izzy's life history, for example, with the analysis of the ways institutions express and foster that culture.

The Gleyzele tey in Philadelphia provided me with abundant material for thought about how Yiddish may function in social groups. A model that I find useful to explain what I saw is that of a "community of practice" (Lave and Wenger 1991: 100). A community of practice comes together for a specific purpose, and learning occurs only where there is negotiation about participation on the part of newcomers. It is the group situation itself that teaches members about communication in Yiddish and the strength of group values. The group may stimulate an individual or group to relate to cultural memories in new ways, but that activity is strictly facilitated by the group practice of Yiddish conversation. Cultural knowledge is located in the lived-in world, which is socially structured, and learning takes place through participation in this world (see Lave and Wenger 1991: 49, 51, 98).

Through my own membership in these "communities of practice," I have learned how to be a teacher. I shunned the role of leader in the first sessions of the Gleyzele tey and rejected the title of teacher, but I have since learned how important it is for older people to be with others who listen to them and their stories. I was first exposed to the skill of listening, as it were, through my grandparents and their friends. My work with the elderly helped me become a more competent listener and a different kind of university teacher. As a beginning lecturer, I filled my class notes with reports of all the findings of experiments in cell and molecular biology. I now know that students develop understanding by reacting to and retelling narratives, by expressing their doubts, questions, and convictions. In South Philadelphia I learned that a teacher is one who listens.

By acknowledging the wisdom of active listening, I have paid attention to those who are silent in Yiddish. Indeed, from this generation where silence in Yiddish predominated, a renaissance is occurring. The Yiddish speakers in this book are living out their lives after the Holocaust. Perhaps, the best-known metaphor for the endurance of Yiddish lies in the words of the Yiddish poet, H. Leivik, who wrote: "Ikh bren un ikh bren un ikh ver nit farbrent" (I burn and I burn, but I am not extinguished; Rozhanski 1984: 32). In this spirit, one of the members of the Gleyzele tey wrote: "Join us in the re-birth of Yiddish; and enjoy yet unconceived Bubba Mysses from today's Bubbas, as the water boils" (*JCC Beacon*, June 1985, p. 14).

In December 1985, a nineteen-year-old neighborhood resident set fire to the South Philadelphia senior center. Extensive damage forced activities to be moved temporarily to the Albert Einstein Hospital Daroff Division. Living then in Massachusetts, I wrote an appeal for the organized Philadelphia Jewish community to rebuild the center: "My dream is that sometime soon this JCC Center will once again be a cultural center for Jewish children. . . . The Jewish community must rebuild at Marshall and Porter Sts. It is urgent for us not to forget these elderly Jews. Many center members are in their 60s, and we must provide Jewish communal services for them for decades to come in South Philadelphia" (*Jewish Exponent*, January 24, 1986, 29). Making such a public statement marked a turnabout for me, from low-profile participant-observer eighteen months earlier to outspoken activist.

The Philadelphia Jewish community did rebuild the Center. Five years later, the new Center director again asked the members of a Yiddish discussion group what it was about Yiddish that kept it going. And the arguments continued. One member answered: "It's the universal language of all dispersed Jewish people. It goes back a thousand years." But a second member deferred, tongue in cheek: "I wouldn't know myself. I don't go back that far" (*Philadelphia Inquirer*, February 24, 1991, 1-A).

Appendixes

Map of the Neighborhood

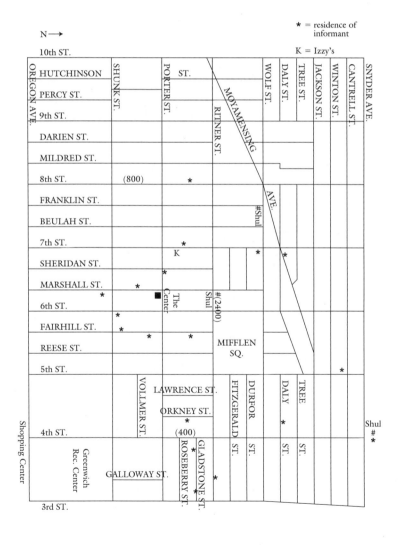

Information About the Residents[1]

Yiddish name	Sex	Age	Place of birth	Parents' place of birth	Age upon arrival in U.S.	Occupation/Employer
Basye A.	F	66	Chester, Penn.	U.S. (of Hungarian Jewish extraction), Ukraine	—	upholstery store, inspector
Beyle	F	60	S. Phila.	Ukraine	—	clerical, sales
2Blumke	F	74	S. Phila.	Ukraine	—	pocketbook factory worker
Dveyre	F	83	Great Britain	Lithuania, Ukraine	1	administrative secretary
Elke	F	66	S. Phila.	Ukraine	—	salesperson
2Ester A.	F	72	S. Phila.	Poland	—	city office worker
Ester-Beyle	F	66	S. Phila.	Ukraine	—	real estate office
2Ester-Sosye	F	83	Ukraine	Ukraine	3	factory office, housewife
2Feygl-Asye	F	66	S. Phila.	Ukraine	—	factory, cleaning store
2Itke	F	62	S. Phila.	Lithuania	—	housewife
Izhak	M	77	Transylvania	Transylvania	20	linoleum store proprietor
Izzy	M	75	S. Phila.	Belorussia	—	luncheonette proprietor, insurance sales, food sales
2Khatshe	M	100	Belorussia	Belorussia	27	baker
Libe	F	72	Poland	Poland	17	linoleum store, housewife
2Leye	F	78	New York City	Ukraine (Volhynia)	—	office worker, housewife
Marye	F	75	Ukraine	Ukraine	65	housewife

Yiddish name	Sex	Age	Place of birth	Parents' place of birth	Age upon arrival in U.S.	Occupation/Employer
[2]Moyshe B.	M	67	New York City	Greece, Turkey	—	clothing sales
[2]Reyzl	F	72	S. Phila.	Ukraine	—	bank clerk
[2]Rive-Rukhl	F	69	S. Phila.	Ukraine	—	millinery worker, housewife
[2]Rivke A.	F	74	Ukraine	Ukraine	12	landlady, housewife
[2]Rivke B.	F	74	S. Phila.	Ukraine	17	homecare for sick patients, housewife
[2]Roze	F	72	S. Phila.	Ukraine	—	hospital secretary, waitress
[2]Shmiel-Leyb	M	86	Ukraine	Ukraine	3	worker in soup factory
Shmuel-Am	M	71	S. Phila.	Ukraine	—	paperhanger
Sure A.	F	73	Ukraine	Ukraine	10	bookkeeper, housewife
[2]Surele	F	86	Great Britain	Poland	2	salesperson in department store
[2]Tsipe-Khashe	F	69	Baltimore	Lithuania	—	high school English teacher
[2]Yankl A.	M	81	Ukraine	Ukraine	17	plumber, union organizer
[2]Yankl B.	M	75	S. Phila.	Ukraine	—	sales
Yisrul	M	95	Ukraine (Volhynia)	Ukraine (Volhynia)	17	carpenter

1. All 30 of the people in this list took part in conversations with the investigator that were tape-recorded in 1985.
2. Member of the *Gleyzele tey* group.

Glossary of Yiddish Terms Used in the English Text

English Spelling*	Standard Yiddish Transcription	Definition
	anshey	synagogue in which members come from same European hometown
	beys yesoymim	orphan asylum
challah	khale	bread, prepared with eggs, that is eaten on shabbos
daven	davn	pray
erev shabbos	erev shabes	Friday evening
	gubernye	province in Czarist Russia
Hasid (pl. Hasidim, adj. Hasidic)	khosid (khsidim, khsidish)	adherent of religious groups founded by Israel Baal Shem Tov; currently regarded as an ultra-Orthodox Jew
hazan	khazn	cantor
	hoykhe fentster	high society
kaddish	kadish	prayer for the dead
kapote	kapote	long black coat
kashrus	kashris	the dietary laws
kiddush	kidish	blessing over the wine
landsleit	landslayt	fellow townspeople
landsmanshaft	landsmanshaft	association of fellow townspeople
	melamed	teacher of children
milchigs	milkhiks	dairy food
minyan	minyen	quorum for prayer
	moyshev-zkeynim	old age home
oneg shabbat	oyneg shabes	Friday evening celebration ushering in the Sabbath
	opshprekher	exorcist
rebbe	rebe	Hasidic rabbi, teacher
rebbitzin	rebitsin	rabbi's wife
seder	seyder	traditional ceremonial meal at Passover
shabbos	shabes	Sabbath
shames	shames	sexton of synagogue
shochet	shoykhet	ritual slaughterer of animals
shtetl	shtetl	small town
shul	shul	synagogue

English Spelling*	Standard Yiddish Transcription	Definition
siddur	sider	prayer book
talis	talis	prayer shawl
Talmud Torah	talmid toyre	religious school for children
tfillin	tfilin	phylacteries
Torah	toyre	scroll containing the Pentateuch
yeshiva	yeshive	institution of higher Talmudic learning
yiddishkeit	yidishkayt	Jewishness
yizkor	yizker	memorial service
yom tov	yontif	holiday

* Variant closest to Yiddish transcription, as listed in *Webster's Third New International Dictionary of the English Language, Unabridged*.

American Yiddish Voices
Narrative Documents
of Ethnic Culture

See the Note to the Reader at the front of the book for the system used to transcribe Yiddish and for an explanation of the symbols and punctuation used in the following.

1. Feygl-Asye on Belief in God

During a Gleyzele tey session, I try to make peace and recognize both sides, those believing in the power of God and those who are nonbelievers. Feygl-Asye interprets events of brutal destruction of human life as a test of God. Feygl-Asye says, "Me tur nit zindikn kign im (we are not allowed to sin against him), no matter what." Her mother recently died, and she views Ezra's declaration of nonbelief in God as an attack on her own faith. Everyone is silent as she speaks:

Ikh ho derkhgelibt a sakh, bot ikh gleyb in got. Az mayn mame hot gelibt, she surpassed medical science and medical knowledge, vus iz nit gevin miglekh de—a—khob geredt tsim dokter, zug ikh, mir tit anuve vus man mam—I lost her in January, but—, mirn eyn mol geredt vus me indzer dokter hot geholfn zi de—got hot dus getun but indzer dokter hot geholfn arangegibn man mame in in hospitul zeyer fil mul, en m(eh)ot zi gerotevet in ikh ho(b) zi ge(h)at. Tse akht in fertsik yor mir(n) zi sher farlurn, en di dokteyrim hobm gezukt az ey—m(eh)ot zi (ge)meakht an apereyshin in eyber zi vet derlibn biz fuftsik. Finef yor hot men ir farlengert. En ikh hob farlurn man mame en se tit mir vey but man mame iz gegangen tse eyn in nantsik yur. Vus got ken TSAYGN iz meyn vi di dokteyrim in medikl sayins in medikl noledzh en oles— [buzz of general comments]. En ikh GLEYB en vus ikh hob far-lurn ikh ken im nit frign farvus iz man tate gegangen ing in farvus man brider, hot er mir getsaygt, az go—er iz gevin mit mir in ikh ho gehot mayn mame lange yurn, en ikh vil nisht hern az si nishtu ken got. Ikh GLEYB in got. Er ho— [general commotion] er hot mir getsaygt in ibertsaygt az er ken tun vus vus andere konen nisht [buzz of comments; Roze says, "Me darf gleybm"].

I lived through a lot, but I believe in God. If my mother lived, she surpassed med-ical science and medical knowledge, which was not possible de—a—I spoke to the doctor, and I said, I am happy that my moth—I lost her in January, but—, we once spoke how our doctor helped us she de—God did it but our doctor helped admit my mother into the hospital very many times, and they saved her and I had her. At forty-eight I almost lost her, and the doctors said that i—they operated on her and if she would live to fifty. They lengthened her life by five years. And I lost my mother and it hurts me but my mother went when she was ninety-one. What God can SHOW is more than the doctors and medical science and medical knowl-edge and everything—[buzz of comments]. And I BELIEVE and that which I lost I can't ask why my father went so young and why my brother, he showed me, that Go—he was with me and I had my mother for long years, and I do not want to hear that there isn't any God. I BELIEVE in God. He— [general commotion] he showed me and convinced me that he can do what others cannot do [buzz of comments; Roze says, "You have to believe"].

2. Rivke A. on Mothers and Daughters

During a Gleyzele tey session, the group discusses how parents raise boys differently from girls. I pursue with a question, whether daughters aren't emotionally closer to their mothers than sons. Gershon says yes, and Rivke A. tells of a family incident to illustrate the issue:

Lomir dir epes zugn. Man zin iz zeyer git tse mir. Bot, ey—ey—e—em—zey nor, ikh hob gezukt ikh darf koyfn a ring zukt er mam, host zikh tsvey ringen, vus darf-ste a dritn, zug ikh, ikh gey es den trugn? Zukt er, farvuzhe geyst es koyfn? Zug ikh az epes et zekh makhn, a—a—ayl pes avey, zol man shnir ekhet krign. Man shnir e(z) gezesn (h)ot man zin gezukt, her zikh oys mam. Fanensheli vil ikh tun di best vus ikh ken far dir, but az set zan trobl, vet es zan trobl mane shvesterz trobl, zey nemen ker [Roze says, "It's true, it's true"]. A ring zukt er iz git, zit kimen (?) zit dir brengen a sheynem prezint. Bot, zit gikher nemen ker af ir momen vi zit nemen ker af af dir. Therfor zukt er, poisinel zakhn balongt nit tse yir, si balongt tse man shvester. [People agree.]

Let me tell you something. My son is very good to me. But, um um you see, I said I have to buy a ring so he says mom, you have, after all, two rings, why do you need a third, so I say, you think I will wear it? He says, why are you going to buy it? I say if something should happen, I—I—I'll pass away, let my daughter-in-law also get something. My daughter-in-law was sitting there and my son said, listen mom. Financially I will do the best I can for you, but if there will be trouble, it will be my sisters' trouble, they will take care [Roze says, "It's true, it's true"]. A ring he said is good, she'll come (?) she'll bring you a nice present. But, she'll sooner take care of her mother than she'll take care of you. Therefore he said, personal things don't belong to her, it belongs to my sister. [People agree.]

3. Rivke A. on Relations Between Jews and Non-Jews

One of Rivke A.'s narratives was remembered long afterwards by partici-pants of the Gleyzele tey. This narrative raised the group to an emotional height. The group was discussing relations between Jews and non-Jews. Rivke A. asks in English, "Can I say something?" and then proceeds:

Ikh veys nit tsi se rekhtik but azoy hob ikh gereyst mane kinder, akhits riligiyez tse zan darfn ze(y) zan mentshn. Eyb se kimt in a klos emetser vus darf hubm helf ker ikh nit eyb se iz a royter, a shvartser, a peyer, ikh ker erz a MENTSH, a bashefenish fin got. Darfn zey gibn zeyer hilf tsu zey. Eb—a—eyl khil dir tsaygn vi azoy se virkt af a kind. Man yingere tokhter i(z) geganen i—in sku:l, zey hobm graedzhu-veyt tsu oner in dzhuner hay, iz yeder kind hot getrugn a kasazh. Kimt ze aheym zugt, mam, kenst mir gibm man alawens befor, zug ikh, vus darfste dan alawen, zukt ze mam se du a shvarts shiksele, ba indz, ile miz hubm a kasazh. Iz zi darf nor hubm okh hubm a kasazh. Zug ikh di veyst vus man kind, nit nor vil ikh, lozn dir gibm dan alawens ikhl dir gibm a matune far zan a mentsh. Bekoz, ye—tse bi a mentsh iz not onli tu thin- denken af ayer religiyez (?), me darf denken ef a mentsh darf hilf. Kimt ir im nisht frign vus zan naeshinaliti iz, in der malkhume, az e—sol-dotn foln geyt men frign tsi si—a id, a goy, a terk, tse vu:s? Me darf zan a mentsh akhits religiyez.

I don't know if it's right but this is the way I raised my children, besides being re-ligious they have to be human beings. If someone who needs help comes in a class I don't care if it's a red person, a black, a peasant, I care that he's a HUMAN BEING, God's creation. They should help them. If—a—I'll tell you how it influences a child. My younger daughter went to school, they graduated with honors in junior high, and each child wore a corsage. So she comes home and says, mom, could you give me my allowance in advance, I say, why do you need your allowance, she says mom there's a little black non-Jewish girl, in our class, everyone has to have a cor-sage. So she also has to have a corsage. So I say you know what my child, not only will I, let you give your allowance I'll give you a present for being a human being. Because, ye—to be a human being is not only to thin—think of your religious (?), you have to think if a person needs help. You don't go and ask him what his na-tionality is, in the war, if e—soldiers die do you go and ask if it's a Jew, a non-Jew, a Turk, or whatever? You have to be a human being, besides being religious.

4. Beyle on the Stigma Attached to Being a South Philadelphian

The following narrative was recounted to me by Beyle in the presence of her sister, Elke. Conversation has turned to the sensitive topic of the way in which former South Philadelphians look down on those residents who remain. Beyle is animated and tells of a reunion of the *zekste* (Sixth Street). She uses the markers of fast speech, such as abbreviated forms, contractions, and deletions: *ho = hob, ziz = zi iz, mot = me hot, zi ersht = zi iz ersht, tsyir = tsi ir.* She conveys meaning and sarcasm by manipulating her voice quality, for example, by lengthening the vowels and by raising the pitch at these same positions: *oysgepi:tst* (decked out, dressed up) and *ungeshmi:rt* (made up).

Nu, mir zanen gekimen zakh tsineyf, mir hot men glakh derkent, ir hot men derkent, in ikh hob gedarft kikn af zey hob ikh nit gevist, ver siz ver, iz arangekimen eyne oysgepi:tst mit di hekhe liderne buwts, in ungeshmi:rt azey vi zi volt gevin khotsh an ekterise, farbrent dem punim, zeyer sheyn gevin ungetun, zukt zi, in ver bisti? Ikh ho(b) glakh derkent finem kol az ziz fin di hekhe, hekhe fentster. Hob ikh ir gezukt, zug ikh, in ver bisti? Az zi hot mir oysgeredt ver zi iz, ikh ho(b) nit gegleybt az dus iz zi. Zukt zi, di veyst, siz gevin zeyer zeyer git az m(eh)ot mir gerifn, bot ikh bin zakh gevin on di Riviere, iz zi gevin . . . Zi(z) ersht gekimen fin di Riviere far dem shtikl lontshn dortn . . .

Bot zi hot zakh avekgezetst bold aleyn, zi zol nit zitsn mit indz, zug ikh tsi ir, vi voynstu:? Zukt zi, Pen Vae:li. Zukt zi, in vi voynsti, zug ikh, ikh bin nokh in der zekster. Ot zi zakh a vorf getun efsher trug ikh laz af zikh in zey krikhn af ir. Zukt zi tsyir bekoz ziz, aefter awl, ziz, gevin ba mir di eltste. Zukt zi (?), vi voynsti? Zukt zi, ikh voyn nit in shtut, ikh voyn in Seynt Tames. Azey loste dan shvester voynen in Sowth Filadelfye? Didn't she? [Beyle turns and addresses this last question to Elke.]

So, we assembled together, they recognized me right away, they recognized her, but I had to look at them and I still didn't know, who is who, someone came in decked out in high leather boots, and made up as though she was an actress at the very least, her face tanned, very well dressed, she says, "And who are you?" Right off I recognized from the voice that she's from high high society. So I told her, I say, "And who are you?" When she told me who she is, I didn't believe that was she. She says, "You know, it was very very good that they called me, but I was on the Riviera," that's where she was . . . She just arrived from the Riviera for that bit of a luncheon over there . . .

But she sat herself down alone right away, she shouldn't have to sit with us, I say to her, "Where do you live?" She says, "Penn Valley." She says, "And where do you live," I say, "I am still on Sixth Street." She jumped away in case I was carrying lice on my body and they might crawl on her. She says to her [Beyle's sister] because she's, after all, she's, she was the eldest. She says (?), "Where do you live?"

She says, "I don't live in the city, I live in Saint Thomas." "This is how you allow your sister to live in South Philadelphia?" Didn't she? [Beyle turns and addresses this last question to Elke.]

5. Ester-Beyle on Her Mother's Food Preparations for Shabbos

Ester-Beyle recreates for me and her husband, Shmuel-Arn, as we sit in their living room, the aromas and tastes she remembers upon coming home from school on Friday afternoon:

E.-B.: Ziz gevin a balebuste in a zeyer gite kekhin, e—gekent bakn zeyer git. Kho(b) gekimen fin skul yedn fraytik, ikh, siz nor gevin eyn brider. Ikh aleyn bin ikh gegangen in hayskul. Iz e— bin ikh gekimen fraytik fin skul. Az zi(ho)t mir gehert araynki-men. Zi(ho)t shoyn u(p)getsoygn di e—liver finem tshikn, aend zit dos arayngeleykt in der zup. In zi(ho)t gehat a kayzer rol aen ven ikh ho(b) gekimen fraytik, dos iz di ershte zakh vus zi(ho)t mir gegibn fin skul, iz a tshikn liver ersht u(p)gekokht, ersht u(p)gekokht git, he, he, he [laughs], dus iz gevin geshmak.

R. P.: A maykhl, wow.

E.-B.: Aen di dayningrum tish fin ek tse ek iz gevin ungebakn, aler-ley kofi keyks mit bilkes. En di brider hobm gekimen aen gen-imen aheym.

R. P.: Aheym.

E.-B.: Tsu der vayb.

R. P.: Fraytik hobm zey gekent kimen.

E.-B.: Yedn fraytik. O yo. Zeym nish gegesn dortn far diner, bot zeym aheymgenimen vus mame hot u(p)gebakn.

E.-B.: She was a good housekeeper and a really good cook, e—she could bake very well. I came from school every Friday, I, there was only one brother. Only I went to high school. Uh—so I came from school on Friday. When she heard me come in. She had already removed the liver from the chicken, and she put it into the soup. And she had a kaiser roll, and when I came Friday, this is the first thing that she gave me from school, a chicken liver freshly cooked, just well cooked, he, he, he [laughs], that was delicious.

R. P.: A delicacy, wow.

E.-B.: And the dining room table from end to end was full of baked things, all sorts of coffee cakes and rolls. And my brothers came and took things home.

R. P.: Home.

E.-B.: To their wives.

R. P.: They were able to come Friday.

E.-B.: Each Friday. Oh yes. They didn't eat dinner there, but they took home what my mother baked.

6. Elke on Not Recognizing Her Own Name in School

In her living room, Elke recounts to me with ease a narrative from the early years. She tells of the problems of a Yiddish-speaking child in the English-language public school:

English hob ikh nit geredt, khob nor gevist Yidish. Zi rift Ellen, Ellen, Ellen, in ikh entfer nit. Khob nit gevist az dus iz man numen. Flig men mir gibn peyperz ale tug nemen aheym. Kho(b) gebrakht di peyperz aheym. Di mome hot genimen di payperz tsim zeydn, "Vus ken zan?" Biz man onkl, man momes brider, er hot gezukt, s'iz shon, frier iz gevin fin titsher, nakherz gevin fin printsipl, "Ikh entfer nit tsi man numen, ikh ken nit lernen." Hot men shon farshtonen. Man onkl hot geshribm krik, a leter, az ikh ken nit redn English in ikh farshtey nit, derfar entfer ikh nit. Hot men mir ungefangen in d(e)r(h)eym knakn in kop, dus iz dan numen, dus iz dan numen, dus iz dan numen, dus iz dan numen, biz vonen s'iz arangeki-men in kepele. In ikh gey shen in skuwl nokh amul. In epes, in, der tsveyter tsi driter—bin gegangen—promoted, m(eh)ot mir promoted. Ikh gey fin eyn klaes tsi an ondern. Enyhaw, khob ungefongen lernen, in ikh hob gelernt git.

I didn't speak English, I only spoke Yiddish. She calls Ellen, Ellen, Ellen, and I don't answer. I didn't know that that was my name. They used to send papers home with me every day. I brought the papers home. My mother took the papers to my grandfather, "What can be the matter?" Until my uncle, my mother's brother, he said, it's already, first it was from the teacher, then from the principal, "I don't answer to my name, I can't learn anything." They understood already. My uncle answered in a letter, that I can't speak English and I don't understand, therefore I don't answer. At home they started banging it into my head, this is your name, this is your name, this is your name, this is your name, until it entered my little head. And I am attending school again. And for some reason, in the second or third I went—promoted, I was promoted. I go from one class to the next. Anyhow, I started to learn, and I studied well.

7. Elke on Being a Manipulative Little Girl

In her living room, Elke tells a story dealing with her youngest years:

E.: Bot, a di hoyz vi mir(?)n arangemuft, vi mir voynen yetst, iz man momes shvester hot gehot. In eyn mul iz man mome gevin in hospitl, in ikh bin gegan—gekimen du farn tuk mit man tonte, man momes shvester. In der zeyde hot ir gezukt, ir numen iz ekhet gevin Elke. In er hot ir gezukt. Zolst vatshn dem kind. Man tontes gevin zeyer a fensi densi, in zi hot gehot roks in hoyz. Dus iz di gishekhte vus Beyle hot gevolt ikh zol akh zugn.

R. P.: Yeah.

E.: In ikh bin arayngekimen in hoyz. Ikh bin gevin a gite kind, bot ikh hob epes ifgeheybm dem rok, man tonte ot ungefangen shrayen af mir. In ikh(h)ob gemeynt az zi geyt mir shlugn, hob ikh ir gezukt, "zolst mir nit tshepn, ikhln zugn dem zeydn." Zukt zi, "vey iz mir, zolst nit zugn dem zeydn. Zuk dem totn gurnit. Veyste vus, a(z) diz zan a gite kind in gurnit zugn gi ekh dir keyfn a daymind ring." Zu ikh, "far shuwr di geyst mir keyfn a ring?" Zukt zi, "ye ikhln dir keyfn a—" aen azeyt zi getun. Abi zi hot mir gekeyft dem daymind, hob ikh sheyn dertseylt dem zeydn.

R. P.: hi-hi [laugh]

E.: Vus s'hot zakh pasirt, bekos ert gevolt visn vi kimt a(z) zi git mir az zi hot mir gekeyft a daymind ring? Frig sheyn nit vus ert ir gegibn mitn daymind ring in onem daymind ring. Nakher vin di mome iz a—aroysegekimen fin hospitl hot man tote gekeyft di hoyz, fin man tonte, in zi hot avekgemuft. Mir(hob)n gehot gite yurn du, urim zanen mir gevin.

E.: But, the house to which we moved, where we now live, had belonged to my mother's sister. And one time my mother was in the hospital, and I went—came here for a day with my aunt, my mother's sister. And my grandfather told her, her name was also Elke. And he told her. You should watch the child. My aunt was a very fancy-dancy, and she had rugs in the house. This is the story Beyle wanted me to tell you.

R. P.: Yeah.

E.: And I entered the house. I was a good child, but somehow I lifted the rug, my aunt started to scream at me. And I thought that she was going to hit me, so I told her, "You shouldn't bother me, I'll tell grandpa." She says, "Woe is me, don't tell grandpa. Don't tell my father anything. You know what, if you'll be a good child and say nothing I will buy you a diamond ring." I say, "For sure you will buy me a ring?" She says, "Yeh I will buy you a—," and that is what she did. As soon as she bought me the diamond, I went and told my grandfather.

R. P.: hi-hi [laugh]

E.: What took place, because he wanted to know how come she's giving me—that she bought me a diamond ring? Don't ask what he gave her with the diamond ring and without the diamond ring. Afterwards when my mother left the hospital my father bought the house, from my aunt, and she moved away. We had good years here, we were poor.

8. Tsipe-Khashe on Her Mother's Hallucination

This narrative of Tsipe-Khashe's was part of a conversation with me in an office in the senior center. She related the hallucination of her mother upon her sister's birth, which occurred right after her mother learned that her own mother was dead:

Mayn mame ot oysgefunen az ir muter iz teyt a epes a a monet tsi vintsiker zi geven akht monatn in e—ke—leyber in e—zit geshvengert. Iz e—be—ba—ke—kemat in nayntn monet (h)ot zi oysgefunen az ir muter i—geshtorbm. Iz e—zi zokt az e—e—, ven e—e—zit gedarft zi(z) gegangen tsu kind, i—ge—ven zit gehat mayn shvester, iz geven aze—azey gring. Zis aroys un zit gezen ir muters e—gestanen in a korner, un ir ir muter(ho)t ir gezokt zit zayn olrayt, alsding iz gut, ye no: zis zit forgeshtelt. Un derfar gedenk ikh az ir muter iz shen nit geven ven mayn shvester iz geborn gevorn.

My mother found out that her mother was dead a about a a month or less she was eight months in e—ke—labor in e—she was pregnant. So e—be—ba—al—almost in her ninth month she found out that her mother died. So e—she says that e—e—, when e—e—she had to she was ready to give birth, when she had my sister, it was so—so easy. She came out and she saw that her mother e—was standing in a corner, and her her mother told her she'd be all right, everything is okay, you know sh—she imagined it. And therefore I remember that her mother was dead already when my sister was born.

9. Reyzl on How Her Parents Saved Her Brother's Life

Reyzl reminisces to me in her living room:

R.: I.z, may tate gezukt tsu may mame, "di veyst vus Perl . . . Er geyt shtarbm. Dus geredt fin may brider, Duvidl . . . Der dokterz geveyn, der noys iz geveyn in zey zugn, me ken gunisht tin far im, siz zeyer a groyse epedemik du in der velt, aend i—me darf epis tin. Ikh vil epis tin vus mot getun, in Yurop . . . " Aen ikh gedenk. Ert (?) mistom geveyn efsher af der ershte(r) malkume hob ikh ge—mistom gedarft veyn zibm akht yur. Bot di zakhn, gedenkn in kop bekoz, siz vi a a mirikl. Mot genemt tsvey, gaelvinayzt shislekh. Eyne iz geveyn mit gezatine voser in eyne i(z) geveyn mit kolte vaser. In m(h)ot im genemin m(h)ot im

geleygt in di heyse voser m(h)ot im geleygt in di kalte vaser,
bekoz zeym gedenkt i(n) zeyer gedaenk er geyt nisht leybm,
eniwey so. hobm zey genemt a tshaens. Zey ho(b)m, im ge-
kyurt. Bekoz mit yurn krik, ven indz gehot Prezdent Ruzvelt,
in may mame ot dertseylt de manse, hobm zey gevolt may
mame zol geyin af de reydiyo, en zugn vus zi hot getun. Hot
may mame gezukt vos iz geveyn git far ir kind, zi ot nit gevis
un zi hot nit gevey denkt ez duz volt geveyn git, far an anders.
I mit yurn shpeyter ven may bride gegon in de tsveyte malkume, mot im genemin but erz nor geveyn in di arme, zeks
monatn bekoz, se hot im ibergeblibm fin dos infint peraelisis a
fis vus di artsh hot ofgeheypt azoy, aen er hot nit gekent e tin
de eksersayziz.

R. P.: A vinder vos me hot im genemen a

R.: Mot im genemen, but mot im distshardzhd.

R. P.: So zey hobm im gerotevet.

R.: Ye, ye

R. P.: Siz a groyse zakh.

R.: Dus fleg zayn zeyer a groyse tapik.

R. P.: Un er iz geven a yingl. Er iz geven zeyer ying.

R.: Ye. O. Zeyer zeyer ying shur. E—, o may gad, bot e—, ikh
gedenk dus ye no fi(n) redn, e—di manses a sakh manses may
tate hot mir gezukt, azoy vi e—, ez me fleyg e—krign a shtikele haltsn in hont, hot men genemt a shte— a, in der teyg hot
men geyuzt Felz Naeftha so—sop vus ikh denk siz gehot kar-
balik aesid in es. Me fleyg nemin a shtikele zeyf i me fleyg
tsileygn vi dus halts iz a arayngegan in finger, in m(h)ot es
arimgevisht mit a shmate, in dus fleyg aroys e—nemen di e—
de halts . . . Ye no dus dedu, bobe refiyes bot

R. P.: It works.

R.: Ikh, vus nokh gedenk ikh? Ikh gedenk . . .

R.: So., my father said to my mother, "You know what Perl . . . He's
going to die. He was speaking about my brother, Duvidl . . .
The doctor came, the nurse came and they said, there's nothing that can be done for him, there's a very big epidemic in the
world, and i—we have to do something. I want to do something that was done, in Europe . . . " And I remember. He (?)
it was probably maybe after the First World War so I wa—probably had to was seven-eight years old. But these things, are remembered in your head because, it's like a a miracle. They took
two, galvanized bowls. One was full of boiling water and one
was with cold water. And they took him and put him in the hot

water and they put him in the cold water, because they thought in their minds that he was not going to live, anyway so they took a chance. They cured him. Because years ago, when we had President Roosevelt, and my mother told the story, they wanted my mother to be on the radio, and tell what she did. And my mother said what was good for her child, she did not know— and she did not know—think that that would be good, for someone else's child. Years later when my brother went into the Second World War, they took him but he was only in the army six months because, he was left after the infant paralysis with a foot whose arch lifted so, and he couldn't do the exercises.

R. P.: It's a wonder that they took him a

R.: They took him, but they discharged him.

R. P.: So they saved him.

R.: Yeah, yeah.

R. P.: It's a big thing.

R.: That used to be a very big topic.

R. P.: And he was a boy. He was very young.

R.: Yeah. Oh. Very very young sure. E—, oh my God, but e—, I only remember this from talking, and the stories a lot of stories my father told me, like e—, when you used to get a little piece of wood in your hand, you took a st—a, in those days they used Fels Naphtha so—soap which I think contained carbolic acid. You used to take a little piece of soap and you would put it where the wood had gone into the finger, and you rubbed it around with a rag, and that removed the wood . . . You know those th—grandma remedies but

R. P.: It works.

R.: I, what else do I remember? I remember . . .

Notes

Chapter One

1. Labov calls this the observer's paradox: "The aim of linguistic research in the community must be to find out how people talk when they are not being systematically observed: yet we can only obtain these data by systematic observation" (1972a: 209).

2. I was concerned, however, about how the residents would view me. Would I be accepted as an insider or rejected as an outsider? I was reminded of Helan Page, an African American anthropologist, who, during her fieldwork in an African American town in the Midwest, was seen by the residents as an outsider who acted white (Page 1988: 176).

3. The standard Yiddish is *hoykhe fentster*; *hekhe* is the common form for Jews from northern Ukraine.

4. Merritt notes that "instances in which it can be established that recipients and analytic overhearers have essentially equal access to this mutual biographical context can thus be seen to be of special methodological interest (1979: 122).

5. See Chapter 8, "Who's Accommodating Whom?"

6. I used the collections of the American Jewish Archives and the American Jewish Periodical Center, Cincinnati; the Yivo Archives, New York City; and the Philadelphia Jewish Archives Center at the Balch Institute for Ethnic Studies and the Urban Archives at Temple University, Philadelphia.

7. The Neighborhood Center Collection is part of the holdings of the Philadelphia Jewish Archives Center at the Balch Institute for Ethnic Studies. It is of special interest because the senior center that was the focus of my study was in part a successor organization to the original branch of the Neighborhood Center. The Neighborhood Center is the topic of a dissertation by Greifer (1948) and recent research by E. Rose (1994).

Chapter Two

1. The Yiddish first names used in the text refer to residents with whom I conversed during my fieldwork. The translations from Yiddish to English are mine. "Jerusalem" in this quotation should not be confused with the appellation for an

earlier small settlement of Eastern European Jews in the northern Port Richmond section of Philadelphia. Many English words originating from Yiddish and Hebrew are included in *Webster's Third New International Dictionary of the English Language, Unabridged* (Springfield, Mass.: E. and C. Merriam Company, 1981).

2. *Litvish* is an adjective referring to the Jewish language and culture area *lite*, which was much larger than the Lithuanian state between the two world wars and included Belorussia, parts of northeastern Poland, and Latvia. Stereotypes associated with *litvaks* include being learned in Jewish texts and traditions and being cold and rational, rather than emotional and boisterous. It is viewed as the region with the most prestigious East European Jewish language and culture.

3. See, e.g., Bernheimer, ed., 1905: 51–52; Greifer 1948: 487; 1958: 5; B. Rosen, ed. 1938; Rotman 1980: 7; Varbero 1973: 261; and Whiteman 1973: 246. The estimated figures are not exactly comparable: the geographic borders used to define South Philadelphia were not identical in all cases; some figures specify Russian-born residents, assuming them to be Jewish, and exclude Austrian (Galician) immigrants. A study undertaken by the Albert Einstein Medical Center—Daroff Division (Rotman 1980) involved face-to-face interviews with 758 South Philadelphia Jews and estimated the local Jewish population at three to four thousand. This study focused mainly on the health needs of the Jewish population served by the local medical center, which is operated under Jewish communal auspices. Since this study was conducted only a few years before I began my work in the area, some of the quantified survey data were helpful in complementing my qualitative findings. I thank Norma Rotman for providing me with a copy of her final report.

4. Harry Beitchman, manuscript in Philadelphia Jewish Archives Center at the Balch Institute, Accessions 120 and 123, "History of the Hungarian Synagogue—Chevra Emunas Israel Ohev Sholom" (c. 1967), 1, 4–5.

5. "The major challenge to neighborhood as a demographic-physical construct as well as a viable social network comes from organizations and institutions (firms and bureaucracies) whose routine functioning reorganizes urban space. The stranger to fear may not be the man of different ethnicity on the street corner, but a bank president or property management executive of irrelevant ethnicity far from view" (Logan and Molotch 1987: 111).

6. See Lisa Hostein, "Flames Damage Seniors' Center, Not Their Spirit," *Jewish Exponent*, December 20, 1985, 5, 64; Hostein, "Probe into Fire Continues After Arrest," *Jewish Exponent*, December 27, 1985, 5; Rakhmiel Peltz, "Leave the Jewel Where It Is," *Jewish Exponent*, January 24, 1986, 29, 37; and *Jewish Exponent*, "Multi-Service Center Will Be Rebuilt," June 27, 1986, 5, 59.

7. See Leslie Alper, "'Glezele tey': In South Philly Yiddish Still Thrives," *Jewish Exponent*, June 7, 1985, 31, 36; "FJA Funds Programs for Jewish Elderly," *Jewish Exponent*, December 7, 1984, 19; "Center City Senior Groups Begin Project to Feed Needy," *Jewish Exponent*, December 28, 1984, 1; and "Senior Adults Create Food Closet," *Jewish Exponent*, March 29, 1985, 15.

8. Dorette Rota, "Mix Old and Young: Fun," *South Philadelphia Review East*, April 25, 1985, 14E, 20E; Rota, "This Artist Never Sees His Work," *South Philadelphia Review East*, May 9 1985, 29E, 30E.

9. According to a neighborhood newspaper feature on South Philadelphia, the litmus test for "real South Philadelphians" was studded with characteristics of Italian American culture, but it did not make any reference to aspects of American Jewish culture (Dorette Rota, "It Ain't Sauce in South Philly: And Real South Philadelphians Know That and More," *South Philadelphia Review East*, August 8, 1985, 1, 46). Likewise, a brochure for tourists coming to the area trumpeted an array of sights and restaurants mostly associated with Italian American life, but the sole mention of Jews relegated them to the annals of history: "Throughout the 19th and early 20th century, successive waves of Italian and Jewish immigrants arrived at Pier 53" (City of Philadelphia 1985).

10. Greifer (1948: 322) says Jews lived on Fourth and Fifth Streets and Italians from Sixth through Ninth Streets in 1948 (see map, Appendix A). The map appended to his dissertation, obtained from the Philadelphia Housing Association (Philadelphia Foreign-Born Population, 1940 Census), shows that the distribution Greifer claimed is valid for ward 1; in ward 39, however, the southern part of Southeast Philadelphia south of Mifflin Street, the Jewish territory was larger. Italians resided west of Ninth Street, and there were Jews as far east as Second and Third Streets. This east-west distribution also reflects the current pattern: most Jews now reside in the southern part of Southeast Philadelphia, south of Snyder Avenue, between Third and Eighth Streets.

Chapter Four

1. *Kropeve* means "nettle," and perhaps this is the word that belongs in the saying.

2. See Chapter 2, note 2, on the Jewish language and culture area *lite*.

3. In Matisoff's typology of ready-made Yiddish phrases that vent the speaker's emotions, "bono-petitive psycho-ostensive expressions" state the wish for good things to happen (Matisoff 1979: 4, 17)

4. "Jewish" is the common designation for the Yiddish language in the English speech of South Philadelphia Jews. However, I rarely heard this term used in their Yiddish speech; in Yiddish speech, the Yiddish language was referred to as "yidish" or "idish."

Chapter Five

1. Students of identity formation during the life cycle have formulated theories that address how some identities intensify and others recede at different stages of life (Obeyesekere 1975: 256; Simic 1985; Weibel-Orlando 1988: 329).

2. Stoller reemphasizes the vital advantages of long-term relationships in fieldwork. A Songhay native told him: "Today you are learning about us, but to understand us, you will have to grow old with us." Stoller attributes the breakthroughs in his work to his mastery of the language of his subjects and to lasting friendships built on mutual trust (Stoller 1989: 6, 10).

3. I estimate that I came in contact with upwards of four hundred residents of

South Philadelphia in some sort of social situation in which both the residents and I were speakers and listeners. In my files I have notes on 123 individuals whom I know by name. In addition, I spoke with most of the approximately two hundred active Center members, members of synagogues, Jewish and non-Jewish shoppers on the zibete and at the shopping center and other stores, and friends, neighbors, and family members of people with whom I became acquainted. As a result of the deaths of eldery Jews since 1980, the population has declined, and I assume the total number of South Philadelphia Jews to be somewhat less than the three to four thousand estimated by Rotman (1980: vii).

4. This sample is not necessarily representative of the whole Jewish population, only of the social networks I identified.

5. See Appendix D for the full Yiddish text.

6. Studies in the United States documented an increase in intermarriage for Jews and non-Jews from 20 percent in the 1920's to nearly 40 percent in the early 1980's. Moreover, as late as the 1940's, more than 60 percent of Americans at large disapproved of such marriages, whereas by 1980 almost 80 percent approved (Mayer 1985: 7, 48).

7. Cf. Keller's prediction that such a population might be willing to ignore ethnic and status differences in order to get help and fight loneliness (1968: 162).

Chapter Seven

1. "Sephardic" refers to the descendants of Jews who lived in Spain before their expulsion in 1492. They spoke Judezmo, whereas Ashkenazic Jews spoke Yiddish.

2. Standard Yiddish grammar requires an inversion of the verb, which would appear in the first position in the second clause: Oyb der pots shteyt, geyt der kop.

3. Instead of *vern*, the verbs usually used in this phrase are *lign* (lie, assume a horizontal position, die), and *hobn* (have) followed by a name or pronoun.

Chapter Eight

1. Standard Yiddish grammar would require the second clause to contain the second person singular nominative pronoun: *nisht du mir*, not *nisht dir mir*.

2. There were only two instances of convergence that related to dialectally specific phonological or lexical items:

My form	Informant's usual form	Gloss	Informant
leynen	leyzn	read	Izhak
man	mon	husband	Rivke B.

Rivke B. realized both [a] and [o] for this vowel (vowel 11 in the Yiddish proto-vowel system; Herzog 1965: 161), although [o] was more prevalent. (See Note to the Reader for usual pronunciation of Yiddish vowels.)

The following list shows the divergence in response to my choice of lexical item:

My form	Informant's form	Gloss	Informant
zitsung	miting (Eng. borrow.)	meeting	Yisrul
pleytim	bezhnitses (Russ. borrow.)	refugees	Yankl A.
ale	ile	all	Yankl A.
ufgehodevet	oysgehodevet	raised children	Reyzl
iberlebung	ekspiryens (Eng. borrow.)	experience	Reyzl
muzík	myúzik (Eng. borrow.)	music	Reyzl

The following example illustrates divergence both phonologically and syntactically in response to my speech:

R. P.: Ober ir hot gehat a gute dzhab. (But you had a good job.)
E.-S.: Ye, ikh ho(b) gehot, ye kho gehot a gitn dzhab. (Yeah, I had, yeah I had a good job.)

My statement had applied the rules for the case endings of adjectives in Yiddish, treating *dzhab* as a feminine noun. In response, Ester-Sosye used the usual adjectival case ending associated with the masculine accusative. In addition, she retained the [i] of her dialect for pronouncing the adjective *git* as well as the [o] for the past participle *gehot*, although I had used other phonological variants. The pronunciation [gut] seems to have spread beyond the northeastern dialect, perhaps reinforced by the English "good." In several instances residents responded to my *git* with *gut*, which is not characteristic of their dialect (e.g, Roze, Yisrul). This observation on the spread of the form *gut* (good) is reinforced by data from the Language and Culture Atlas of Ashkenazic Jewry, Columbia University (M. Herzog, personal communication).

In the following incidents, in response to my questions, the residents realized a phonological form different from the one I used:

My form	Informant's usual form	Gloss	Informant
freg (n)	frig	ask	Beyle
voynt	veynt	resides	Dveyre, Itke
gekumen	gekimen	came	Surele
farkoyft	farkeyft	sold	Izzy
fareyn	ferayn	landsmanshaft	Sure B.
noent	novnt (followed by nuvnt)	near	Feygl-Asye
nomen	numen	name	Itke

Ferayn, a modern borrowing from German, is the widespread term in Philadelphia for landsmanshaft, or Jewish fraternal organization, associated with a European hometown.

Chapter Nine

1. The contact of Yiddish with other languages and cultures in lands of immigration has been discussed for French, Spanish, and Portuguese (Levinski 1942; Lazdeyski 1941; Kutshinski 1941; M.V. 1941). Little research has been done on spoken Yiddish, but there is some evidence that Yiddish speech borrowed substantially from Russian in the Soviet Union after the Revolution (Zaretski 1930; 1931; Shtif 1930; Tsvayg 1930).

2. This example notwithstanding, I do not wish to imply that switches or borrowings serve only to fill lexical gaps. The lexicographer Mark, in planning a comprehensive dictionary, actually discussed the practical question of what should qualify as a word in the Yiddish language for inclusion in the dictionary. His conclusion was that it should be "every word used by a group of Jews while they think and speak Yiddish" (Mark 1958: 298).

3. In standard Yiddish, *mentsh* would be preceded by the definite article in both instances. Ester's usage seems to reflect English usage. This phrase is a word-for-word translation of the English, "God did not make man, man made God."

4. This is not to say that Yiddish is not also a source of expression of strong emotions. One of the least fluent Yiddish speakers was Basye B. Although she understood Yiddish, her participation in Yiddish in the Gleyzele tey conversation group consisted largely of word-for-word translations from English. During a phone conversation I had with her when she was in the hospital, which took place mostly in English, Basye B. expressed anger that Center members did not call her: "Ikh kak zey on" (I shit on them), she exclaimed. Nevertheless, when residents were speaking Yiddish, they often used English to express intense feelings.

5. *A keyshl* in standard Yiddish.

6. A Russian word; in Yiddish: *gevelb, kleyt, krom*.

7. I have found such usage in the diary of Glikl of Hameln, written between 1690 and 1720, and in collections of tales recorded in the field by folklorists. For example, in Glikl's diary, equivalents from the Germanic and Hebraic and Aramaic components are found together, *in der velt . . . beoylem haze* (*Die Memoiren der Glückel von Hameln*, ed. David Kaufmann, Frankfurt am Main, 1896, p. 1). In Yiddish folktales collected in the field, equivalents from Russian and Yiddish, Russian and Hebrew, and Hebraisms and elements of the Germanic component appear together:

Wasche Prewoss choditjestub—Woss farlangt ir (What do you wish)
mi daf-l'daf—midoske l'doske (from cover to cover)
hint—klowim (dogs)
an oreman—a oni w'ewjejn (a poor man)
darzejlen fun schejschess j'mejbrejschiss—ret un ret un ret (talks endlessly)
finster—chejschech (dark) (Immanuel Olsvanger, *Rosinkess mit Mandlen: Aus der Volksliteratur der Ostjuden: Schwanke, Erzahlungen, Sprichworter und Ratsel*. 2d ed. [Basel: Verlag der Schweizerischen Gesellschaft für Volkskunde, 1931], pp. 118, 120–21, 98, 99, 286, 41, 23, 287).

fakh—melokhe (trade) (Shmuel Lehman, "Ganovim un gneyve," in *Bay undz yidn*, ed. M. Vanvild, Warsaw, 1923, p. 69).

tsuzamen—beshutfes (together) (Y.-L. Kahan, "Mayses un mesores," in *Yidisher folklor* [*Filologishe shriftn*, vol. 5], Vilna: Yivo, 1938, p. 168).

8. For example, in locations exhibiting the northeastern European dialect, "calves' foot jelly" is termed *fisnoge* or *fisribe*, a compound in which each component means "foot." Another example is the use of *bald zaras* (soon) in the Polish Yiddish dialect (from the Language and Culture Atlas, Columbia University, personal communication, M. Herzog).

9. Note that Tsipe-Khashe, whose parents came from Lithuania, realized deviations from the general Yiddish patterns of hissing and hushing sibilants, pronouncing "soldiers," which is borrowed from English, with a hissing affricate, *soldzerz*. Such pronunciation was characteristic in Lithuania at the beginning of the century. I discuss this phenomenon later in this chapter.

10. The verb "to move" is not generally borrowed; when it is, it is used to refer to a change of residence, not to a change in the location of an object—e.g., to move a chair.

11. South Philadelphia–born children of immigrants demonstrated many examples of borrowing and loan translation from Yiddish into English speech— for example, "My father-in-law used to hit me up" (watch over me) and "they used to tsiter over me" (to be nervous about —Itke), "when it kimts me on" (when I get an urge —Sheyndl), "let him be well" (translation of the common Yiddish parenthetical wish, *zol er zayn gezunt* —Blumke).

It has been claimed that the English-language behavior of American Jews reflects the Yiddish in their background. Two sociolinguistic investigations of face-to-face interaction in the English conversation of small groups of American Jews characterized the conversation as fast-moving (Tannen 1981) and argumentative (Schiffrin 1984). These studies were limited to a single dinner conversation in the former case and living-room meetings of one small group of neighbors in the latter case. Thus, these authors have made broad generalizations about "New York Jewish" and "Jewish" style based on extremely limited observation. The present study analyzed Yiddish speech in private conversations with residents and in the Gleyzele tey group discussions. Although some simultaneous speaking or speech overlap occurred in the former situations and some arguing in the latter setting, it was not possible to conclude that those properties were characteristic of Yiddish speech, or for that matter Jewish speech, in South Philadelphia.

12. According to Tabak, "Preliminary data indicate that a large minority of Philadelphia Jews came from the Ukraine in general and from Kiev province and immediately adjoining areas in particular" (1983: 51).

13. Trudgill describes dialect mixing as a process in which accommodation is apparent on the lexical level but stylistic variability is evident; phonetically intermediate forms are not present (1986: 59–60, 108–10).

14. In the numbering scheme of the *Language and Culture Atlas of Ashkenazic*

Jewry, this corresponds to vowel 12 in the Yiddish proto-vowel system, and the re-alizations are represented as u_{12} and o_{12}, respectively (Herzog 1965: 161).

15. In South Philadelphia the designation "Russian" applied almost exclusively to Jews from Ukraine.

16. In the northeastern or *litvish* dialect, the verbal prefix would be pronounced [op]. The verb *shmadn* is used with humor intended.

17. The vowel i_{25}, common to South Philadelphia and to the Yiddish in north-ern Ukraine, was not observed in Itke's speech. The vowel o_{11}, realized by most Ukrainian Yiddish speakers, was pronounced by Itke as *kolte* (cold), but she real-ized a_{11} in *gehat* (had), *tate* (father), *andere* (other), *khazer* (pig), not as Ukrainian Yiddish speakers would talk: *gehot, tote, ondere, khozer*. For example, she referred to her sister-in-law as a *kolte englishe khazer* (a cold English pig). In addition, she exhibited most commonly the deviation from northeastern Yiddish o_{12} and vari-able deviation from $u_{51, 52}$. See Peltz (1990a: 61–62).

18. The phenomenon of *sabesdiker losn*, pronounced in general in Yiddish as *shabesdiker loshn*, refers to the phonetic realization of /s/ and /š/ and the parallel hissing and hushing voiced sibilants and affricates in northeastern Yiddish. The most significant phonetic data based on fieldwork are found in Veynger (1928; 1929). His findings may be summarized as follows: The appearance of hissing phones, where hushing occurs in general Yiddish, is more common than the con-verse. Hushing is especially conditioned by a following /i/. Intermediary sounds are realized. The phenomenon occurs to the greatest extent in the Kovne-Vilna re-gion. The phenomenon is absent in the southwestern part of the Northeastern Yiddish dialect area. Variation was observed within the population at one location and for different words realized by a single individual. Historical issues are treated by U. Weinreich (1952), and the phonetic data, including information from the Lanaguage and Culture Atlas of Ashkenazic Jewry, are summarized by Peltz (1982).

Chapter Ten

1. Of some relevance to the present study is the demonstration of differences in phonological variables in English across ethnic groups (LaFerriere 1979). Labov's early sociolinguistic research focused on how the identity of three ethnic groups related to the awareness of a phonological feature (1972a: 1–42). In his subsequent work, he studied attitudinal differences toward New York City speech among eth-nic groups (Labov 1982: 351–53). An array of studies showed that positive feelings toward one's own language usually reflect the fact that language is a marker of a desirable group identity (Saville-Troike 1989: 200–204). Frake's ethnographic work describes how language differences are dimensions of ethnic differentiation and ranking (1980a; 1980b). In New Guinea, communities purposely cultivate lin-guistic difference as a marker of group identity (Kulick 1992: 2). Stereotypes are conveyed by style of speech and language choice (Taylor 1977: 68; Williams 1983). Edwards (1985) provides a comprehensive review of language and ethnic iden-tity, concluding that although language is an important part of group identity, a sense of group continuity can be maintained without necessarily retaining an

original language variety. Scollon and Scollon, drawing on their work on inter-ethnic communication, define an ethnic group as a communicative system that persists in the face of outside pressure and change (1981: 194–98). My research is concerned with the dynamics of the persistence and change of language and group identification.

Chapter Eleven

1. Other instances indicate that Roth (1991: 16) knew better than to use a German pronoun and an auxiliary verb that no Yiddish or German speaker would use: "Gehen vir voinen du? In Nev York?" "Nein, Bronzeville. Ich hud dir schoin geschriben."

2. National Yiddish Book Center Summer Institute, Hampshire College, June 27, 1986.

3. Northampton, home of Smith College, is a city of 30,000, with a Jewish population that numbers about 2,000. The one synagogue has a membership of 300 families. Most of the older members were born in Northampton or Springfield, children of immigrants. None of the original East European immigrants are alive. In 1986, for the first time in the history of the local synagogue, Congregation B'nai Israel, a group of members mostly between the ages of 65 and 75, established a seniors group. See Peltz 1991: 196–98.

Chapter Twelve

1. Because of my focus on the generation of children of immigrants, I generally neglect for the present purposes the kindred research concerns of ethnic group language, culture, and identity of African Americans, Native Americans, and deaf Americans. In dealing with the ethnicity of immigrant groups, historians and sociologists have largely adhered either to theories of assimilation into the "melting pot," which accepts the dislodging and disappearance of the group-specific heritage, or ethnicization, which postulates the alteration yet retention of group-specific culture through mixing and blending with the ways of the dominant group. For a recent discussion of these issues, see Morawska 1994. Relatively little has been done to chart a theoretical middle ground, to emphasize the similarities in the two theoretical approaches, or to integrate the analysis of multiple and overlapping identities.

2. As McGoldrick writes, "To understand ethnic norms, one must maintain a developmental perspective on both variations in family life cycle patterns and the impact that immigration has on families over succeeding generations" (1993: 342).

3. Treatises that purport to review Yiddish in America have described social institutions, such as the press, without mentioning spoken language (Shtarkman 1939; Doroshkin 1969). There has been no extensive publication of texts of spoken Yiddish analogous to the early work on American Norwegian (Haugen 1953). Interview projects with American Yiddish speakers either recorded only English (Myerhoff 1978a) or neglected to present aspects of Yiddish language (Mintz

1968). One study, however, has discussed language choice and switching (Kirshen-blatt-Gimblett 1972: 330–84). Much of the extant research analyzes macrosociology (J. Fishman 1965; Gertner, Fishman, Lowy, and Milan 1983; Lowy et al. 1983; J. Fishman, ed., 1985). Only Heilman's microsociolinguistic study examines language in a natural setting (1983: 160–200). Other reports present the results of formal linguistic tests and questionnaires (Slobin 1963; Jochnowitz 1968; Ronch, Cooper, and Fishman 1969).

Slobin was not interested in how the informants spoke in America, but in how they had spoken Yiddish in Europe. He designed his questions to "reinstate the set of speaking Yiddish in its native environment in the past . . . establishing the set of viewing social relations through the eyes of a young person from the perspective of middle- or old-age" (1963: 195–96). The largest archive of Yiddish spoken by American immigrants has been compiled in the Language and Culture Atlas of Ashkenazic Jewry at Columbia University (Herzog 1965, 1992; Herzog et al. 1969); however, from this collection it would be difficult to tell how Yiddish is spoken in neighborhoods and families in America.

4. In the Jewish communities I have studied, only in Northampton are younger generations present, children and grandchildren of Jews from other locations who have chosen Northampton as home. But the opportunities for intergenerational education are few.

5. The Florida newsletter is *Undzer shtime—Our Voice*, published by the Circle of Yiddish Clubs, Jewish Community Center, Plantation, Florida; the Peninsula Jewish Community Center of Belmont, California (near San Francisco) publishes a similar newsletter, *Der bay: The Golden Gate to the Yiddish Community*.

6. This phenomenon is evidence that: "The primary function of language is formative or rhetorical. . . . This enables the crafting, the social construction of certain devices, particularly *ways* of speaking . . . for use in co-ordinating and sequentially ordering complex and intricate activities (and their outcomes) among large numbers of people over large distances and long times" (Shotter 1989: 148–49).

7. "Experience and memory of the social world are powerfully structured not only by deeply internalized and narrativized conceptions of folk psychology but also by the historically rooted institutions that a culture elaborates to support and enforce them" (Bruner 1990: 57).

Bibliography

Aguilar, John L. 1981. "Insider Research: An Ethnography of a Debate." In Donald A. Messerschmidt, ed., *Anthropologists at Home in North America*, pp. 15–28. Cambridge, Eng.: Cambridge University Press.

Amoss, Pamela T. 1981. "Cultural Centrality and Prestige for the Elderly: The Coast Salish Case." In Christine L. Fry, ed., *Dimensions: Aging, Culture, and Health*, pp. 47–63. South Hadley, Mass.: Bergin and Garvey.

Anderson, Roger W. 1989. "The 'Up' and 'Down' Staircase in Secondary Language Development." In Dorian, ed., 1989, pp. 385–94.

Aronowitz, Stanley. 1992. *The Politics of Identity: Class, Culture, Social Movements*. New York: Routledge.

———. 1993. *Roll Over Beethoven: The Return of Cultural Strife*. Middletown, Conn.: Wesleyan University Press.

Barth, Fredrik. 1969. "Introduction." In Fredrik Barth, ed., *Ethnic Groups and Boundaries*, pp. 9–38. Boston: Little, Brown.

Beckett, Samuel. 1956. *Malone Dies*. Translated from French by the author. New York: Grove Press.

Bender, Thomas. 1978. *Community and Social Change in America*. Baltimore, Md.: The Johns Hopkins University Press.

Berger, H. 1956. *Di geshikhte fun der leybor layseum bavegung in Filadelfye*. Philadelphia: Labor Educational Center.

Berk-Seligson, Susan. 1986. "Linguistic Constraints on Intrasentential Code-switching: A Study of Spanish/Hebrew Bilingualism." *Language in Society* 15: 313–48.

Berman, Rochel, Audrey S. Weiner, and Gella S. Fishman. 1986. "Yiddish: It's More Than a Language: In-Service Training for Staff of a Jewish Home for the Aged." *Journal of Jewish Communal Service* 62: 328–34.

Bernheimer, Charles, ed. 1905. *The Russian Jew in the United States*. Philadelphia: John C. Winston Co.

Briggs, Charles L. 1985. "The Pragmatics of Proverb Performances in New Mexican Spanish." *American Anthropologist* 87: 793–810.

Bruner, Jerome. 1990. *Acts of Meaning*. Cambridge, Mass.: Harvard University Press.

Butler, Robert N. 1963. "The Life Review: An Interpretation of Reminiscence in the Aged." *Psychiatry* 26: 65–76.

————. 1970. "Looking Forward to What?: The Life Review, Legacy, and Excessive Identity Versus Change." *American Behavioral Scientist* 14: 121–28.

Chrisman, Noel J. 1976. "Secret Societies and the Ethics of Urban Fieldwork." In Michael A. Rynkiewich and James P. Spradley, eds., *Ethics and Anthropology: Dilemmas in Fieldwork*, pp. 135–47. New York: John Wiley.

Christian, Barbara. 1990. "The Race for Theory." In JanMohamed and Lloyd, eds., 1990b, pp. 37–49.

Cicourel, Aaron V. 1985. "Text and Discourse." *Annual Review of Anthropology* 14: 159–85.

City of Philadelphia. 1985. *South Philadelphia*.

Clyne, Michael G. 1984. "The Decade Past, the Decade to Come: Some Thoughts on Language-Contact Research." *International Journal of the Sociology of Language* 45: 9–20.

Cohen, Oscar, and Stanley Wexler, eds. 1987. *'Not the Work of a Day': Anti-Defamation League of B'nai B'rith Oral Memoirs*. New York: Anti-Defamation League of the B'nai B'rith.

Coleman, Peter G. 1991. "Ageing and Life History: The Meaning of Reminiscence in Late Life." In Shirley Dex, ed., *Life and Work History Analysis: Qualitative and Quantitative Developments*, pp. 120–43. London: Routledge.

Connerton, Paul. 1989. *How Societies Remember*. Cambridge, Eng.: Cambridge University Press.

Coupland, Nikolas, and Jon F. Nussbaum, eds. 1993. *Discourse and Lifespan Identity*. Newbury Park, Calif.: Sage Publications.

Coupland, Nikolas, Justine Coupland, and Howard Giles. 1991. *Language, Society and the Elderly: Discourse, Identity and Ageing*. Oxford, Eng.: Blackwell.

Coupland, Nikolas, Jon F. Nussbaum, and Alan Grossman. 1993. "Introduction: Discourse, Selfhood, and the Lifespan." In Coupland and Nussbaum, eds., 1993, pp. x–xxviii.

Cronen, Vernon E., Victoria Chen, and W. Barnett Pearce. 1988. "Coordinated Management of Meaning: A Critical Theory." In Young Y. Kim and William B. Gudykunst, eds., *Theories in International Communication*, pp. 66–98. Newbury Park, Calif.: Sage Publications.

Davies, Bronwyn, and Rom Harre. 1990. "Positioning: The Discursive Production of Selves." *Journal of the Theory of Social Behaviour* 20: 43–63.

Dawidowicz, Lucy, ed. 1967. *The Golden Tradition: Jewish Life and Thought in Eastern Europe*. New York: Holt, Rinehart, and Winston.

De Camp, David. 1971. "Toward a Generative Analysis of a Post-Creole Speech Continuum." In Dell Hymes, ed., *Pidginization and Creolization of Languages*, pp. 349–70. Cambridge, Eng.: Cambridge University Press.

De Vos, George. 1975. "Ethnic Pluralism: Conflict and Accommodation." In De Vos and Romanucci-Ross, eds., 1975b, pp. 5–41.

De Vos, George, and Lola Romanucci-Ross. 1975a. "Ethnicity: Vessel of Meaning and Emblem of Contrast." In De Vos and Romanucci-Ross, eds., 1975b, pp. 363–90.

————, eds. 1975b. *Ethnic Identity: Cultural Continuities and Change*. Palo Alto, Calif.: Mayfield Publishing Co.

di Leonardo, Micaela. 1984. *The Varieties of Ethnic Experience: Kinship, Class, and Gender Among California Italian-Americans*. Ithaca, N.Y.: Cornell University Press.

Doi, Mary L. 1991. "The Transformation of Ritual: The Nisei 60th Birthday." *Journal of Cross-Cultural Gerontology* 6: 153–63.

Dorian, Nancy C. 1981. *Language Death: The Life Cycle of a Scottish Gaelic Dialect*. Philadelphia: University of Pennsylvania Press.

———. 1982a. "Linguistic Models and Language Death Evidence." In Obler and Menn, eds., 1982, pp. 31–48.

———. 1982b. "Defining the Speech Community to Include Its Working Margins." In Romaine, ed., 1982, pp. 25–33.

———, ed. 1989. *Investigating Obsolescence: Studies in Language Contraction and Death*. Cambridge, Eng.: Cambridge University Press.

Doroshkin, Milton. 1969. *Yiddish in America: Social and Cultural Foundations*. Rutherford, N.J.: Fairleigh Dickinson University Press.

Dubin, Murray. 1996. *South Philadelphia*. Philadelphia: Temple University Press.

Eastman, Carol M. 1992a. "Codeswitching as an Urban Language-Contact Phenomenon." In Eastman, ed., 1992b, pp. 1–17.

———, ed. 1992b. *Codeswitching*. Clevedon, Eng.: Multilingual Matters.

Eastman, Carol M., and Thomas C. Reese. 1981. "Associated Language: How Language and Ethnic Identity Are Related." *General Linguistics* 21: 109–16.

Eckert, Penelope. 1984. "Age and Linguistic Change." In David I. Kertzer and Jennie Keith, eds., *Age and Anthropological Theory*, pp. 219–33. Ithaca, N.Y.: Cornell University Press.

Edwards, John. 1985. *Language, Society and Identity*. Oxford, Eng.: Basil Blackwell.

Elshtain, Jean B. 1995. *Democracy on Trial*. New York: Basic Books.

Emery, Olga B. 1985. "Language and Aging." *Experimental Aging Research* 11: 3–61.

Erikson, Erik H. 1968. "Life Cycle." In David L. Sills, ed., *International Encyclopedia of the Social Sciences*. Vol. 9, pp. 286–92. New York: Macmillan and Free Press.

———. 1975. *Life History and the Historic Moment*. New York: W. W. Norton.

Erikson, Erik H., Joan M. Erikson, and Helen Q. Kivnik. 1986. *Vital Involvement in Old Age*. New York: W. W. Norton.

Escobar, Arturo. 1993. "The Limits of Reflexivity: Politics in Anthropology's Post-Writing Culture Era." *Journal of Anthropological Research* 49: 377–91.

Fabian, Johannes. 1990. *Power and Performance: Ethnographic Explorations Through Proverbial Wisdom and Theater in Shaba, Zaire*. Madison: University of Wisconsin Press.

Ferguson, Charles A. 1982. "Simplified Registers and Linguistic Theory." In Obler and Menn, eds., 1982, pp. 49–66.

Fillmore, Charles J. 1979. "On Fluency." In Charles J. Fillmore, Daniel Kempler, and William S. Y. Wang, eds., *Individual Differences in Language Ability and Language Behavior*, pp. 85–101. New York: Academic Press.

Fishman, Joshua A. 1965. *Yiddish in America*. The Hague: Mouton.

———. 1980. "Theoretical Issues and Problems in the Sociolinguistic Enterprise."

Annual Review of Applied Linguistics 1: 161–67.

———. 1981. "The Sociology of Yiddish: A Foreword." In Joshua A. Fishman, ed., *Never Say Die!*, pp. 1–97. The Hague: Mouton.

———, ed. 1985. *The Rise and Fall of the Ethnic Revival: Perspectives on Language and Ethnicity*. Berlin: Walter de Gruyter.

Fishman, Shikl. 1982. "Yidish, modernizatsye un reetnifikatsye: An ernster un faktndiker tsugang tsu der itstiker problematik." *Afn shvel* 248: 1–7.

Frake, Charles O. 1980a. "Languages in Yakan Culture." In *Language and Cultural Description*, pp. 233–52. Stanford, Calif.: Stanford University Press.

———. 1980b. "The Genesis of Kinds of People in the Sulu Archipelago." In *Language and Cultural Description*, pp. 311–32. Stanford, Calif.: Stanford University Press.

Frakes, Jerold C. 1989. *The Politics of Interpretation: Alterity and Ideology in Old Yiddish Studies*. Albany: State University of New York Press.

Freeman, Moses. 1929. *Fuftsik yor geshikhte fun yidishn lebn in filadelfye*. Philadelphia: Mid-City Press.

Gal, Susan. 1989. "Lexical Innovation and Loss: The Use and Value of Restricted Hungarian." In Dorian, ed., 1989, pp. 313–31.

Gallaher, Art, and Harland Padfield, eds. 1980. *The Dying Community*. Albuquerque: University of New Mexico Press.

Gans, Herbert J. 1979. "Symbolic Ethnicity: The Future of Ethnic Groups and Cultures in America." *Ethnic and Racial Studies* 2: 1–20.

Geertz, Clifford. 1973. *The Interpretation of Cultures*. New York: Basic Books.

———. 1983. *Local Knowledge: Further Essays in Interpretive Anthropology*. New York: Basic Books.

Gelfand, Donald E. 1982. *Aging: The Ethnic Factor*. Boston: Little, Brown.

Gerson, Kathleen, C. Ann Stueve, and Claude S. Fischer. 1977. "Attachment to Place." In Claude S. Fischer et al., eds., *Networks and Places: Social Relations in the Urban Setting*, pp. 139–61. New York: Free Press.

Gertner, Michael H., Joshua A. Fishman, Esther G. Lowy, and William G. Milan. 1983. "Language and Ethnicity in the Periodical Publications of Four American Ethnic Groups." *Multilingua* 2: 83–99.

Gibson, Margaret. 1988. *Accommodation Without Assimilation: Sikh Immigrants in an American High School*. Ithaca, N.Y.: Cornell University Press.

Giddens, Anthony. 1990. *The Consequences of Modernity*. Stanford, Calif.: Stanford University Press.

———. 1991. *Modernity and Self-Identity: Self and Society in the Late Modern Age*. Stanford, Calif.: Stanford University Press.

Giles, Howard. 1979. "Ethnicity Markers in Speech." In Klaus R. Scherer and Howard Giles, eds., *Social Markers in Speech*, pp. 251–89. Cambridge, Eng.: Cambridge University Press.

Giles, Howard, and Nikolas Coupland. 1991. *Language: Contexts and Consequences*. Pacific Grove, Calif.: Brooks/Cole.

Gilman, Sander. 1986. *Jewish Self-Hatred: Anti-Semitism and the Hidden Language of the Jews*. Baltimore, Md.: The Johns Hopkins University Press.

Glazer, Nathan, and Daniel P. Moynihan. 1963. *Beyond the Melting Pot*. Cambridge, Mass.: MIT Press.

Golab, Caroline. 1977. *Immigrant Destinations*. Philadelphia: Temple University Press.

Goldstein, Sidney, and Calvin Goldscheider. 1968. *Jewish Americans: Three Generations in a Jewish Community*. Englewood Cliffs, N.J.: Prentice-Hall.

Green, Eugene. 1962. "Yiddish and English in Detroit." Ph.D. diss., University of Michigan.

Greifer, Julian L. 1948. "Neighborhood Center—a Study of the Adjustment of a Cultural Group in America." Ph.D. diss., New York University.

———. 1958. MS in Neighborhood Center collection, Philadelphia Jewish Archives Center, Balch Institute for Ethnic Affairs, Philadelphia, MSS 10/3, Box 1, Folder 1. Draft of address to the tenth anniversary celebration of the Neighborhood Center South.

Gupta, Akhil, and James Ferguson. 1992. "Beyond 'Culture': Space, Identity, and the Politics of Difference." *Cultural Anthropology* 7: 6–23.

Gutmans, T. 1958. "Di shprakh fun a yidisher radyo-stantsye in Nyu-York." *Yidishe shprakh* 18: 65–72.

Gysels, Marjolein. 1992. "French in Urban Lubumbashi Swahili: Codeswitching, Borrowing, or Both." In Eastman, ed., 1992b, pp. 41–55.

Hakuta, Kenji. 1986. *Mirror of Language: The Debate on Bilingualism*. New York: Basic Books.

Halbwachs, Maurice. 1992 [1925]. "The Social Frameworks of Memory." In Maurice Halbwachs, *On Collective Memory*, pp. 35–189. Ed., trans. Lewis A. Coser. Chicago: University of Chicago Press.

Hannerz, Ulf. 1992. *Cultural Complexity: Studies in the Social Organization of Meaning*. New York: Columbia University Press.

Hare, Paul, Edgar F. Borgatta, and Robert F. Bales. 1955. *Small Groups: Studies in Social Interaction*. New York: Alfred A. Knopf.

Harre, Rom. 1989. "Language Games and Texts of Identity." In John Shotter and Kenneth J. Gergen, eds., *Texts of Identity*, pp. 20–35. London: Sage Publications.

Harshav, Benjamin. 1990. *The Meaning of Yiddish*. Berkeley: University of California Press.

Harshav, Benjamin, and Barbara Harshav, eds. 1986. *American Yiddish Poetry: A Bilingual Anthology*. Berkeley: University of California Press.

Hartsock, Nancy. 1990. "Rethinking Modernism: Minority vs. Majority Theories." In JanMohamed and Lloyd, eds., 1990b, pp. 17–36.

Haugen, Einar. 1950. "The Analysis of Linguistic Borrowing." *Language* 26: 210–31.

———. 1953. *The Norwegian Language in America*. Vol. 2. Philadelphia: University of Pennsylvania Press.

———. 1977. "Norm and Deviation in Bilingual Communities." In Hornby, ed., 1977, pp. 91–102.

———. 1989. "The Rise and Fall of an Immigrant Language: Norwegian in America." In Dorian, ed., 1989, pp. 61–73.

Heilman, Samuel C. 1983. *The People of the Book*. Chicago: University of Chicago Press.

Heller, Monica. 1988. "Introduction." In Monica Heller, ed., *Codeswitching: Anthropological and Sociolinguistic Perspectives*, pp. 1–24. Berlin: Mouton de Gruyter.

Hellerstein, Kathryn. 1988. "A Question of Tradition: Women Poets in Yiddish." In Lewis Fried, ed., *Handbook of American-Jewish Literature*, pp. 195–237. New York: Greenwood Press.

Herzog, Marvin I. 1965. *The Yiddish Language in Northern Poland*. The Hague: Mouton.

———. 1969. "Yiddish in the Ukraine: Isoglosses and Historical Inferences." In Marvin I. Herzog, Wita Ravid, and Uriel Weinreich, eds., 1969.

———, ed. 1992. *The Language and Culture Atlas of Ashkenazic Jewry*. Vol. 1. Tübingen: Max Niemeyer Verlag.

Herzog, Marvin I., Wita Ravid, and Uriel Weinreich, eds. 1969. *The Field of Yiddish*. 3d collection. The Hague: Mouton.

Hewitt, John P. 1989. *Dilemmas of the American Self*. Philadelphia: Temple University Press.

Hindle, Donald M. 1979. "The Social and Situational Conditioning of Phonetic Variation." Ph.D. diss., University of Pennsylvania.

Hoffman, Gerard, and Joshua A. Fishman. 1971. "Life in the Neighborhood." *International Journal of Comparative Sociology* 12: 85–100.

Holzberg, Carol. 1982. "Ethnicity and Aging: Anthropological Perspectives on More Than Just the Minority Elderly." *Gerontologist* 22: 249–57.

Hornby, Peter A., ed. 1977. *Bilingualism: Psychological, Social and Educational Implications*. New York: Academic Press.

Howe, Irving. 1946. "The Lost Young Intellectual: A Marginal Man, Twice Alienated." *Commentary* 2: 361–67.

———. 1982. *A Margin of Hope: An Intellectual Autobiography*. New York: Harcourt Brace Jovanovich.

Hummon, David M. 1990. *Commonplaces: Community Ideology and Identity in American Culture*. Albany: State University of New York Press.

Inoue, Yashusi. 1982. *Chronicle of My Mother*. Trans. Jean O. Moy. Tokyo: Kodansha International.

Irvine, Judith. 1985. "Status and Style in Language." *Annual Review of Anthropology* 14: 557–86.

Itskovits, H. 1944. "A zitsung oyf a reynem yidish." *Yidishe shprakh* 4: 114–20.

JanMohamed, Abdul R., and David Lloyd. 1990a. "Introduction: Toward a Theory of Minority Discourse: What Is to Be Done?" In JanMohamed and Lloyd, eds., 1990b, pp. 1–16.

———, eds. 1990b. *The Nature and Context of Minority Discourse*. New York: Oxford University Press.

Jochnowitz, George. 1968. "Bilingualism and Dialect Mixture Among Lubavitcher Hasidic Children." *American Speech* 43: 182–200.

Joffe, Judah A. 1936. "Yidish in amerike." *Yivo-bleter* 10: 127–45.

———. 1943. "The Development of Yiddish in the United States." In *The Universal Jewish Encyclopedia*, Vol. 10, pp. 601–2.

Joselit, Jenna Weissman. 1994. *The Wonders of America: Reinventing Jewish Culture 1880–1950*. New York: Hill and Wang.

Kaminsky, Marc. 1984. "The Uses of Reminiscence: A Discussion of the Formative Literature." In Marc Kaminsky, ed., *The Uses of Reminiscence: New Ways of Working with Older Adults*, pp. 137–56. New York: Haworth Press.

———. 1992. "Story of the Shoebox: The Meaning and Practice of Transmitting Stories." In Thomas R. Cole, David D. Van Tassel, and Robert Kastenbaum, eds., *Handbook of the Humanities and Aging*, pp. 307–27. New York: Springer.

Karp, Florence Berman. 1983. *Roses in December: A Memoir of My Parents*. Pittsburgh, Penn.: Wolfson.

Kaufman, Sharon. 1981. "Cultural Components of Identity in Old Age." *Ethos* 9: 51–87.

Keller, M. Jean, and Mary Ann McArdle. 1985. "Establishing Intergenerational Exchange Opportunities." *Activities, Adaptation and Aging* 7: 31–43.

Keller, Suzanne. 1968. *The Urban Neighborhood*. New York: Random House.

Kellogg, Susan. 1990. "Exploring Diversity in Middle-Class Families: The Symbolism of American Ethnic Identity." *Social Science History* 14: 27–41.

Kertzer, David I. 1988. *Ritual, Politics, and Power*. New Haven, Conn.: Yale University Press.

Kertzer, David I., and Jennie Keith, eds. 1984. *Age and Anthropological Theory*. Ithaca, N.Y.: Cornell University Press.

Kirshenblatt-Gimblett, Barbara. 1972. "Traditional Storytelling in the Toronto Jewish Community." Ph.D. diss., Indiana University.

———. 1973. "Toward a Theory of Proverb Meaning." *Proverbium* 22: 821–27.

———, ed. 1986. *Folksongs in the East European Jewish Tradition*, booklet accompanying sound recording. Global Village Music GVM 117.

Klepfisz, Irena. 1994. "*Di mames, dos loshn*/The Mothers, the Language: Feminism, *Yidishkayt*, and the Politics of Memory." *Bridges* 4: 12–47.

Knight, Lisa, Rakhmiel Peltz, and Susan Pintzuk. 1983. "The 17th Street Area: The Jews of South Philadelphia." Unpublished paper, Linguistics Department, University of Pennsylvania.

Krause, Corinne Azen. 1979. *Grandmothers, Mothers and Daughters: An Oral History Study of Ethnicity, Mental Health, and Continuity of Three Generations of Jewish, Italian, and Slavic-American Women*. New York: Institute on Pluralism and Group Identity of the American Jewish Committee.

Kroskrity, Paul V. 1985. "Language Death in Western Mono." Paper presented at the Annual Meeting of the American Anthropological Association, Washington, D.C.

———. 1993. *Language, History, and Identity: Ethnolinguistic Studies of the Arizona Tewa*. Tucson: University of Arizona Press.

Kulick, Don. 1992. *Language Shift and Cultural Reproduction: Socialization, Self, and Syncretism in a Papua New Guinean Village*. Cambridge, Eng.: Cambridge University Press.

Kutshinski, Meyer. 1941. "Yidish un di landshprakhn in latayn-amerike: portugezishe elementn in yidish." *Yivo-bleter* 18: 207–14.

Labov, William. 1972a. *Sociolinguistic Patterns*. Philadelphia: University of Pennsylvania Press.

———. 1972b. *Language in the Inner City: Studies in the Black English Vernacular*. Philadelphia: University of Pennsylvania Press.

———. 1982. *The Social Stratification of English in New York City*. 3d ed. Washington, D.C.: Center for Applied Linguistics.

———. 1984. "Field Methods of the Project on Linguistic Change and Variation." In John Baugh and Joel Sherzer, eds., *Language in Use: Readings in Sociolinguistics*, pp. 28–53. Englewood Cliffs, N.J.: Prentice-Hall.

Labov, William, and Joshua Waletzky. 1967. "Narrative Analysis." In June Helm, ed., *Essays on the Verbal and Visual Arts*, pp. 12–44. Seattle: University of Washington Press.

Laferriere, Martha. 1979. "Ethnicity in Phonological Variation and Change." *Language* 55: 603–17.

Lambert, Wallace E. 1977. "The Effects of Bilingualism on the Individual: Cognitive and Sociocultural Consequences." In Hornby, ed., pp. 15–27.

Landesman, Alter F. 1969. *Brownsville*. 2d ed. New York: Bloch.

Lasch, Christopher. 1978. *The Culture of Narcissism*. New York: Basic Books.

———. 1995. *The Revolt of the Elites and the Betrayal of Democracy*. New York: W. W. Norton.

Lash, Scott, and Jonathan Friedman, eds. 1992. *Modernity and Identity*. Oxford, Eng.: Basil Blackwell.

Lasson, Robert. 1984. "It's Fourth St.—of Another Time." *Jewish Exponent*, February 24, 48–49.

Lave, Jean, and Etienne Wenger. 1991. *Situated Learning: Legitimate Peripheral Participation*. Cambridge, Eng.: Cambridge University Press.

Lazdeyski, Khayim. 1941. "Yidish un di landshprakhn in latayn-amerike: shpanishe elimentn in yidish." *Yivo-bleter* 18: 204–7.

Le Page, R. B., and Andree Tabouret-Keller. 1985. *Acts of Identity: Creole-Based Approaches to Language and Ethnicity*. Cambridge, Eng.: Cambridge University Press.

Lehiste, Ilse. 1975. "The Attitude of Bilinguals Toward Their Personal Names." *American Speech* 50: 30–35.

Leibowitz, N. 1931. "Die Uebersetzungstechnik der judisch-deutschen Bibelübersetzungen des XV. und XVI. Jahrhunderts, dargestellt an den Psalmen." *Beiträge zur Geschichte der deutschen Sprache und Literatur* 55: 377–463.

Levinski, M. 1942. "Frantseyzishe verter inem parizer yidish." In A. Tsherikover, ed., *Yidn in frankraykh*, pp. 193–204. New York: Yivo.

Liebkind, Karmela. 1989a. "Introduction." In Liebkind, ed., 1989c, pp. 1–5.

———. 1989b. "Conceptual Approaches to Ethnic Identity." In Liebkind, ed., 1989c, pp. 25–40.

———, ed. 1989c. *New Identities in Europe: Immigrant Ancestry and the Ethnic Identity of Youth*. Hants, Eng.: Gower.

Light, Leah L., and Shirley A. Albertson. 1988. "Comprehension of Pragmatic Implications in Young and Older Adults." In Light and Burke, eds., 1988, pp. 133–53.

Light, Leah L., and Deborah M. Burke, eds. 1988. *Language, Memory, and Aging*. Cambridge, Eng.: Cambridge University Press.

Linde, Charlotte. 1993. *Life Stories: The Creation of Coherence*. New York: Oxford University Press.

Lloyd, David. 1993. *Anomalous States: Irish Writing and the Post-Colonial Moment*. Durham: Duke University Press.

Logan, John R., and Harvey L. Molotch. 1987. *Urban Fortunes: The Political Economy of Place.* Berkeley: University of California Press.

Lowenstein, Steven M. 1989. *Frankfurt on the Hudson: The German-Jewish Community of Washington Heights, 1933–1983, Its Structure and Culture.* Detroit: Wayne State University Press.

Lowenthal, David. 1985. *The Past Is a Foreign Country.* Cambridge, Eng.: Cambridge University Press.

Lowy, Esther G., Joshua A. Fishman, Michael H. Gertner, Itzek Gottesman, and William G. Milan. 1983. "Ethnic Activists View the Ethnic Revival and Its Language Consequences." *Journal of Multilingual and Multicultural Development* 4: 237–54.

Luborsky, Mark R., and Robert L. Rubinstein. 1990. "Ethnic Identity and Bereavement in Later Life: The Case of Older Widowers." In Sokolovsky, ed., 1990, pp. 229–40.

M. V. 1941. "Yidish un di landshprakhn in latayn-amerike." *Yivo-bleter* 18: 203–4.

McGoldrick, Monica. 1993. "Ethnicity, Cultural Diversity, and Normality." In Froma Walsh, ed., *Normal Family Processes*, pp. 331–60. New York: Guilford Press.

McGoldrick, Monica, John K. Pearce, and Joseph Giordano, eds. 1982. *Ethnicity and Family Therapy.* New York: Guilford Press.

Malamut, J. 1942–43. *Filadelfyer yidishe anshtaltn un zeyere firer.* Philadelphia.

Marcus, George. 1992. "Past, Present and Emergent Identities: Requirements for Ethnographies of Late Twentieth-Century Modernity Worldwide." In Lash and Friedman, eds., 1992, pp. 309–30.

Mark, Yudl. 1938. "Yidishe anglitsizmen." *Yorbukh fun amopteyl fun yivo* 1: 296–321.

———. 1941. "Fun der redaktsye." *Yidishe shprakh* 1: 1–2.

———. 1958. "Vos iz a vort fun der yidisher shprakh?" In Yudl Mark, ed., *Yuda A. Yofe-bukh*, pp. 287–98, New York: Yivo.

Mascia-Lees, Frances, Patricia Sharpe, and Colleen Ballerino Cohen. 1989. "The Postmodernist Turn in Anthropology: Cautions from a Feminist Perspective." *Signs* 15: 7–33.

Matisoff, James A. 1979. *Blessings, Curses, Hopes, and Fears: Psycho-Ostensive Expressions in Yiddish.* Philadelphia: ISHI.

Mayer, Egon. 1979. *From Suburb to Shtetl: The Jews of Boro Park.* Philadelphia: Temple University Press.

———. 1985. *Love and Tradition: Marriage Between Jews and Christians.* New York: Plenum Press.

Mendele Mokher Sforim. 1967. "Notes from My Literary Biography." In Dawidowicz, ed., 1967, pp. 273–80.

Merritt, Marilyn. 1979. "Building 'Higher' Units and Levels: The Case for the Strategic Locus of Observation." In Paul R. Clyne, William F. Hanks, and Carol L. Hofbauer, eds., *The Elements: A Parasession on Linguistic Units and Levels*, pp. 19–31. Chicago: Chicago Linguistics Society.

Middleton, David, and Derek Edwards, eds. 1990. *Collective Remembering.* London: Sage Publications.

Milroy, James, and Lesley Milroy. 1985. *Authority in Language: Investigating*

Language Prescription and Standardisation. London: Routledge and Kegan Paul.

Milroy, Lesley. 1980. *Language and Social Networks*. Oxford, Eng.: Basil Blackwell.

Mintz, Jerome R. 1968. *Legends of the Hasidim*. Chicago: University of Chicago Press.

Miron, Dan. 1973. *A Traveler Disguised: The Rise of Modern Yiddish Fiction in the Nineteenth Century*. New York: Schocken Books.

Moerman, Michael. 1993. "Ariadne's Thread and Indra's Net: Reflections on Ethnography, Ethnicity, Identity, Culture, and Interaction." *Research on Language and Social Interaction* 26: 85–98.

Moffatt, Michael. 1992. "Ethnographic Writing About American Culture." *Annual Review of Anthropology* 21: 205–29.

Moore, Deborah Dash. 1980. *At Home in America: Second Generation New York Jews*. New York: Columbia University Press.

———. 1994. *To the Golden Cities: Pursuing the American Jewish Dream in Miami and L.A.* New York: Free Press.

Morawska, Eva. 1994. "In Defense of the Assimilation Model." *Journal of American Ethnic History* 13: 76–87.

Moreno, Jacob L. 1953. *Who Shall Survive?* Revised ed. New York: Beacon House.

Myerhoff, Barbara. 1978a. *Number Our Days*. New York: E. P. Dutton.

———. 1978b. "A Symbol Perfected in Death: Continuity and Ritual in the Life and Death of an Elderly Jew." In Myerhoff and Simic, eds., 1978, pp. 163–205.

———. 1980. "Life History Among the Elderly: Performance, Visibility and Remembering." In Kurt W. Back, ed., *Life Course: Integrative Theories and Exemplary Populations*, pp. 133–53. Boulder, Colo.: Westview Press.

———. 1987. "Life, Not Death in Venice: Its Second Life." In Harvey E. Goldberg, ed., *Judaism Viewed from Within and from Without: Anthropological Studies*, pp. 143–69. Albany: State University of New York Press.

———. 1988. "Surviving Stories: Reflections on *Number Our Days*." In Jack Kugelmass, ed., *Between Two Worlds: Ethnographic Essays on American Jewry*, pp. 265–94. Ithaca, N.Y.: Cornell University Press.

Myerhoff, Barbara, and Jay Ruby. 1982. "Introduction." In Jay Ruby, ed., *A Crack in the Mirror: Reflexive Perspectives in Anthropology*, pp. 1–35. Philadelphia: University of Pennsylvania Press.

Myerhoff, Barbara, and Andrei Simic, eds. 1978. *Life's Career—Aging*. Beverly Hills, Calif.: Sage Publications.

Myers-Scotton, Carol. 1992. "Comparing Codeswitching and Borrowing." In Eastman, ed., 1992b, pp. 19–39.

———. 1993a. *Social Motivations for Codeswitching: Evidence from Africa*. Oxford, Eng.: Clarendon Press and Oxford University Press.

———. 1993b. *Duelling Languages: Grammatical Structure in Codeswitching*. Oxford, Eng.: Clarendon Press and Oxford University Press.

Neumann, J. H. 1938. "Notes on American Yiddish." *Journal of English and Germanic Philology* 37: 403–21.

Niger, Sh. 1912–13. "Shtudyes tsu der geshikhte fun der yidisher literatur. A. Di yidishe literatur un di lezerin." In Sh. Niger, ed., *Der pinkes*, pp. 85–138. Vilna:

B. A. Kletskin Farlag (reprinted in Niger, Sh. 1959. *Bleter geshikhte fun der yidisher literatur*, pp. 35–107. New York: Congress for Jewish Culture).

———. 1941. "Lomir zey kashern (a briv in redaktsye)." *Yidishe shprakh* 1: 21–24.

Noble, Shlomo. 1943. *Khumesh-taytsh: An oysforshung vegn der traditsye fun taytshn khumesh in di khadorim*. New York: Yivo.

Obeyesekere, Gananath. 1975. "Sinhalese-Buddhist Identity in Ceylon." In De Vos and Romanucci-Ross, eds., 1975b, pp. 231–58.

Obler, Loraine, and Lisa Menn, eds. 1982. *Exceptional Language and Linguistics*. New York: Academic Press.

Ochs, Elinor. 1988. *Culture and Language Development: Language Acquisition and Language Socialization in a Samoan Village*. Cambridge, Eng.: Cambridge University Press.

Padden, Carol A. 1990. "Folk Explanation in Language Survival." In Middleton and Edwards, eds., 1990, pp. 190–202.

Page, Helan. 1988. "Dialogic Principles of Interactive Learning in the Ethnographic Relationship." *Journal of Anthropological Research* 44: 163–81.

Parmentier, Richard J. 1985. Review of *Kuna Ways of Speaking: An Ethnographic Perspective*, by Joel Sherzer. *American Ethnologist* 12: 161–62.

Parush, Iris. 1994. "Readers in Cameo: Women Readers in Jewish Society of Nineteenth-Century Eastern Europe." *Prooftexts* 14: 1–23.

Peltz, Rakhmiel. 1982. "The Sibilants of Northeastern Yiddish: The Phonetic Data." Unpublished paper. Linguistics Department, Columbia University.

———. 1990a. "Spoken Yiddish in America: Variation in Dialect and Grammar." In *Studies in Yiddish Linguistics*, ed. Paul Wexler, pp. 55–73. Tübingen: Max Niemeyer Verlag.

———. 1990b. "Di politik fun forshn di geredte shprakh in di fareynikte shtatn un in sovetn-farband." *Oksforder yidish* 1: 141–58.

———. 1990c. "The Changing Ethnic Identity of the New Jewish Elderly." *Journal of Aging and Judaism* 5: 65–69.

———. 1991. "Ethnic Identity and Aging: Children of Jewish Immigrants Return to Their First Language." In *Language and Ethnicity*, ed. James Dow, pp. 183–205. Philadelphia: John Benjamins.

Polanyi, Livia. 1989. *Telling the American Story: A Structural and Cultural Analysis of Conversational Storytelling*. Cambridge, Mass.: MIT Press.

Polenberg, Richard. 1980. *One Nation Divisible: Class, Race, and Ethnicity in the United States Since 1938*. New York: Penguin Books.

Poplack, Shana. 1978. "Dialect Acquisition Among Puerto Rican Bilinguals." *Language in Society* 7: 89–103.

———. 1980. "'Sometimes I'll Start a Sentence in Spanish y Termino en Espanol': Toward a Typology of Code-Switching." *Linguistics* 18: 581–618.

Porter, Jack. 1958. "Differing Features of Orthodox, Conservative and Reform Jewish Groups in Metropolitan Philadelphia." Ph.D. diss., Temple University.

Prince, Ellen. 1987. "Sarah Gorby, Yiddish Folksinger: A Case Study of Dialect Shift." *International Journal of the Sociology of Language* 67: 83–116.

Rayfield, J. R. 1970. *The Language of a Bilingual Community*. The Hague: Mouton.

Rempusheski, Veronica F. 1988. "Caring for Self and Others: Second Generation

Polish American Elders in an Ethnic Club." *Journal of Cross-Cultural Gerontology* 3: 223–71.

Rodriguez, Richard. 1983. *Hunger of Memory: The Education of Richard Rodriguez.* New York: Bantam Books.

Romaine, Suzanne, ed. 1982. *Sociolinguistic Variation in Speech Communities.* London: Edward Arnold.

Ronch, Judah, Robert Cooper, and Joshua Fishman. 1969. "Word Naming and Usage Scores for a Sample of Yiddish-English Bilinguals." *Modern Language Journal* 53: 232–35.

Roosens, Eugeen E. 1989. *Creating Ethnicity: The Process of Ethnogenesis.* Newbury Park, Calif.: Sage Publications.

Rosaldo, Renato. 1989. *Culture and Truth: The Remaking of Social Analysis.* Boston: Beacon Press.

Rose, Dan. 1989. *Patterns of American Culture: Ethnography and Estrangement.* Philadelphia: University of Pennsylvania Press.

———. 1990. *Living the Ethnographic Life.* Newbury Park, Calif.: Sage Publications.

Rose, Elizabeth. 1994. "From Sponge Cake to *Hamentashen*: Jewish Identity in a Jewish Settlement House, 1885–1952." *Journal of American Ethnic History* 13: 3–23.

Rosen, Ben, ed. 1938. *Jewish Education to the Fore.* Philadelphia: Associated Talmud Torahs of Philadelphia.

Rosen, Phillip. 1983. "German Jews vs. Russian Jews in Philadelphia Philanthropy." In Murray Friedman, ed., *Jewish Life in Philadelphia: 1830–1940*, pp. 198–212. Philadelphia: ISHI.

Roth, Henry. 1991 [1934]. *Call It Sleep.* New York: Noonday Press.

Rothstein, D. G. 1983. "Developing a Voluntary Neighborhood Intergenerational Program." *Journal of Jewish Communal Service* 60: 48–62.

Rotman, Norma. 1980. *Health Needs Assessment and Social History of the Jewish Population of South Philadelphia.* Philadelphia: Albert Einstein Medical Center, Daroff Division.

Rowe, John W., and Robert L. Kahn. 1987. "Human Aging: Usual and Successful." *Science* 237: 143–49.

Rozhanski, Shmuel, ed. 1984. *In der yidisher literatur: Tsu a nayem lebn.* Buenos Aires: Literatur-gezelshaft baym yivo in argentine.

Russell, Joan. 1982. "Networks and Sociolinguistic Variation in an African Urban Setting." In Romaine, ed., 1982, pp. 125–40.

Sanders, Scott Russell. 1993. *Staying Put: Making a Home in a Restless World.* Boston: Beacon Press.

Sanjek, Roger. 1990. "Fire, Loss, and the Sorcerer's Apprentice." In Roger Sanjek, ed., *Fieldnotes: The Makings of Anthropology*, pp. 34–44. Ithaca, N.Y.: Cornell University Press.

Saul, Jack M. 1983. "Jewish Ethnic Identity and Psychological Adjustment in Old Age." Ph.D. diss., Boston University.

Saunders, R., and P. W. Davis. 1974. "Some Problems in Amerindian Second Language Pedagogy." *Etudes de Linguistique Appliquée* 15: 34–42.

Saville-Troike, Muriel. 1989. *The Ethnography of Communication.* 2d ed. Oxford, Eng.: Basil Blackwell.

Scherer, Klaus R. 1979. "Personality Markers in Speech." In Klaus R. Scherer and Howard Giles, eds., *Social Markers in Speech*, pp. 147–209. Cambridge, Eng.: Cambridge University Press.

Schiffrin, Deborah. 1984. "Jewish Argument as Sociability." *Language in Society* 13: 311–35.

Schmidt, Annette. 1985. *Young People's Dyirbal: An Example of Language Death from Australia*. Cambridge, Eng.: Cambridge University Press.

Schuman, Howard, and Jacqueline Scott. 1989. "Generations and Collective Memories." *American Sociological Review* 54: 359–81.

Scollon, Ron, and Suzanne B. K. Scollon. 1981. *Narrative, Literacy and Face in Interethnic Communication*. Norwood, N.J.: Ablex.

Scotton, Carol Myers, and William Urey. 1977. "Bilingual Strategies: The Social Functions of Code-switching." *International Journal of the Sociology of Language* 13: 5–20.

Seitel, Peter. 1976. "Proverbs: A Social Use of Metaphor." In Dan Ben-Amos, ed., *Folklore Genres*, pp. 125–43. Austin: University of Texas Press.

Seliger, Herbert. 1989. "Deterioration and Creativity in Childhood Bilingualism." In Kenneth Hyltenstam and Loraine Obler, eds., *Bilingualism Across the Lifespan: Aspects of Acquisition, Maturity, and Loss*, pp. 173–84. Cambridge, Eng.: Cambridge University Press.

Seyfer Hazikorin: Souvenir Journal Commemorating the Celebration of the Fortieth Anniversary of the Yeshiva Mishkan Israel and Central Talmud Torah. 1934. Philadelphia.

Shaffir, William. 1985. "Some Reflections on Approaches to Fieldwork in Hassidic Communities." *Jewish Journal of Sociology* 27: 115–34.

Shotter, John. 1989. "Social Accountability and the Social Construction of 'you.'" In John Shotter and Kenneth J. Gergen, eds., *Texts of Identity*, pp. 133–51. London: Sage Publications.

Shtarkman, Moyshe. 1939. "Tsu der geshikhte fun yidish in amerike." *Yorbukh fun amopteyl fun yivo* 2: 181–90.

Shtif, N. 1930. *Yidishe stilistik*. Kiev: Tsenterfarlag.

———. 1967. "How I Became a Yiddish Linguist." In Dawidowicz, ed., pp. 257.

Silverman-Weinreich, Beatrice. 1978. "Towards a Structural Analysis of Yiddish Proverbs." *Yivo Annual of Jewish Social Science* 17: 1–20.

Simic, Andrei. 1978. "Introduction: Aging and the Aged in Cultural Perspective." In Myerhoff and Simic, eds., 1978, pp. 9–22.

———. 1985. "Ethnicity as a Resource for the Aged: An Anthropological Perspective." *Journal of Applied Gerontology* 4: 65–71.

Skorupski, John. 1976. *Symbol and Theory: A Philosophical Study of Theories of Religion in Social Anthropology*. Cambridge, Eng.: Cambridge University Press.

Slobin, Dan. 1963. "Some Aspects of the Use of Pronouns of Address in Yiddish." *Word* 19: 193–202.

Smolicz, J. J. 1983. "Modification and Maintenance: Language Among School-Children of Italian Background in South Australia." *Journal of Multilingual and Multicultural Development* 4: 313–37.

Sokolovsky, Jay, ed. 1990. *The Cultural Context of Aging: Worldwide Perspectives*. New York: Bergin and Garvey.

Sollors, Werner. 1986. *Beyond Ethnicity: Consent and Descent in American Culture*. New York: Oxford University Press.

———. 1989. "Introduction: The Invention of Ethnicity." In Werner Sollors, ed., *The Invention of Ethnicity*, pp. ix–xx. New York: Oxford University Press.

Sorin, Gerald. 1990. *The Nurturing Neighborhood: The Brownsville Boys Club and Jewish Community in Urban America, 1940–1990*. New York: New York University Press.

Spivak, Gayatri Ch. 1988. "Can the Subaltern Speak?" In Cary Nelson and Lawrence Grossberg, eds., *Marxism and the Interpretation of Culture*, pp. 271–313. Urbana: University of Illinois Press.

Stoller, Paul. 1989. *The Taste of Ethnographic Things: The Senses in Anthropology*. Philadelphia: University of Pennsylvania Press.

———. 1994. "Ethnographies as Texts/Ethnographers as Griots." *American Ethnologist* 21: 353–66.

Stubbs, Michael. 1983. *Discourse Analysis: The Sociolinguistic Analysis of Natural Language*. Chicago: University of Chicago Press.

Suttles, Gerald D. 1968. *The Social Order of the Slum: Ethnicity and Territory in the Inner City*. Chicago: University of Chicago Press.

———. 1972. *The Social Construction of Communities*. Chicago: University of Chicago Press.

Svensson, Frances. 1974. "Language as Ideology: The American Indian Case." *Etudes de Linguistique Appliquée* 15: 60–68.

Tabak, Robert. 1983. "Orthodox Judaism in Transition." In Murray Friedman, ed., *Jewish Life in Philadelphia 1830–1940*, pp. 48–63. Philadelphia: ISHI.

———. 1990. "The Transformation of Jewish Identity: The Philadelphia Experience, 1919–1945." Ph.D. diss., Temple University.

Tannen, Deborah. 1981. "New York Jewish Conversational Style." *International Journal of the Sociology of Language* 30: 133–49.

———. 1984. *Conversational Style: Analyzing Talk Among Friends*. Norwood, N.J.: Ablex.

Taylor, Donald M. 1977. "Bilingualism and Intergroup Relations." In Hornby, ed., 1977, pp. 67–75.

Tedlock, Barbara. 1991. "From Participant Observation to the Observation of Participation: The Emergence of Narrative Ethnography." *Journal of Anthropological Research* 47: 69–94.

Tedlock, Dennis. 1983. *The Spoken Word and the Work of Interpretation*. Philadelphia: University of Pennsylvania Press.

Thakerar, Jitendra N., Howard Giles, and Jenny Cheshire. 1982. "Psychological and Linguistic Parameters of Speech Accommodation Theory." In Colin Fraser and Klaus R. Scherer, eds., *Advances in the Social Psychology of Language*, pp. 205–55. Cambridge, Eng.: Cambridge University Press.

Thomas, Rosemary Hyde. 1979. "Some Aspects of the French Language of Old Mines, Missouri." Ph.D. diss., Saint Louis University.

Toll, William. 1982. *The Making of an Ethnic Middle Class: Portland Jewry over Four Generations*. Albany: State University of New York Press.

Troike, Rudolph C. 1970. "Receptive Competence, Productive Competence, and

Performance." In James E. Alatis, ed., *Linguistics and the Teaching of Standard English to Speakers of Other Languages or Dialects*, pp. 63–73. Washington, D.C.: Georgetown University Press.

Trudgill, Peter. 1986. *Dialects in Contact*. Oxford, Eng.: Basil Blackwell.

Tsvayg, A. R. 1930. "Lingvotekhnisher ekizm." *Di yidishe shprakh* 21–22: 49–52.

Van Langenhove, Luk, and Rom Harre. 1993. "Positioning and Autobiography: Telling Your Life." In Coupland and Nussbaum, eds., 1993, pp. 81–99.

Varbero, Richard A. 1973. "Philadelphia's South Italians in the 1920s." In A. Davis and M. Haller, eds., *The Peoples of Philadelphia*, pp. 255–75. Philadelphia: Temple University Press.

———. 1975. "Urbanization and Acculturation: Philadelphia's South Italians." Ph.D. diss., Temple University.

Varenne, Herve. 1986. "'Drop in Anytime': Community and Authenticity in American Everyday Life." In Herve Varenne, ed., *Symbolizing America*, pp. 209–28. Lincoln: University of Nebraska Press.

Veynger, M. 1928. "Vegn yidishe dialektn." *Tsaytshrift* 2–3: 614–52.

———. 1929. *Yidishe dialektologye*. Minsk.

Vincent, Joan. 1991. "Engaging Historicism." In Richard G. Fox, ed., *Recapturing Anthropology: Working in the Present*, pp. 45–58. Sante Fe, N.M.: School of American Research Press.

Waters, Mary C. 1990. *Ethnic Options: Choosing Identities in America*. Berkeley: University of California Press.

Weber, Lennard. 1962. MS in Mt. Sinai Hospital, Philadelphia, file, American Jewish Archives, Cincinnati. Unpublished letter from the president of the medical staff, Albert Einstein Medical Center, Southern Division, to Earl Perloff, December 5.

Weibel-Orlando, Joan. 1988. "Indians, Ethnicity as a Resource and Aging: You Can Go Home Again." *Journal of Cross-Cultural Gerontology* 3: 323–48.

———. 1990. "Grandparenting Styles: Native American Perspectives." In Sokolovsky, ed., 1990, pp. 109–25.

———. 1991. *Indian Country, L.A.: Maintaining Ethnic Community in Complex Society*. Urbana: University of Illinois Press.

Weinreich, Max. 1938. "Daytshmerish toyg nit." *Yidish far ale* 1: 97–106.

———. 1941. "Vegn englishe elementn in undzer kulturshprakh." *Yidishe shprakh* 1: 33–46.

———. 1971. "Di yidishe klal-shprakh in der tsveyter helft 20stn yorhundert." *Yidishe shprakh* 30: 2–18.

———. 1980. *History of the Yiddish Language*. Trans. Shlomo Noble. Chicago: University of Chicago Press.

Weinreich, Peter. 1989a. "Conflicted Identification: A Commentary on Identity Structure Analysis Concepts." In Liebkind, ed. 1989c, pp. 219–36.

———. 1989b. "Variations in Ethnic Identity: Identity Structure Analysis." In Liebkind, ed., 1989c, pp. 41–75.

Weinreich, Uriel. 1952. "*Sabesdiker losn* in Yiddish: A Problem of Linguistic Affinity." *Slavic Word* 8: 360–77.

———. 1953. *Languages in Contact*. New York: Linguistic Circle of New York.

———. 1958. "Nusakh hasofrim haivri-yidi." *Lishoneynu* 22: 54–66.

———. 1968. *Modern English–Yiddish Yiddish–English Dictionary.* New York: McGraw-Hill.

———. 1971. *College Yiddish.* 5th ed. New York: Yivo.

———. 1972. "Dos normirn a shprakh: prat-faln un oysfirm." *Yidishe shprakh* 31: 1–11, 48–54.

———. 1973. "Yiddish Language." *Encyclopedia Britannica.* 14th ed. 23: 893.

Weissler, Chava. 1987. "The Traditional Piety of Ashkenazic Women." In Arthur Green, ed., *Jewish Spirituality.* Vol. 2, *From the Sixteenth-Century Revival to the Present,* pp. 245–75. New York: Crossroad.

———. 1991. "Prayers in Yiddish and the Religious World of Ashkenazic Women." In Judith R. Baskin, ed., *Jewish Women in Historical Perspective,* pp. 159–81. Detroit: Wayne State University Press.

White, Geoffrey M. 1987. "Proverbs and Cultural Models: An American Psychology of Problem Solving." In Dorothy Holland and Naomi Quinn, eds., *Cultural Models in Language and Thought,* pp. 151–72. Cambridge, Eng.: Cambridge University Press.

Whiteman, Maxwell. 1973. "Philadelphia's Jewish Neighborhoods." In A. Davis ' and M. Haller, eds., *The Peoples of Philadelphia,* pp. 231–54. Philadelphia: Temple University Press.

———. 1977. "Western Impact on East European Jews: A Philadelphia Fragment." In Randall M. Miller and Thomas D. Marczik, eds., *Immigrants and Religion in Urban America,* pp. 117–37. Philadelphia: Temple University Press.

Williams, Frederick. 1983. "Some Research Notes on Dialect Attitudes and Stereotypes." In Ralph A. Fasold, ed., *Variation in the Form and Use of Language: A Sociolinguistics Reader,* pp. 354–69. Washington, D.C.: Georgetown University Press.

Williams, Michael R. 1985. *Neighborhood Organizations: Seeds of a New Urban Life.* Westport, Conn.: Greenwood Press.

Wilpert, Czarina. 1989. "Ethnic and Cultural Identity: Ethnicity and the Second Generation in the Context of European Migration." In Liebkind, ed., 1989c, pp. 6–24.

Wireman, Peggy. 1984. *Urban Neighborhoods, Networks, and Families: New Forms for Old Values.* Lexington, Mass.: Lexington Books.

Wolf, Christa. 1984. *Patterns of Childhood.* New York: Noonday Press.

Wolfson, Nessa. 1976. "Speech Events and Natural Speech: Some Implications for Sociolinguistic Methodology." *Language in Society* 5: 189–209.

Woodward, Kathleen. 1986. "Reminiscence and the Life Review: Prospects and Retrospects." In Thomas R. Cole and Sally Gadow, eds., *What Does It Mean to Grow Old?: Reflections from the Humanities,* pp. 135–61. Durham, N.C.: Duke University Press.

———. 1991. *Aging and Its Discontents: Freud and Other Fictions.* Bloomington: Indiana University Press.

Woolard, Kathryn A. 1985. "Language Variation and Cultural Hegemony: Toward an Integration of Sociolinguistic and Social Theory." *American Ethnologist* 12: 738–48.

Yancey, William L., and Ira Goldstein. 1985. *The Jewish Population of the Greater Philadelphia Area*. Philadelphia: Federation of Jewish Agencies of Greater Philadelphia.

Yuval-Davis, Nira. 1994. "Identity Politics and Women's Ethnicity." In Valentine M. Moghdam, ed., *Identity Politics and Women: Cultural Reassertions and Feminisms in International Perspective*, pp. 408–24. Boulder, Colo.: Westview Press.

Zaretski, A. 1930. "Problemen fun yidisher lingvotekhnik." *Di yidishe shprakh* 20: 1–10.

———. 1931. "Derlernt di sotsyale diferentsiatsye in Yidish." *Afn shprakhfront* 26–27: 69–80.

Zelinski, Elizabeth M. 1988. "Integrating Information from Discourse: Do Older Adults Show Deficits?" In Light and Burke, eds., 1988, pp. 117–32.

Zukin, Sharon. 1992. "Postmodern Urban Landscapes: Mapping Culture and Power." In Lash and Friedman, eds., 1992, pp. 221–47.

Index

In this index an "f" after a number indicates a separate reference on the next page, and an "ff" indicates separate references on the next two pages. A continuous discussion over two or more pages is indicated by a span of page numbers, e.g., "57–59." *Passim* is used for a cluster of references in close but not consecutive sequence.

Library of Congress Cataloging-in-Publication Data

Peltz, Rakhmiel
    From immigrant to ethnic culture : American Yiddish in South Philadelphia /
Rakhmiel Peltz.
        p.   cm. — (Stanford studies in Jewish history and culture)
    Includes bibliographical references and index.
    ISBN 0-8047-3020-2 (cloth)—ISBN 0-8047-3167-5 (paper)
    1. Jews—Pennsylvania—Philadelphia—Social life and customs. 2. Yiddish
language—Dialects—Pennsylvania—Philadelphia. 3. South Philadelphia
(Philadelphia, Pa.)—Social life and customs. 4. Philadelphia (Pa.)—Ethnic
relations. I. Title. II. Series.
    F158.9.J5P45   1998
    974.8'11004924—dc21   97-11999
                                                     CIP
                                                      r97

Original printing 1998
Last figure below indicates year of this printing:

07 06 05 04 03 02 01 00 99 98